Unemployment
in the Urban Core

Stanley L. Friedlander
assisted by
Robert Shick
foreword by
Eli Ginzberg

Conservation of Human Resources Studies—
Columbia University

The Praeger Special Studies program—utilizing the most modern and efficient book production techniques and a selective worldwide distribution network—makes available to the academic, government, and business communities significant, timely research in U.S. and international economic, social, and political development.

Unemployment in the Urban Core

An Analysis of Thirty Cities with Policy Recommendations

Praeger Publishers   New York   Washington   London

PRAEGER SPECIAL STUDIES IN U.S. ECONOMIC, SOCIAL, AND POLITICAL ISSUES

PRAEGER PUBLISHERS
111 Fourth Avenue, New York, N.Y. 10003, U.S.A.
5, Cromwell Place, London S.W.7, England

Published in the United States of America in 1972
by Praeger Publishers, Inc.

Library of Congress Catalog Card Number: 72-85976

Printed in the United States of America

This report was prepared for the Manpower Administration, U.S. Department of Labor, under research contract number 81-34-68-44 authorized by Title I of the Manpower Development and Training Act. Since contractors performing research under Government sponsorship are encouraged to express their own judgment freely, the report does not necessarily represent the Department's official opinion or policy. Moreover, the contractor is solely responsible for the factual accuracy of all material developed in the report.

This is an important book because of the questions it addresses, the findings it presents, and the policy recommendations that flow therefrom. This Foreword will discuss the relationship of the present effort and the ongoing program of manpower research being conducted by the Conservation of Human Resources Project, Columbia University; the research methodology that the author used; and the bearing of his principal findings on our understanding of contemporary labor markets and improved guidelines for manpower policy.

In the early 1969s, the conservation project realized that it should shift its theretofore almost exclusive focus on manpower macrostudies at the national and international level to explorations of local labor markets. The staff reached this conclusion because it found that the only way it could respond to the New York City Planning Commission's request for assistance was in analyzing the structure and functioning of the local labor market. National trends set parameters of growth and change but it was clear that every large city and every region was responding to unique forces in its immediate environment. The difficulties of local implementation of the federally financed new manpower legislation—Manpower Development Training Act, Neighborhood Youth Corps, Job Corps, Operation Mainstream— gave added impetus to our shifting attention to local labor markets.

Within the last several years the conservation project has published a series of studies whose focus has been the urban or the metropolitan labor market. Among the most important are the following: Manpower Strategy for the Metropolis (Columbia, 1968); The Metropolitan Economy (Columbia, 1970); and New York Is Very Much Alive— A Manpower View, (in press; New York: McGraw-Hill).

The present study by Stanley Friedlander assisted by Robert Shick is an important addition to the published work of the conservation project on disaggregative research focused on the city and the metropolitan community. Initiated in 1967, the basic research was completed by 1970. Friedlander made an oral report to the staff of the U.S. Department of Labor—the sponsor of the research—at that time. The delay in publication was the result of the extensive rewriting that was necessary to eliminate the mathematical and statistical symbolism throughout the manuscript, which reflected the use of various econometric models. I was convinced that the subject, analysis, and conclusions were of sufficient moment to warrant the onerous and difficult task of rewriting the story in straightforward prose. Otherwise, the book would have been interesting to a small audience of the initiated, and only a minority of them have any interest in manpower research. The rewriting went through two stages: Friedlander undertook the initial effort, and Gladys Topkis, a professional editor, produced the finished version. This version demands no technical expertise. It presents the details of an important empirical investigation in simple declarative sentences. It is our hope, and expectation, that a book which considers urban unemployment in the nation's thirty largest cities will engage the attention of the business, labor, minority, and political leadership in these key cities, as well as that of the community of social scientists. If the tragic human waste and dangerous political instability of widespread urban unemployment are to be contained and reduced, an enlightened and concerned citizenry must attend to these problems.

The author, using data for 1960, a year of recession, and 1966, a year of prosperity, seeks to determine the principal factors responsible for the significant differences in urban unemployment among the nation's thirty largest cities. The census data for 1960 are, of course, more complete than the data for 1966, which are derived from the special urban employment survey funded by the U.S. Department of Labor. Data from the 1966 survey were made available to Friedlander through the cooperation of the Council of Economic Advisers and the Census Bureau.

A supplemental resource that Friedlander developed was a series of interviews conducted in Harlem, New York, in the summer of 1968 by three minority group students who had attended his classes at City College. The interviewers sought out young men and young women between the ages of eighteen and twenty-four, who were not full-time students, who did not have full-time jobs, and who were not in the armed forces, to determine how they spent their time and how they were supporting themselves. These interviews yielded rich materials and insights into the problems of unemployed young blacks, which are reported and analyzed in Chapter 6.

The three faces of urban unemployment with which this book is primarily concerned are the central city, the slum areas within central cities, and youth unemployment in the slums. A fourth dimension that is threaded through the entire analysis is the problem of unemployment among nonwhites, primarily blacks in these large cities.

By using data for a year when the economy was in recession and a year during which it enjoyed marked prosperity, the author is able to pinpoint the factors responsible for differential unemployment among the nation's major cities. As his detailed findings indicate, a factor may be important under one set of economic conditions but not when the cycle is in another phase. However, because he has confined his analysis to a short time period, he has not been able to

consider the structural changes within the American economy, especially after the end of World War II, such as suburbanization,
education, race relations, internal migration, occupational trends, and
other factors that affect the performance of national and urban labor
markets. Although to ignore structural changes carries a price,
Friedlander was probably wise to opt in favor of a more intensive
analysis of a shorter time frame.

No analysis can rise above the level of data available to the
researcher. In many instances the author had to make do with both
quantitatively and qualitatively indifferent information. The most
significant lack is valid measures of educational achievement, health,
and crime. Despite these handicaps, which afflict most investigations
of the contemporary scene, his basic analysis and findings are firmly
anchored in data that can stand up to critical inspection.

So much for his approach. For an overview of his findings, the
reader is referred to Chapter 7, in which the highlights of the study
are summarized. He may also want to pay attention to the concluding
sections of Chapters 3, 4, and 5. We will limit ourselves here to
calling attention to those findings which run counter to the conventional
wisdom:

1. Rapid employment growth, high educational achievement by
minorities, or limited job dispersal to the suburbs are not correlated
with relatively low unemployment rates, particularly among nonwhites,
slum residents, and ghetto youth.

2. If low educational achievement is a significant factor in urban
unemployment, especially among minorities, the critical consideration
is not how much education the minorities have achieved but rather
the gap between them and the white population. This reflects the fact
that employer specifications keep rising as the educational achievement levels go up and consequently minorities still tend to be hired
last.

3. Intensive residental segregation within the central city is
associated with lower unemployment rates for minority groups. The
explanation for this apparent anomaly may be the improved labor
market information flow among highly segregated minorities.

4. One of the most disturbing findings relates to a relative
worsening in the measures of discrimination affecting minorities
during the 1960's—at least up to 1966. While minorities in 1966 were
represented in the higher occupational levels in greater absolute
numbers than in 1960, their relative position had worsened.

5. Although employment growth is a necessary condition to
reduce urban unemployment to tolerable proportions and to bring
down the excessively high rates afflicting minorities, slum dwellers,
and youth, it is not a sufficient condition. A critical finding was that

the rapid growth in total employment had no appreciable effect on the unemployment rates of ghetto youth. And an even more surprising finding was that employment growth was occasionally associated with a rising unemployment rate among slum dwellers—an anomaly that could be explained by the characteristics of the people living in the slums, large in-migration, and particularly the segmented labor market, which continued to keep most slum dwellers at arm's length from the burgeoning jobs.

6. Some economists have strong views about the effect of wage structures and wage changes (minimum wage legislation) on unemployment. The present study found that cities characterized by relatively high wage structures also tend to have high unemployment rates among slum youth, which reflect the direct impact of wages on the demand for labor and a great number of discriminatory employment practices that tend to be associated with high wage industries, such as those in which trade unions are strongly entrenched.

7. A complementary finding is that cities with high wages had relatively low slum unemployment rates among all slum dwellers, which is a clear warning that intervening structural factors, such as segmentation of the labor market, may outweigh the significance of wages as a determining element in the employment of this group.

8. Cities differ noticeably in their industrial structure. In both 1960 and 1966 those central cities characterized with above average employment in highly cyclical industries tended to have above average unemployment rates. In the prosperous year, 1966, cities with above average employment in construction, manufacturing, and finance had above average slum unemployment. The explanation for this seems to be that these fields tend to have more selective and controlled hiring practices. Confirmation of this finding is suggested by the fact that high retail employment is generally associated with below average urban and slum unemployment.

9. Probably the most tantalizing finding of the entire study was the unequivocal demonstration that a high rate of crimes against property is correlated with lower unemployment rates for minorities and slum dwellers. It may not be easy for a law-abiding citizenry to accept, but this finding, reinforced by the field interviews, points to the fact that many people on the periphery of society view illicit and illegal work as an alternative to unemployment or marginal jobs and, therefore, give up the search for regular employment.

There is no point in detailing more of the author's findings. These few should suffice to whet the appetite of even the most sophisticated or jaded student of urban America. Here is a mine of important, useful, relevant information about the unemployment experiences of our nation's largest cities, their nonwhite populations, their slum dwellers, and their ghetto youth.

Friedlander, unlike many of his academic confreres, is n
hesitant to move from the realm of analysis to that of policy. I
concluding chapters, he draws a large number of conclusions fr
study, as well as from his reflections about related aspects of urban
and national economics, and sets forth a bill of particulars for public
policy. It does not matter whether the reader agrees with Friedlander's
recommendations; it is more important that he outline an alternative
set of policies that would be responsive to the pathology the author has
illuminated and analyzed. It would be an easy out to find fault with the
author's specific and general recommendations on the ground that they
are not substantiated by his earlier analysis, that their costs and benefits
have not been calculated, and that the negative impacts of particular
policies have been disregarded. However, the critical reader must
joust not with the author but with the problems he is addressing.

Even after I persuaded Friedlander to revise the first draft of
his recommendations and to specify and clarify them, I disagreed with
many of his formulations. But if we remember that these formulations
are presented to encourage early action by the public to come to grips
with pressing social and economic problems that endanger the Republic
and doom millions of its citizens to a life without promise or achievement, disagreements about details are less important than agreement
about the directions where constructive actions must be developed.

In these concluding paragraphs I will summarize the principal
directions for constructive public policies that are discussed at length
in the author's last chapter.

Friedlander begins with a strong plea for a new mix of federal
macropolicies, aimed at reducing the present high level of unemployment, circa 6 percent, to an interim goal of 4.5 percent by the end of
1972, to be followed by reductions between 3.5 to 3 percent, with an
aim of eventually running the American economy with no more than
2.5 percent unemployment. It is his view that the inflationary dangers
of such a policy can be contained by effective—and continuing—policies
that will help check the oligopolistic price and wage increases of large
corporations and powerful trade unions. As he sees it, the appallingly
high unemployment rates characteristic of urban minorities, slum
dwellers, and ghetto youth cannot be significantly reduced unless the
growth of the economy is sufficiently rapid to depress the general
unemployment rate to a low figure. One may disagree about his
specific targets but it would be difficult to fault him on his orientation.

His second recommendation is a sweeping claim for a vastly
expanded program of public service employment. Now that Congress
has taken the plunge in the Emergency Employment Act of 1971—$2.25
billion for 145,000 public service jobs over a two-year period—
Friedlander suggests that with a $10-billion child care program
leading to 1.4-million public service jobs, the potentiality would

contribute to the improved development of the nation's human resources by creating a large number of jobs, many of which could be filled, surely after training, by the unemployed and underemployed urban minorities. Again, one may be restive about the ease with which Friedlander moves past the fiscal implications of so large a program, while being sympathetic to his underlying position of using public monies to create new constructive employment.

His third thrust for remedial action relates to education. He makes a strong plea for the radical reform of elementary and particularly secondary education, with an aim of raising the capabilities of its graduates, particularly those from inner city schools, who today often leave after ten to twelve years with little knowledge and less skill. His specific recommendations include more work-study programs, more career counseling, more and better vocational curricula, more community involvement, and other conventional if not proved proposals. But again, his recommendations for reform at this level and at the college level, where he advocates experimentation with income supplementation for students from low-income homes, open admissions, and vouchers, are less important than his deeply felt and poignantly expressed convictions that, short of major reforms, the educational system will continue to shortchange young people from disadvantaged backgrounds who most need to acquire useful knowledge and marketable skills.

Another proposal relates to the restructuring of second-chance opportunities, which, at present, are confined primarily to enabling the disadvantaged to enter one or another federally funded manpower training program. While he is not opposed to manpower training as a remedial effort to help many of the poorly educated and unskilled youth and adults who have failed to profit from the educational system, Friedlander stresses the importance of helping these individuals to get jobs, especially in environments where they will be able to advance from beginning jobs as they acquire skills and competence at work. In short, Friedlander asks for a much closer linkage than presently exists between training, job placements, and job promotions. To ensure job promotions for minority groups, he recommends the use of subsidies to private employers who will hire, retain, and promote disadvantaged persons and a substantial expansion of public service jobs, which, he argues, would be well suited to the needs of these groups, while the work that they would perform would be useful to their cities and the nation.

Finally, he urges more energetic efforts at the reduction and elimination of discrimination, particularly job discrimination, but also discrimination in housing, schooling, and the other critical aspects of the society and economy that directly or indirectly affect the development and utilization of the human resources of minority groups.

Friedlander correctly states that, unless more and faster progress is made to lower and remove the artificial barriers that block minority groups from the desirable opportunities available to the white population, there is little prospect that their unemployment rates will be significantly reduced. To this end he suggests that the major governmental agencies concerned with the enforcement of antidiscrimination statutes be strengthened by an increase in their budgets, which will permit them to expand their personnel, and by providing the Equal Employment Opportunity Commission with the right to issue cease and desist orders. Once again, the skeptic might question whether, if all these recommended steps were taken, the outcome would necessarily be the erosion of discrimination. The odds are that this would not be the near-term outcome. Nevertheless, the critic should either outline a preferred program of action or support the author. Clearly, discrimination contributes to high unemployment rates among nonwhites, and although the best designed antidiscrimination programs do not promise immediate or total solutions, additional corrective actions must be instituted.

All of Friedlander's recommendations are addressed primarily to the federal government, although in some areas, particularly education, he acknowledges important roles for state and local governments. The author singles out for special attention the roles of city governments in urban renewal, welfare, and the control of crime. With respect to the last, he urges that much that is now in violation of the law—prostitution, gambling, even access to drugs—be legalized in the hope that by such action public morality would not be weakened but the position of the poor strengthened. Again, these issues are complex, and well-informed and well-intentioned persons differ. But Friedlander's thrust points to the desirability that the public make some hard choices. There is little to commend the status quo. Much more is advocated in this free-swinging last chapter, but no recommendation is more significant than Friedlander's final comment, which puts the issue bluntly: either the American people face up to the cancerous condition of urban unemployment and seek radical therapy or they risk the demise of their society.

The goal of full employment was reached in 1966. Manpower and economic policies were working effectively, and from a national perspective we had made great progress. The unemployment rate had reached 3.8 percent, the lowest since the Korean war. Prices were relatively stable, and the gross national product was rising rapidly. Despite this prosperity, many areas of the country were experiencing substantial unemployment. Moreover, subgroups of the American labor force had unemployment rates paralleling the unemployment of the Great Depression. Amidst this prosperity civil disorders and urban riots racked many large cities during the 1960's. The Kerner Commission on Civil Disorders, after extensive studies, highlighted the critical problem of unemployment and its concentration in cities and slum areas. The seeds of destruction were rooted in the unemployment of urban and slum dwellers. Alienation from the mainstream of American society and isolation and segregation in the labor market grew into despair and frustration. The intensity of these feelings erupted into aggression and destruction. Today, in 1972, these explosive conditions have worsened.

Stimulated by the severity of the unemployment problems of the cities, I decided to undertake an exploratory study to investigate the factors related to unemployment in cities and slums and among non-whites and slum youth. It was appalling to learn how little we knew of the determinants of urban unemployment. A major reason was the paucity of data to analyze the operation of a local labor market. The data problems were so severe that local, state, and federal government officials did not know the unemployment rates of major cities in the United States. Yet, policies and programs were developed at a record-breaking pace, based on limited knowledge of these employment problems in the cities.

Acknowledgment of this serious gap in information occurred in 1966, when the U.S. Department of Labor initiated a major survey of twelve urban slum areas. The following year, the Labor Department obtained additional data on urban labor markets and unemployment from special tabulations of the current Population Survey. These new data sources provided the foundation for this exploratory study. At the time these two sets of data were the extent of materials available to study urban labor markets. Despite the fact that we are a highly urbanized nation, it was equally difficult to collect other city data representing factors thought to influence or affect unemployment. We are a nation of Standard Metropolitan Statistical Areas and not of cities. Therefore, data on these independent factors, such as crime and health, are crude and not very reliable. The quantity and quality of the data dictated the type of methodology employed. As a result of the data limitations, the analysis is confined to two distinct time periods—1960, a recession year, and 1966, a year of rapid economic growth and low unemployment. While the data is aged the analysis of the determinants of unemployment is unaffected. Unemployment in the cities existed in both prosperity and recession, and the level of unemployment in 1972 resembles the conditions of 1960. Moreover, even if full employment should return by 1973, all cities and slums will not share in the benefits. The findings of the research are relevant and useful in solving the unemployment concentrated in major urban labor markets. However, a word of caution is necessary. The results of the analysis are not conclusive and are not to be taken as definitive. Great care should be exercised in using these findings for the development of public policy. Nevertheless, the findings are useful in questioning conventional views, dispelling accepted myths, and stimulating much needed future research and data collection. In some cases the findings should generate some serious thinking on programs and policies in the manpower area. This is especially true at the present time, with the passage of the Emergency Employment Act, the introduction of the Administration's Manpower Revenue-Sharing legislation, and the reorganization of the Cooperative Area Manpower-Planning systems. All of these programs if they are to be successful require planning and programming at the local level. These activities are based on the understanding and knowledge of the operation of these local labor markets. Effective evaluation and sound planning require data and research for these local labor markets. All our current efforts at decentralized manpower planning, programming, and evaluation will not be successful unless and until we acquire a better understanding of the complex forces affecting these urban labor markets. It is my hope that this study will stimulate future research on urban labor markets so that every American will enjoy the right to work and earn a decent living.

A research project of this size and nature requires the cooperation and commitment of many people. While it is impossible to list all those who have indirectly contributed to the project, special acknowledgments are in order to those who made major contributions.

First, recognition to the contribution of capital is essential. Without the financial support of the U.S. Department of Labor, Manpower Administration, Office of Research and Development, and the encouragement and patience of its director, Howard Rosen, this study would never have been undertaken. Members of the staff of the Office of Research and Development made constructive criticisms of the manuscript.

Equally important was the labor contribution of Eli Ginzberg, director of the Conservation of Human Resources Project, who provided me with expert guidance and valuable suggestions to improve the manuscript at every stage of development. Moreover, his patience was beyond the call of duty.

By far the greatest contribution to the project was made by my research associate, Robert Shick, who was responsible for the substantial task of data collection and processing. His many substantive suggestions greatly improved the quality of the research. His dilligence and commitment shortened the time of production and made the completion a reality.

The transformation of the research into a readable manuscript benefited greatly from the talented skills of Gladys Topkis, who reorganized and edited the manuscript.

I would like to thank my research assistants who were involved in the collection and processing of the data: George Edelbaum, Peter Friedlander, Susan Ginsberg, Frank Jones, Martin Suda, and Lenore Swenson. I would also like to express my appreciation to the interviewers in the survey of Harlem youth: Edward Fabre, Diane Lewis, and Aubrey Williams. A special debt of gratitude is owed to the last of the research assistants, Virginia Thomas, who contributed significantly to the difficult task of the final preparation of the manuscript.

Two persons who were invaluable in helping to secure the data utilized in this study were Howard Stambler of the U.S. Bureau of Labor Statistics and Daniel Levine of the U.S. Bureau of the Census.

I would also like to take this opportunity to thank my colleagues at the Conservation of Human Resources Project at Columbia University, especially Gretchen Maclachlan and Marcia Freedman for their advice, guidance, and friendship, and Charles Brecher for a critical and constructive reading of the manuscript. I would like to thank Charlotte Frick, who provided valuable secretarial services throughout the study.

Many thanks to my parents for laying the foundation for all of my productive efforts. And finally, I want to thank my wife, Naomi, and my son, Michael, for their understanding and cooperation. Time foregone is time lost forever.

CONTENTS

LIST OF TABLES

Unemployment in the Urban Core

INTRODUCTION: SELECTIVE PROSPERITY

Many observers of contemporary America have noted the striking paradox of rapid economic growth and simultaneous urban decay; of rising incomes and standards of living side by side with persistent poverty; of great scientific and technological achievements in space and medicine coexisting with polluted air and water, decaying housing, and deteriorating sanitation and transportation services; of rising levels of both education and training and crime and drug addiction. This study explores one facet of these complex anomalies in the disparity between the high level of national prosperity that prevailed during much of the 1960's and the marked lack of prosperity that characterized selected portions of the population, as reflected in varying rates of unemployment. The centers of our largest cities are the site and the symbol of this paradoxical situation.

During the decade of the 1960's the American economy created millions of new jobs and raised the standard of living of millions of families. For the last seven years of the decade, from 1963 to 1969, the economy expanded continuously, chalking up a record of uninterrupted and unparalleled progress.

Stimulated by several pieces of landmark legislation, beginning with the Manpower Development and Training Act of 1962 and the Revenue Act of 1964 and by the large increase in government expenditures due primarily to the escalation of the Vietnam war in 1965, the economy achieved a major victory against the high level of unemployment that had afflicted the American labor force since the recession of 1958. The drop in unemployment was clear and decisive: the rate fell from 6.7 percent in 1961 to 3.5 percent in 1969, even lower than the 4 percent earlier designated as the full employment goal by the President's Council of Economic Advisors.[1]

The success of government policies in stimulating the economy was noteworthy and impressive. However, close to the pinnacle of success, in 1967, when unemployment was only 3.8 percent and prices were increasing at 2.9 percent per annum,[2] it became obvious that significant pockets of poverty and unemployment remained. Despite the impressive performance of the national economy, the fruits of economic progress were not equally distributed to all communities and to all families in the nation. Great variations existed among labor markets and among the several ethnic and age groups of the population. Many cities were far above the full employment target, while some local labor markets did even better than the national rate. From a disaggregated point of view of urban labor markets, then, the benefits of economic expansion were not complete.

Furthermore, the rate of unemployment often conceals the extent of maladjustment in a given labor market. Workers may be underemployed, i.e., employed in jobs that do not fully utilize their skills, training, and experience. Part-time workers may be unsuccessful seekers of full-time work. Frustrated job hunters may drop out of the labor force, thus artificially depressing the unemployment rate and concealing the true extent of excess labor. Hidden or disguised unemployment may operate in casual and family-operated employing units, where work sharing provides employment of a largely unnecessary and unproductive nature. And data collection may be inadequate, not accurately counting people who do not have a permanent residence or who do not wish to be enumerated for a variety of reasons. Nevertheless, the measured rate of unemployment does provide a valid approximation of at least relative unemployment in the labor markets of large cities.

SCOPE OF THE STUDY

This study attempts to analyze the key factors that account for the failure of many local labor markets to perform their primary function of producing and providing employment for all those who are able and willing to work. Why do some urban labor markets perform effectively, while others are characterized by high rates of unemployment?

An equally important objective is to discover why the residents of slum areas in our largest cities have vastly different labor market experiences and, more specifically, why nonwhites and slum youth in urban areas differ in their rates of unemployment. A better understanding of how urban labor markets operate and why some perform satisfactorily and others do not will lead to better allocation of scarce government resources and to improvement of policies and programs to alleviate and reduce urban unemployment and urban poverty. This, in turn, should provide policy guidance for ameliorating some of the most pressing problems of urban America.

Among the policy issues illuminated by this study are the questions of whether the government should emphasize an intensified educational program or a strong antidiscrimination program. Should local governments try to promote economic development of the ghetto or to change the industrial structure of their economy? Should educational programs attempt to raise nonwhite levels absolutely, or should they concentrate on narrowing the gap in education between whites and nonwhites? Should we develop relocation programs to house minority groups in suburbs, or should we promote improved transportation systems from city to suburb? What would be the consequences for urban unemployment of intensified efforts to curb crime and narcotics addiction and to improve the health of urban residents? Should we have a national migration program to keep people in rural areas, or should we facilitate more migration into our urban centers?

In order to answer these questions, it is necessary to move beyond analysis of the national economy toward a disaggregated view of the operation of local urban labor markets. Despite the paucity of acceptable data, it is critical to examine these markets, for they are the focus of the major unemployment problems of a prosperous, full-employment economy, along with the governmental machinery and funds to implement policies and programs designed to solve these problems. As the study evolved it became apparent that the differences among urban labor markets made it important to address the unique characteristics of the labor market and labor force in these diverse cities rather than generalize national policies and programs.

In order to observe how the state of the national economy affects urban labor markets and the rate of unemployment among various subgroups of the labor force, we selected two time periods, 1960 and 1966. These years provide significantly different national economic conditions: 1960 was a year of recession and a high national unemployment rate, and 1966 was a year of rapid economic growth and prosperity, with a low national rate of unemployment.*

---

*Although throughout the text we will refer to the two years of study as 1960 and 1966, in several instances these do not represent the actual years in which the data were recorded. The discrepancies refer to data for the industrial structure in terms of employment shares by industry, which actually apply to 1959 and 1966, and labor force statistics (unemployment, labor force participation, and population) by individual city, which actually apply to 1960 and 1967. The decision to present the data in this manner was made for the following reasons: First, in studying the interaction of employment structure and changes in unemployment, it is known that the two factors do not interact simultaneously, but rather a time lag exists in the relationship.

The study, therefore, examines the thirty most populous cities in
the United States as of 1960,[3] focusing particularly on sixteen slum
areas in eleven of these cities. In 1960 there were 33,971,319 people
in these cities, or 18.9 percent of the U.S. population. By 1966 the
population had increased to 35,347,900, or 18.0 percent of the U.S.
population.[4] The cities and their unemployment rate in 1960 and 1966
are shown in Table 1-1. The rates of the sixteen slum areas in 1960
and 1966 are shown in Table 1-2.

As we have noted, in a period when the U.S. economy was growing
rapidly and the national unemployment rate dropped substantially, the
cities of the nation did not experience a proportionate or uniform reduction in unemployment. As Table 1-1 indicates, four of the thirty
largest cities in the United States actually had an increase in their
unemployment rate, and in the other twenty-six cities, decreases in
unemployment were not equally distributed. In 1960, the unemployment
rates ranged from a low of 3.3 percent in Dallas to a high of 9.9 percent
in Detroit. By 1966 the range had increased, from a low of 2.0 percent
in Columbus and San Antonio to a high of 10.2 percent in Newark. The
mean unemployment rate among the thirty cities decreased between

---

The industrial structure of a city in one year influences that city's
employment rate at a later date. Second, as will be discussed later,
the scarcity of data for cities or close geographical approximations
of cities limited our choice of lag periods to one year (instead of two
or three years); a one-year lag was necessitated by the nature of the
most appropriate data. Employment by industry data from County
Business Patterns, a publication of the U.S. Bureau of the Census,
were available for 1959 and 1966. Labor force status data were
available for 1960 from the U.S. Census of Population and for 1967
from data collected by the U.S. Department of Labor, supplemented
by special tabulations prepared specifically for this study.

In order to enhance the readability of this manuscript, it was
decided to simply refer to all data as that for 1960 and for 1966, that
is, where the industrial structure for cities refers to 1960, the data
are actually for 1959, and where the data for labor force status refers
to 1966, they are actually for 1967. This also refers to data for the
United States: where national industrial structure data appear as that
for 1960, they represent data for 1959, and national labor force status
data, which appear as that for 1966 represent data for 1967.

Finally, data from the special tabulations prepared for this
study were used to calculate the educational attainment of the population in cities and will appear as those for 1966 instead of 1967, the
actual year of reference.

TABLE 1.1

City Unemployment Rates, 1960 and 1966
(percent)

City	1960	1966
New York	5.2	4.1
Chicago	5.4	4.3
Los Angeles	6.4	6.6
Philadelphia	6.5	4.4
Detroit	9.9	5.2
Baltimore	6.5	5.5
Houston	4.3	3.7
Cleveland	7.5	5.8
Minneapolis-St. Paul	4.3	2.6
Washington, D.C.	4.1	2.1
St. Louis	5.4	6.6
Milwaukee	4.6	4.0
San Francisco	6.7	6.3
Boston	5.0	3.5
Dallas	3.3	2.5
New Orleans	5.6	4.3
Pittsburg	8.1	5.2
San Antonio	5.2	2.0
San Diego	7.0	5.6
Seattle	6.1	2.6
Buffalo	8.5	6.4
Cincinnati	5.9	3.1
Memphis	4.6	4.0
Denver	3.6	3.5
Atlanta	3.6	3.8
Indianapolis	4.7	2.7
Kansas City	5.0	2.9
Columbus	5.4	2.0
Phoenix	4.7	3.3
Newark	8.2	10.2

Note: Unemployment rates are for cities and include the city of Long Beach with Los Angeles and the city of Oakland with San Francisco for both 1960 and 1966. In 1960 the unemployment rate for Kansas City includes the cities of Kansas City, Kansas, and Kansas City, Missouri, while in 1966 the unemployment rate includes only the city of Kansas City, Missouri. Unemployment rates for 1960 are for all persons aged fourteen and over, while data for 1966 are for all persons aged sixteen and over.

Source: 1960: Census Tracts, U.S. Bureau of the Census, U.S. Census of Population, Final Reports PCH (1)—8, 13, 18, 21, 26, 27, 28, 32, 34, 38, 40, 63, 64, 70, 82, 89, 92, 93, 103, 104, 105, 116, 117, 118, 131, 134, 136, 137, 142, and 166. 1966: Paul O. Flaim, "Jobless Trends in 20 Large Metropolitan Areas," Monthly Labor Review (U.S. Department of Labor, Bureau of Labor Statistics) Vol. XCI, No. 5 (May 1968); U.S. Department of Labor, Bureau of Labor Statistics, unpublished data supplied by the Bureau of Labor Statistics, 1968; and U.S. Bureau of the Census, special tabulations prepared by the Bureau of the Census, 1969, based on annual averages from the "Current Population Survey of 1967."

TABLE 1.2

Slum Area Unemployment Rates, 1960 and 1966
(percent)

City	1960	1966
Harlem	7.7	8.1
East Harlem	8.2	9.0
Brooklyn	7.0	6.2
Philadelphia	15.0	11.0
St. Louis	9.8	12.9
San Antonio	9.0	8.1
Phoenix	9.7	13.2
New Orleans	8.0	10.0
San Francisco	11.9	11.1
Boston	7.2	6.9
South Chicago	13.3	5.3
West Chicago	13.0	5.5
Cleveland	11.0	11.5
East Los Angeles	8.1	7.4
South Los Angeles	11.0	10.7
Oakland	13.1	13.0

Note: Unemployment rates are for the same geographic areas in 1960 and 1966, as defined by census tracts. The unemployment rates were recorded in the years as listed, except for Cleveland, which was recorded in April 1965; South and East Los Angeles, which were recorded in November 1965; and Oakland, which was recorded in May-August, 1966. All unemployment rates are for persons aged fourteen years and over.

Source: 1960: Census Tracts, U.S. Bureau of the Census, U.S. Census of Population, Final Reports PCH (1)—8, 13, 18, 21, 26, 27, 28, 32, 34, 38, 40, 63, 64, 70, 82, 89, 92, 93, 103, 104, 105, 116, 117, 118, 131, 134, 136, 137, 142, and 166; 1966: "Urban Employment Survey of 1966," unpublished data prepared by the U.S. Department of Labor, Bureau of Labor Statistics; "Characteristics of Selected Neighborhoods in Cleveland, Ohio: April 1965," U.S. Bureau of the Census, Current Population Reports, Series P-23, No. 21 (Washington, D.C., 1967); "Characteristics of the South and East Los Angeles Areas: November 1965," U.S. Bureau of the Census, Current Population Reports, Series P-23, No. 18 (Washington, D.C., 1966); and "Housing and Population, Tabulations From the 701 Household Survey of Oakland, Revised August 1968," University of California, Berkeley, Survey Research Center (Berkeley: University of California Press, 1968).

1960 and 1966, from 5.7 percent to 4.3 percent, while the national rate fell from 5.5 percent to 3.8 percent.

The cities that experienced the largest reductions in unemployment from 1960 to 1966 were primarily heavy manufacturing cities located in the Midwest; yet one of the few cities experiencing increased unemployment was St. Louis, Missouri, a manufacturing center.

A characteristic of the urban labor market that may account for differences among cities in unemployment rates is the variation in these cities in the nonwhite share of the labor force. Table 1-3 shows the percentage of the labor force in each of the thirty largest cities that was nonwhite in 1960 and 1966. A more direct measure of disequilibrium in the labor market than the percent of nonwhites in the labor force of a city in the unemployment rate among the nonwhite labor force and the ratio of the nonwhite rate to the white unemployment rate. (See Table 1-4.) No clear pattern emerges: cities that had the highest unemployment rates did not consistently have the highest nonwhite unemployment rates or the highest ratios of nonwhite to white employment.

The cities exhibited extremely wide variations in the ratio of the nonwhite to white unemployment rates (see Table 1-4) in both 1960 and 1966, with the variations widening in a period of full employment. Although direct comparisons may be somewhat inaccurate (because 1966 rates are for total white and nonwhites, while male rates were used in 1960 because total nonwhite rates were not available), it appears that nonwhites in most cities were worse off compared to whites in prosperous 1966 than in 1960's recession. Although nonwhite unemployment rates were lower in 1966 than in 1960, white rates declined even more.

The relative position of nonwhites worsened in twenty-one cities, with the greatest deterioration occurring in San Antonio, Pittsburgh, St. Louis, Cleveland, and Detroit. Apparently these cities, with the exception of San Antonio, dominated by heavy manufacturing sectors, had substantial white unemployment in the recession of 1960. During the recovery these skilled workers were quickly reabsorbed into factory production. The gains made by the nonwhites, most of them unskilled, were more modest, and the ratio therefore deteriorated. It may also be that more nonwhites had become discouraged and dropped out of the labor force in the recession of 1960 and then reentered in the boom of 1966, keeping nonwhite unemployment high relative to white.

Unemployment rates for nonwhites declined in all but five cities in our thirty-city sample, while four cities showed no appreciable improvement for nonwhites. In contrast, eight cities experienced at least a four-point decline in the nonwhite unemployment rate, marking substantial progress.

TABLE 1.3

Nonwhite Share of the Labor Force:
Cities, 1960 and 1966
(percent)

City	1960	1966	Percent Change
New York	14.5	16.5	13.8
Chicago	20.1	27.1	34.8
Los Angeles	15.4	19.1	24.0
Philadelphia	25.8	29.7	15.1
Detroit	25.7	33.7	31.1
Baltimore	32.4	46.7	44.1
Houston	23.0	26.9	17.0
Cleveland	26.9	35.8	33.1
Minneapolis-St. Paul	2.8	1.7	-39.3
Washington, D.C.	55.7	66.5	19.4
St. Louis	24.9	40.2	61.4
Milwaukee	7.4	13.0	75.7
San Francisco	18.7	31.2	66.8
Boston	9.5	15.8	66.3
Dallas	18.5	18.2	- 1.6
New Orleans	33.6	44.8	33.3
Pittsburgh	15.4	20.0	29.9
San Antonio	8.4	2.8	-66.7
San Diego	6.9	8.1	17.4
Seattle	8.0	16.2	102.5
Buffalo	12.0	15.7	30.8
Cincinnati	20.8	28.9	38.9
Memphis	33.5	32.0	- 4.5
Denver	6.8	12.4	82.4
Atlanta	35.3	40.1	13.6
Indianapolis	20.0	27.0	35.0
Kansas City	17.2	20.4	18.6
Columbus	15.9	21.3	34.0
Phoenix	5.1	9.1	78.4
Newark	32.5	43.9	35.1

Note: Unemployment rates are for cities and include the city of Long Beach with Los Angeles and the city of Oakland with San Francisco for both 1960 and 1966. In 1960 the unemployment rate for Kansas City includes the cities of Kansas City, Kansas, and Kansas City, Missouri, while in 1966 the unemployment rate includes only the city of Kansas City, Missouri. Unemployment rates for 1960 are for all persons aged fourteen and over, while data for 1966 are for all persons aged sixteen and over.

Source: 1960: Census Tracts, U.S. Bureau of the Census, U.S. Census of Population, Final Reports PCH (1)—8, 13, 18, 21, 26, 27, 28, 32, 34, 38, 40, 63, 64, 70, 82, 89, 92, 93, 103, 104, 105, 116, 117, 118, 131, 134, 136, 137, 142, and 166. 1966: Paul O. Flaim, "Jobless Trends in 20 Large Metropolitan Areas," Monthly Labor Review (U.S. Department of Labor, Bureau of Labor Statistics), Vol. XCI, No. 5 (May 1968); U.S. Department of Labor, Bureau of Labor Statistics, unpublished data supplied by the Bureau of Labor Statistics, 1968; and U.S. Bureau fo the Census, special tabulations prepared by the Bureau fo the Census, 1969, based on annual averages from the "Current Population Survey of 1967."

TABLE 1.4

Ratio of Nonwhite to White Unemployment Rates: Cities, 1960 and 1966
(percent)

| City | 1960 | | 1966 | |
	Male Nonwhite Unemployment Rate	Ratio of Male Nonwhite to Male White Unemployment Rate	Total Nonwhite Unemployment Rate*	Ratio of Total Nonwhite to Total White Unemployment Rate
New York	6.9	1.47	5.3	1.36
Chicago	10.8	2.82	8.2	2.83
Los Angeles	9.8	1.65	9.1	1.52
Philadelphia	11.1	2.22	7.5	2.42
Detroit	18.2	2.41	9.8	3.38
Baltimore	10.1	1.93	8.0	2.29
Houston	7.2	2.05	6.3	2.25
Cleveland	12.7	2.17	10.1	3.48
Minneapolis-St. Paul	9.2	1.85	—	—
Washington, D.C.	5.4	1.89	2.8	3.50
St. Louis	8.9	2.06	11.3	3.77
Milwaukee	11.6	2.85	7.8	2.17
San Francisco	9.7	1.85	9.6	1.96
Boston	7.9	1.41	6.2	2.21
Dallas	6.1	2.27	4.6	2.00
New Orleans	9.7	2.12	7.2	3.60
Pittsburgh	17.0	2.24	13.2	4.40
San Antonio	6.2	1.19	7.8	4.33
San Diego	10.4	1.60	4.3	0.75
Seattle	11.3	1.86	3.4	1.42
Buffalo	16.4	2.12	14.3	2.80
Cincinnati	11.6	2.48	5.7	2.59
Memphis	7.5	2.54	7.9	3.76
Denver	5.7	1.67	4.2	1.20
Atlanta	4.1	1.27	5.5	2.12
Indianapolis	7.6	2.02	3.5	1.46
Kansas City	9.1	1.86	4.7	1.96
Columbus	10.7	2.19	3.5	2.33
Phoenix	10.8	2.33	1.9	0.56
Newark	9.7	1.67	14.2	2.09

*Nonwhite unemployment rates for cities were only available for males in 1960.

Note: Unemployment rates are for cities and include the city of Long Beach with Los Angeles and the city of Oakland with San Francisco for both 1960 and 1966. In 1960 the unemployment rate for Kansas City includes the cities of Kansas City, Kansas, and Kansas City, Missouri, while in 1966 the unemployment rate includes only the city of Kansas City, Missouri. Unemployment rates for 1960 are for all persons aged fourteen and over, while data for 1966 are for all persons aged sixteen and over.

Source: 1960: Census Tracts, U.S. Bureau of the Census, U.S. Census of Population, Final Reports PCH (1)—8, 13, 18, 21, 26, 27, 28, 32, 34, 38, 40, 63, 64, 70, 82, 89, 92, 93, 103, 104, 105, 116, 117, 118, 131, 134, 136, 137, 142, and 166. 1966: Paul O. Flaim, "Jobless Trends in 20 Large Metropolitan Areas," Monthly Labor Review (U.S. Department of Labor, Bureau of Labor Statistics) Vol. XCI, No. 5 (May 1968); U.S. Department of Labor, Bureau of Labor Statistics, unpublished data supplied by the Bureau of Labor Statistics, 1968; and U.S. Bureau of the Census, special tabulations prepared by the Bureau of the Census, 1969, based on annual averages from the "Current Population Survey of 1967."

In summary, nonwhites have not had a substantial improvement
in their relative unemployment, despite enormous employment gains
nationwide. There were even greater variations in nonwhite unemployment rates among the cities in 1966 than in 1960. Nonwhite unemployment rates were considerably above the 4 percent full-employment
target in twenty-five of the thirty cities; one-third of the cities had
nonwhite rates more than double the national rate.

WHAT IS A LABOR MARKET?

The data used in the analysis come mainly from the census and
other government surveys. However, wherever possible we have concentrated on a much smaller geographical definition of the relevant
city labor market than is used in these surveys. For example, a great
deal of data on employment are collected by county or Standard Metropolitan Statistical Area (SMSA)* and not by city or region within a city.
The SMSA's are so varied and large that they are not the most useful
concept in analyzing employment and unemployment for members of
the urban labor force.

Traditional concepts of a labor market are usually confined to
geographical areas surrounding a major central business or industrial
district.[5] However, for purposes of analysis and policy making, it is
necessary to define the labor market operationally as "an area in
which a substantial majority of the working force has reasonable access
to places of work." "Reasonable access" should be interpreted in
terms of both transportation charges and costs in time, based on hourly
wages or some valuation of a workers' leisure after working a full
day. For example, a labor market could be defined as an area in which
a worker could reach and return from work in a period of time no
more than one-fourth of his work time and at a transportation cost of

---

*An SMSA includes at least "a) one city with 50,000 or more
inhabitants, or b) two cities having contiguous boundaries and consti-
tuting, for general and social purposes, a single community with a
combined population of at least 50,000, the smaller of which must
have a population of at least 15,000." Source: Standard Metropolitan
Statistical Areas, 1967, Executive Office of the President, Bureau of
the Budget (Washington, D.C., 1967), p. 1.

In addition, our definition of the Boston SMSA is larger than
the conventional one—the spatial distribution calculation used data
for entire counties rather than portions of counties.

no more than one-sixth of his net weekly wages. Knowledge of earnings, transit costs, and travel time required during rush hours would then permit us to map labor market areas for individuals residing in different locations in the central city. For different groups in the labor force of any given geographical area, the size of the labor market will vary according to the benefit/cost ratio of commuting. For example, some executives of large consulting firms and corporations commute daily from New York to Washington; many workers travel for more than one and one-half hours a day and at substantial cost from Long Island to mid- or lower Manhattan. Less skilled workers, earning substantially less, find the cost of reverse commuting prohibitive in relation to their earnings. As a result of cost-versus-earnings calculations, the geographical boundaries of the labor market will differ significantly for different sets of workers in the labor force. This notion is especially relevant in analyzing the reasons for urban unemployment and the differences in the rates of unemployment among cities and the slums of cities.

It has been alleged that the distribution of jobs has shifted away from the central cities to the suburban and exurban rings and, moreover, that the size of the labor force residing in older, dilapidated regions in the core of the city has increased. The result would be a serious mismatch between the location of employment opportunities and the residences of workers. The gap should be measured in terms of the cost to the slum resident of traveling to employment in outlying areas. As we have noted, the size of the labor market confronting an individual worker is in part a function of the cost of commuting between home and workplace measured against the compensation of the jobs. Following this reasoning the labor market—that is, the number of available unemployment opportunities—is much smaller for an unskilled, uneducated worker than for a worker who commands higher wages because of more skill and education.

Current data-collection efforts by the federal government provide information based primarily on SMSA's. Conventional views on regional economic development have continued to focus on the metropolitan area as a unit of analysis and policy. However, there are some serious limitations in using the SMSA data in considering policies for city residents, and particularly for slum residents of central cities.

Over the last fifteen years the trend has been for more and more jobs in the SMSA to be located outside the central city. If this trend continues, as is expected, the SMSA will become increasingly irrelevant as the standard unit of study for policy formulation of employment difficulties in the central city.

The inhabitant of the central city who wishes to work outside his environment is confronted with a two-dimensional predicament:

one of distance and one of time. The distance from the central city to
the boundary of the SMSA can be as great as 100 miles (as for New
York), although the average for our thirty cities was 50 miles. The
time variable is a function of the type of transportation (public or
private) available and the network of roads in the given area. Generally, a person who does not have access to private transportation
cannot afford the cost or time of traveling more than 40 miles to a
place of employment. Thus, the SMSA, although an adequate measure
when making long-run considerations of the economic development of
a labor market area, is not sufficient for the short-run problems of
the urban poor.

It is currently not possible to collect accurate data on employment trends in the thirty largest cities in the nation on an annual
basis. The closest approximation of the industrial structure in city
labor markets and the growth and changes in employment is provided
by the county data collected by the Census Bureau (through its periodic
survey of private employment).* Therefore, we have arbitrarily defined the relevant urban labor market as the county or counties containing the major city of our sample.** In some cases the county or
counties are coterminous with the city, as in the case of New York
City, composed of five counties. In most cases the county is larger
than the city, and the labor market is naturally somewhat larger and
less accessible for urban dwellers. In four instances, Philadelphia,
San Francisco, Cincinnati, and Kansas City, adjacent counties close
to the central city were added to the central city county to approximate

----

*The primary source of employment data utilized in this study
is County Business Patterns, published by the Bureau of the Census.
The data include the following types of employment covered by the
Social Security Program: (a) all covered wage and salary employment
of private nonfarm employers and of nonprofit membership organizations under compulsory coverage, and (b) all employment of religious,
charitable, educational, and other nonprofit organizations covered
under the elective provision of the Federal Insurance Contributions
Act. Data for the following types of employment covered in whole or
in part by the Social Security Program are excluded from the basic
tabulations of County Business Patterns: (a) government employees,
(b) self-employed persons, (c) farm workers, and (d) domestic service
workers (all reported separately). In 1966 approximately two-thirds
of paid civilian employment in the United States was included in the
scope of County Business Patterns.

**For complete (county) definitions of SMSA's, central city labor
markets, and suburban labor markets, see appendix.

the urban labor market. In short, the county data may overstate the employment opportunities and the size of the local labor market. However, they are clearly more relevant and useful than the more accurate and abundant data on SMSA's. In comparing the changes and growth of city and suburban employment, the county data serve as if they were the city employment structure and growth in the remaining portion of the SMSA serves as the reference for suburban growth.

METHODOLOGY AND LIMITATIONS

The research findings presented in the following chapters were based on two quite different techniques: multiple regression analysis and in-depth interviewing. The statistical analysis consisted of the development of a series of models representing clusters of factors believed to be associated with unemployment in the urban labor market. The three models are economic, industrial structure, and structural labor market barriers. Multiple regression analysis was employed to explain the differences in unemployment rates among the thirty cities and sixteen slum areas, as well as among nonwhites in the city and slum youth. The multiple regression analysis reveals the nature and significance of the relationship between selected independent variables and the unemployment rate, thereby providing a basis for the formulation of public policy.

However, there are several limitations in the nature of the data and the methodology that require caution regarding the findings. This is an exploratory study and was not designed to be definitive nor exhaustive in the examination of factors related to urban unemployment. The approach selected was broad, to account for all possible factors in examining unemployment, but lacked precision and depth. The data were crude because of the use of surrogate measures and the lack of reliable disaggregate data. Nevertheless, despite the quality of the data and the limited number of observations and the problems of multicollinearity in the multiple regression analysis, the findings are of value in determining new areas of research and guiding new policies and programs to solve the employment problems of urban dwellers.

Chapter 2 outlines various theories of urban labor markets and presents various labor market factors alleged to contribute to unemployment in the thirty cities in 1960 and 1966. Chapter 3 continues this examination, emphasizing factors related to the characteristics of the labor force. The focus then shifts away from the city and toward specific disadvantaged groups in the urban labor force. Chapter 4 examines the operation and impact of the labor market on residents of the sixteen urban slums in 1960 and 1966. Chapter 5 examines the experiences of youth in these slums during 1966. The statistical analysis of factors contributing to slum youth unemployment is supplemented by interviews of Harlem youth, presented in Chapter 6. Chapter 7 summarizes the major findings, and Chapter 8 discusses the policy questions they raise for federal, state, and local governments concerned with urban unemployment.

2

ECONOMIC FACTORS
IN URBAN UNEMPLOYMENT

Current orthodoxy provides a long list of factors and policies that supposedly cause or can solve the unemployment problem of cities, slums, and particularly the minority groups of the cities. In the early 1960's many economists and government officials believed that rapid economic growth of the country as a whole would be sufficient to provide employment opportunities for all Americans, regardless of their race or ethnicity, education, skills, and location. This opinion is less popular today, but it still has adherents. Other social scientists and government policy makers in the early 1960's adhered to the view that various "structural" barriers—for example, a mismatch between the requirements of jobs and the qualifications of workers, labor immobility, and accelerating technological unemployment—impeded the operation of the labor market and that increasing the aggregate demand would only aggravate the problem by causing prices to rise.

The policies and legislation of the early 1960's reflected both views. As time passed and the unemployment rates of cities and slums did not decline significantly, particularly among blacks, Puerto Ricans, and Mexican-Americans, new theories were advanced to explain and resolve the urban unemployment problem. The educational deficiencies of the labor force were seen as a major causal factor. Racial discrimination, poor health practices, and the availability of income from illegal sources or from welfare were also cited. The growth of suburbs and the dispersion of jobs throughout the new industrial parks of suburban America, away from cities, were also believed to be a cause of urban unemployment.

The current view is that for these and other reasons, unemployment is concentrated in cities, and especially among nonwhite slum residents, and that the plight of the poor is deteriorating, despite national economic growth and prosperity.

Although our findings give partial support to this pessimistic view, they also reveal that it is greatly exaggerated. We have seen that the unemployment rates varied considerably among our sample cities; many cities had extremely tight labor markets, with unemployment rates well below the national average; moreover, nonwhites in some cities had unemployment rates even lower than the national rate. Then, too, some cities improved substantially between 1960 and 1966, although others experienced a significant increase in unemployment rates. Finally, data for 1970 show that, nationally, black unemployment rates have declined over the decade and that blacks have made significant occupational advances.[1] The experience of the most disadvantaged members of the city's labor force, the slum residents, also indicates considerable variation. Nonwhites in most slums, particularly youngsters, had extremely high unemployment when compared with that of nonwhites nationally.

In view of these variations, can we say that major central cities in the United States face similar employment problems? Do slum or ghetto areas within these major cities have the same employment problems as the cities of which they are part, and are the employment problems of slums in all major cities similar? If so, why are the unemployment rates of cities significantly different from each other, and why do slums have much higher unemployment rates than the cities? And why is there such a significant variation in unemployment rates among the slums and ghettos of our major cities? The answers to these and other vital questions depend on an analysis of the labor markets of cities.

Cities may be losing or changing their economic functions. Advances in transportation, communication, commutation patterns, and technology have lessened the need for large concentrations of business firms in small physical areas. Natural resource bases are less important in the manufacturing, processing, and development of final goods; rivers and oceans are less important as transportation facilities. Personal contact can be achieved by a vast telephonic communications network; new highway and airway systems have opened up new lands for the location of businesses; and people seeking quasi-rural life styles are willing to work and live outside the excitement of the urban centers.

The economic foundations of the cities have been weakened by the growth of the suburbs. Many observers, impressed by the increase in employment in the suburbs surrounding our major cities, believe that the suburbs are attracting employers away from the cities and that the cities are doomed to defeat in the competition for jobs. The cities are unable to provide employment to the labor supply housed within their political borders. Tax revenues are not keeping pace with the rising demands for municipal services. The cities cannot cope with the increases in labor supply generated by natural population growth and accelerated by a large influx of uneducated, unskilled, rural migrants of varied background.

However, whether the growth of the suburban labor market has taken place at the expense of the city labor market is not clear. Moreover, even if the answer is affirmative, it is not clear that such a change necessarily contributes to the decay of the city. That is, the growth of suburbia does not necessarily mean a rapid increase in poverty and unemployment in the central city.

Before analyzing the impact of job dispersal on unemployment in the city or on specific groups of the labor force, such as nonwhites, slum residents, and youth, it is essential to examine the industrial structure of the urban labor market and the changes that have occurred during the past decade.

THE INDUSTRIAL STRUCTURE
OF URBAN LABOR MARKETS

The vast differences in the employment patterns of our sample cities reveal fundamental differences in their basic economic structure and functions, as well as in the historical forces influencing these metropolises.

Table 2.1 shows the national distribution of employment among eight industrial categories in 1951, 1962, and 1966. The domination of manufacturing employment over the industrial structure of the economy is clear in all three time periods, despite the slow decline from 1951 to 1966 in the percentage of jobs in the manufacturing sector. The share of retail employment has been the second largest consistently, and it decreased slightly from 1951 to 1966. The fastest growing sector, both in absolute numbers and relative percentage, is services, which now rivals retail for second place.

The proportion of total employment increased in the finance, insurance, and real estate sector and in the wholesale and transportation and public utilities sectors. It decreased in mining. The share of contract construction remained remarkably stable over a fifteen-year period of rapid economic growth.

Table 2.2 shows the industrial mix for our thirty cities for 1960 and 1966.* We see that the labor markets vary widely in the share of

---

*For a list of the counties containing the labor market of each city, see appendix. The addition of all sectors does not total 100 percent due to the omission of the agriculture and mining sectors and a small unclassified category.

TABLE 2.1

The National Economy: Industrial Mix and Percentage
Change in Employment, 1951, 1962, and 1966

(a)
Absolute Employment

Industry and Total Employment	1951	1962	1966
Total Employment	37,496,261	44,155,952	50,265,688
Mining	903,812	902,983	602,522
Contract Construction	2,357,646	3,205,228	3,054,375
Manufacturing	16,127,040	16,413,787	18,772,021
Transportation and Public Utilities	2,670,134	3,010,632	3,364,539
Wholesale Trade	2,768,312	3,239,698	3,593,445
Retail Trade	7,265,708	8,045,023	9,448,976
Finance, Insurance, and Real Estate	1,898,692	2,723,335	3,109,652
Services	3,504,917	6,615,266	8,320,158

(b)
Industrial Mix
(percent)

Industry	1951	1962	1966
Mining	2.41	2.04	1.19
Contract Construction	6.28	7.25	6.07
Manufacturing	43.00	37.17	37.34
Transportation and Public Utilities	7.12	6.81	6.69
Wholesale Trade	7.38	7.33	7.14
Retail Trade	19.37	18.21	18.79
Finance, Insurance, and Real Estate	5.06	6.16	6.18
Services	9.34	14.98	16.55

(c)
Percentage Change in Employment

Industry and Total Employment	1951-62	1951-66	1962-66
Total Employment	+17.76	+ 34.05	+13.83
Mining	- 0.09	- 33.33	-33.27
Contract Construction	+35.95	+ 29.55	- 4.70
Manufacturing	+ 1.77	+ 16.40	+14.36
Transportation and Public Utilities	+12.75	+ 26.00	+11.75
Wholesale Trade	+17.02	+ 29.80	+10.91
Retail Trade	+10.72	+ 30.04	+17.45
Finance, Insurance, and Real Estate	+43.41	+ 63.77	+14.18
Services	+88.74	+137.38	+25.77

Source: 1951: County Business Patterns, U.S. Bureau of the Census and
Bureau of Old Age and Survivors Insurance, cooperative report, First Quarter,
1951, Part 1 (Washington, D.C., 1953); 1962: County Business Patterns, U.S.
Bureau of the Census, First Quarter, 1962, Part I (Washington, D.C., 1963);
1966: County Business Patterns, U.S. Bureau of the Census, CBP-66-1
(Washington, D.C., 1967).

TABLE 2.2

Industrial Mix: Cities, 1960 and 1966
(percent)

(a)
1960

City	Contract Construc-tion	Manufac-turing	Transpor-tation and Public Utilities	Whole-sale	Retail	Finance, Insurance, and Real Estate	Services
New York	3.7	30.9	8.5	10.7	14.2	12.7	18.2
Chicago	4.3	41.2	7.7	9.1	15.5	7.3	14.4
Los Angeles	6.1	39.3	6.4	7.4	16.7	5.8	17.0
Philadelphia	4.4	41.2	7.2	8.9	15.9	7.0	14.9
Detroit	3.6	48.2	6.6	7.1	15.8	5.2	13.2
Baltimore	6.0	31.4	11.6	8.1	19.6	7.8	14.9
Houston	8.6	25.9	10.5	10.9	18.8	6.4	14.2
Cleveland	4.1	47.8	5.9	8.2	14.9	5.0	13.6
Minneapolis-St. Paul	5.6	31.6	8.2	11.1	19.0	7.9	16.1
Washington, D.C.	8.1	8.6	9.5	7.5	24.1	10.9	30.2
St. Louis	4.0	39.5	7.2	10.9	15.2	7.0	15.8
Milwaukee	4.4	50.2	4.9	7.0	16.1	5.4	11.8
San Francisco	6.8	24.6	11.7	11.9	17.2	9.9	17.1
Boston	3.4	23.2	11.3	10.9	17.2	13.3	20.1
Dallas	7.6	30.4	7.6	11.2	18.1	9.1	13.4
New Orleans	7.4	16.0	14.4	12.4	20.5	8.3	18.5
Pittsburgh	5.3	40.6	7.0	8.8	16.3	5.7	15.4
San Antonio	9.8	17.1	6.1	10.7	27.3	8.5	19.0
San Diego	9.2	37.7	5.8	5.1	19.7	5.3	15.5
Seattle	5.7	40.2	7.1	9.7	16.3	6.5	13.3
Buffalo	4.7	44.5	7.3	7.5	18.3	4.6	12.8
Cincinnati	4.4	45.8	6.6	7.8	1.68	5.6	12.5
Memphis	7.1	28.4	7.2	13.2	20.8	6.1	16.6
Denver	6.9	20.4	11.3	12.5	19.3	9.1	18.9
Atlanta	5.8	24.6	11.0	13.5	19.6	9.2	15.3
Indianapolis	4.8	40.8	6.6	8.5	18.9	7.8	12.0
Kansas City	5.8	33.2	9.9	10.6	17.7	7.3	14.6
Columbus	6.1	36.1	6.5	7.8	20.3	7.3	15.3
Phoenix	11.9	22.9	7.7	9.3	21.7	8.2	17.3
Newark	3.6	40.3	9.2	7.4	15.0	10.1	14.0

(Continued)

TABLE 2.2 Contd.

(b)
1966

City	Contract Construc- tion	Manufac- turing	Transpor- tation and Public Utilities	Whole- sale	Retail	Finance, Insurance, and Real Estate	Services
New York	3.3	28.8	9.7	10.1	13.8	12.5	21.4
Chicago	4.2	39.8	7.1	9.0	16.0	7.1	16.5
Los Angeles	5.2	35.9	6.8	7.6	17.4	6.5	19.6
Philadelphia	4.6	37.9	7.4	8.2	15.6	7.5	18.6
Detroit	4.3	45.4	6.3	6.8	15.7	5.5	15.7
Baltimore	5.9	31.0	9.6	8.3	17.8	8.4	18.8
Houston	11.6	23.8	9.9	9.9	17.4	6.2	17.1
Cleveland	4.7	43.5	6.3	8.0	15.6	5.5	16.2
Minneapolis-St. Paul	5.2	32.2	7.2	9.4	19.0	8.0	18.6
Washington, D.C.	7.7	7.8	8.9	7.0	20.9	11.3	35.9
St. Louis	4.8	37.3	8.4	9.7	13.5	7.4	18.7
Milwaukee	4.5	46.9	4.9	6.4	16.7	5.8	14.7
San Francisco	6.7	22.2	11.6	10.5	17.1	11.3	20.0
Boston	4.2	21.0	9.6	9.5	16.5	13.6	25.3
Dallas	6.9	28.9	8.1	11.1	17.9	9.6	15.7
New Orleans	9.0	17.0	15.2	9.9	17.5	7.8	20.4
Pittsburgh	5.8	37.6	6.5	7.4	17.6	5.9	18.5
San Antonio	9.6	17.0	5.4	9.4	25.8	8.9	22.6
San Diego	6.6	26.7	7.3	5.4	24.2	6.5	21.6
Seattle	6.1	37.7	7.5	8.4	16.6	7.0	15.9
Buffalo	4.2	43.2	6.4	6.7	18.6	5.1	15.5
Cincinnati	4.6	42.0	6.5	7.9	16.4	6.0	16.1
Memphis	7.7	27.6	7.0	12.2	19.2	7.3	18.3
Denver	6.3	19.0	11.0	11.6	19.6	9.3	21.4
Atlanta	7.8	21.3	11.3	13.8	17.6	9.9	17.6
Indianapolis	6.2	40.5	6.2	8.7	16.3	7.9	13.8
Kansas City	5.6	31.8	9.4	10.2	18.7	7.6	16.2
Columbus	5.8	33.7	6.3	7.6	20.9	7.7	17.4
Phoenix	7.5	28.1	6.7	7.4	21.6	7.8	19.8
Newark	4.5	35.7	9.8	7.5	15.1	10.3	16.7

Source: 1960: County Business Patterns, U.S. Bureau of the Census and U.S. Bureau of Old Age and Survivors Insurance, cooperative report First Quarter, 1959, Parts 2, 3, 4, 5, 6, 7, 8, 9, and 10 (Washington, D.C., 1961); 1966: County Business Patterns, U.S. Bureau of the Census, CBP-66, 4, 5, 6, 7, 10, 12, 15, 16, 18, 19, 22, 23, 24, 25, 27, 32, 34, 37, 40, 44, 45, 49, and 51 (Washington, D.C., 1967).

the manufacturing sector, from a low of 7.8 percent in Washington, D.C., in 1966 to a high of 46.9 percent in Milwaukee. Moreover, no discernible pattern emerges. Some western cities, such as San Francisco, have very low concentrations of manufacturing employment, while others, such as Seattle, have more than the national share. Even cities of similar age, size, and historic function—e.g., the old eastern seaboard cities of Boston, New York, Philadelphia, and Baltimore— vary considerably in employment patterns. For example, Boston had only 21.0 percent of its labor force engaged in manufacturing employment in 1966, while Philadelphia had 37.9 percent. The only tentative pattern that emerges with respect to the share of manufacturing employment in cities is that midwestern cities tended to approximate the national figure, ranging from 32.2 percent to 46.9 percent in 1966, whereas southern cities, including those in Texas, had shares in manufacturing considerably below the national average.

The cities did not vary so much in the second largest sector of employment, retail, as in manufacturing. St. Louis had the lowest share of retail employment in 1966, with 13.5 percent, while the greatest concentration of retail employment was found in San Antonio, with 25.8 percent. Most of the cities had a smaller concentration of retail employment than the national share.

The third largest sector, services, tended to follow a similar pattern, in that the variations among cities were not large and the cities resembled the nation in the share of employment in the service sector. The one major exception, Washington, D.C., had a share double the national rate, 35.9 percent, because of professional and personal services associated with the functioning of the federal government and the concentration of educational institutions. Boston had the second largest share of services (25.3 percent). San Antonio, San Francisco, New York, New Orleans, San Diego, and Denver had shares between 20 percent and 25 percent. Chicago, Detroit, Dallas, Indianapolis, and Milwaukee had the lowest service sector shares, around 15 percent. In neither services nor the retail sector was there a systematic pattern based on age, size, or location of the city.

Most of the cities in the sample had a larger share of wholesale employment than the national share. The ranges were not large, from San Diego, with a share of 5.4 percent, the only one below the national share, to Atlanta, with a high of 13.8 percent.

City labor markets also tended to have a larger share of finance, insurance, and real estate than the national share. The leading cities in this respect were Boston, San Francisco, New York, Washington, D.C., and Newark, all with more than twice the proportion of jobs in this sector than the national shares.

In contract construction the variations were larger than expected, with New York City having the smallest share, well below the national

average, and Houston the largest. Except for Houston and Washington,
D.C., the nation's ten largest cities had shares of contract construction
below the national share. Southern and southwestern cities had shares
of contract construction well above the national average. This obviously
reflects the rapid growth and development of these cities compared to
the older eastern and midwestern cities.

The largest shares of transportation and public utilities are
found in New Orleans, San Francisco, Denver, Atlanta, Newark, and
Houston.

Economic Growth and Changes in
the Industrial Structure of Cities

Mining was the only sector in the national economy that experienced a decline in absolute employment between 1951-62 and
1951-66. (See Table 2-1.) The largest absolute increases in employment from 1951 to 1966 were in services, manufacturing, and
retail. The largest percentage increases were registered in services,
retail trade, and finance, insurance, and real estate.

A more significant change occurred in the percentage share of
national employment in each sector. Manufacturing was still by far
the largest employer in 1966, but its relative share had declined substantially from 1951 to 1962 and remained stable between 1962 and
1966. Since manufacturing is more cyclically vulnerable than other
sectors, and given the tight labor market in 1951 and the recessed
economy of 1962, the decline in the share of manufacturing employment is not surprising. However, the fact that the share was unchanged in a period of rapid growth of the economy indicates that there
was a structural shift in employment patterns over the past fifteen
years.

From 1951 to 1966 (see Table 2-3), employment in the manufacturing sector decreased in twelve of the thirty cities—New York,
Chicago, Philadelphia, St. Louis, Boston, Pittsburgh, Cleveland, Detroit, Milwaukee, Buffalo, Newark, and Baltimore. These cities have
three salient characteristics in common: (a) they are all older, established urban centers, (b) they are fairly heavily industrialized, and
(c) most are east of the Mississippi River and north of the Mason-
Dixon line. The limited availability of areas for expansion within the
cities, the high cost of land and space for manufacturing sectors, and
the development of miles of new superhighways throughout the northeast contributed to the exodus of manufacturing from these cities into
the suburbs. In the suburban ring (that is, the SMSA less the central
city county or counties) of every city except Pittsburgh, Buffalo, and
Cincinnati, the change in manufacturing employment was upward and

TABLE 2.3

Percentage Change in Employment by Industrial Classification:
Cities and Suburban Rings, 1951-66
(percent)

City	Contract Con-struction	Manufac-turing	Transpor-tation and Public Utilities	Whole-sale	Retail	Finance, Insurance, and Real Estate	Services	Total Employment
New York	-14.8	-15.1	20.0	-3.7	-7.6	23.7	76.3	6.0
Suburban Ring	58.8	110.6	54.7	237.5	144.1	198.1	345.7	142.1
Chicago	21.6	-1.1	27.9	29.2	14.9	31.9	92.8	18.4
Suburban Ring	96.2	79.2	133.4	157.4	71.6	158.8	308.2	97.6
Los Angeles	6.3	63.2	75.0	72.8	55.6	102.6	142.5	69.8
Philadelphia	-10.0	-18.2	-12.7	2.2	-1.9	23.5	128.2	1.6
Suburban Ring	47.6	35.7	82.6	268.9	110.4	134.7	312.0	75.7
Detroit	1.4	-31.3	114.6	25.6	-2.5	51.5	88.1	-9.1
Suburban Ring	176.5	139.6	100.0	277.0	180.0	262.4	402.1	169.1
Baltimore	-23.7	-12.4	-16.9	19.3	-6.9	35.3	129.0	4.9
Suburban Ring	184.6	40.6	369.8	454.6	335.4	334.1	509.8	116.5
Houston	60.0	58.7	80.1	58.1	55.1	141.2	196.6	74.5
Suburban Ring	149.5	23.2	139.7	147.5	34.6	172.7	129.1	56.7
Cleveland	15.0	-6.8	22.3	16.2	16.0	66.5	116.5	14.6
Suburban Ring	157.7	63.6	234.6	210.3	85.6	148.3	321.0	92.5
Minneapolis-St. Paul	19.1	36.9	30.0	24.1	28.9	73.5	171.9	48.0
Suburban Ring	240.4	45.2	94.6	22.0	136.8	187.7	486.6	86.4
Washington, D.C.	-3.0	37.4	27.8	14.9	-15.1	42.4	133.7	32.7
Suburban Ring	186.1	303.2	185.2	788.7	270.8	359.9	614.8	307.6
St. Louis	5.9	-26.5	6.0	-22.3	-34.6	12.1	79.5	-12.0
Suburban Ring	151.4	67.6	68.4	258.5	127.6	214.4	343.3	110.4
Milwaukee	6.4	-6.0	10.3	22.1	22.3	53.0	131.2	13.9
Suburban Ring	307.1	106.9	223.2	292.2	123.1	217.6	173.4	137.3
San Francisco	-5.6	4.3	12.5	5.8	2.3	62.5	75.9	18.2
Suburban Ring	68.0	59.9	233.6	505.4	132.0	222.9	269.7	126.4
Boston	12.4	-24.4	5.9	-18.2	-17.5	43.3	124.7	7.0
Suburban Ring	55.0	21.3	36.0	152.2	66.5	99.3	310.3	59.0
Dallas	19.6	116.4	45.2	58.9	68.0	119.3	161.5	78.8
Suburban Ring	61.5	90.5	34.1	61.8	24.9	106.7	121.4	64.6
New Orleans	37.3	1.9	1.7	20.8	0.9	61.1	115.8	26.8
Suburban Ring	504.5	63.7	321.9	237.3	363.7	798.2	439.6	218.0

(Continued)

25

TABLE 2.3 Contd.

City	Contract Con- struction	Manufac- turing	Transpor- tation and Public Utilities	Whole- sale	Retail	Finance, Insurance, and Real Estate	Services	Total Employment
Pittsburgh	6.9	-17.8	87.0	10.0	3.9	36.9	120.8	3.0
Suburban Ring	57.8	-12.7	48.4	117.9	16.3	71.5	95.4	-0.5
San Antonio	10.4	45.3	11.9	34.6	32.7	112.2	109.2	44.9
Suburban Ring	9.5	37.1	99.7	58.2	34.7	114.0	150.8	96.9
San Diego	17.5	47.6	174.3	75.5	73.5	193.7	195.6	84.1
Seattle	42.0	90.6	23.5	36.0	34.6	73.6	121.7	64.3
Suburban Ring	244.8	26.3	100.5	157.2	65.1	203.9	194.2	73.5
Buffalo	-4.0	-5.9	7.5	18.4	18.2	55.2	136.6	14.1
Suburban Ring	-0.8	-22.3	34.3	39.0	10.2	48.5	182.0	-7.3
Cincinnati	16.6	1.2	26.9	18.7	10.0	44.3	110.3	18.4
Suburban Ring	41.4	-8.6	68.2	104.9	59.3	114.8	165.5	31.2
Memphis	38.1	27.1	37.4	43.0	23.7	101.9	119.7	45.0
Suburban Ring	250.5	151.9	-38.0	81.8	57.2	164.3	270.7	90.6
Denver	-1.5	11.3	45.0	40.4	17.1	97.3	151.9	42.4
Suburban Ring	438.3	703.6	65.2	818.2	370.8	494.1	834.6	488.3
Atlanta	40.9	23.9	71.0	66.3	34.7	133.4	144.4	61.7
Suburban Ring	220.5	364.1	314.7	1177.9	252.5	612.1	436.7	336.6
Indianapolis	58.0	6.1	-2.4	45.6	10.9	82.9	103.8	23.9
Suburban Ring	70.2	34.9	59.2	13.4	84.8	132.9	119.9	60.5
Kansas City	24.4	22.6	47.5	32.0	14.7	51.3	97.4	33.7
Suburban Ring	177.2	827.8	208.5	538.2	278.9	478.1	590.0	377.3
Columbus	31.2	26.9	48.7	49.9	51.6	57.1	162.1	51.3
Suburban Ring	60.9	184.6	55.6	63.6	21.7	104.8	322.0	113.7
Phoenix	73.0	422.8	128.1	140.9	243.6	265.9	306.9	209.4
Newark	4.6	-21.7	24.2	18.0	2.7	17.4	105.6	4.0
Suburban Ring	59.2	42.4	73.5	301.9	73.1	137.2	133.8	68.4

Source: 1951: County Business Patterns, U.S. Bureau of the Census and U.S. Bureau of Old Age and Survivors Insurance, cooperative report, First Quarter, 1951, Parts 2, 3, 4, 5, 6, 7, 8, 9, and 10 (Washington, D.C., 1953); 1966: County Business Patterns, U.S. Bureau of the Census, CBP-66, 4, 5, 6, 7, 10, 12, 15, 16, 18, 19, 22, 23, 24, 25, 27, 32, 34, 37, 40, 44, 45, 49, and 51 (Washington, D.C., 1967).

substantial. The largest increases were registered in the suburban rings of Washington, D.C., Detroit, and New York City.

In contrast to the older northeastern cities, the western and southern cities had substantial increases in manufacturing employment between 1951 and 1966. Phoenix experienced an increase of 422.8 percent in manufacturing employment. Kansas City had an increase in the central city (22.6 percent) but a much larger increase in the suburban ring (827.8 percent). Cincinnati was the only city to have an increase in manufacturing employment in the city but a decrease in the suburban ring. Dallas, Phoenix, Seattle, and Los Angeles had large increases in manufacturing employment in the central city, but the Phoenix, San Diego, and Los Angeles central city county and SMSA boundaries are coterminous, so their employment increases may not reflect true central city growth. Phoenix, San Diego, and Dallas were the fastest growing cities in the United States between 1951 and 1966, as measured by change in employment, with gains of 209.4 percent, 84.1 percent, and 78.8 percent, respectively.

All of the cities, except St. Louis and Detroit, experienced overall increases in employment, as did all the suburban rings, except those of Buffalo and Pittsburgh. Suburban rings experienced substantially greater increases than central cities, except for Pittsburgh and Buffalo and such southwestern cities as Dallas and Houston.

The service sector experienced the largest increases for both central cities and suburban rings, followed by finance, insurance, and real estate. Contract construction experienced a modest increase in employment, except in New York, Philadelphia, Baltimore, and Washington, D.C. Every city in the study, except Philadelphia and Baltimore, had an increase in the transportation and public utility sector.

The smallest employment gains for most cities were registered in the wholesale and retail sectors. Boston, New York, Philadelphia, Washington, D.C., Baltimore, St. Louis, and Detroit were the cities that experienced decreases in the retail sector, and New York, Boston, and St. Louis had decreases in wholesale as well. The suburbanization of American cities and the decline of the central business district can be seen in the enormous increase in retail employment registered in the suburban rings. The largest such increase between 1951 and 1966 occurred in the suburban ring of Denver (370.8 percent). Even better illustrations are Baltimore and Washington, D.C., where the retail sector in the central city had decreases in employment of 6.9 percent and 15.1 percent, respectively, while the suburban rings had increases of 335.4 percent and 270.8 percent, respectively.

Changes in Industrial Mix

Between 1960 and 1966 the manufacturing share of employment has decreased considerably. (See Table 2-4.) Only three cities experienced an increase: Minneapolis-St. Paul, New Orleans, and Phoenix. San Diego had the largest decreases in share (29.2 percent).

In the contract-construction sector fifteen cities experienced a decrease and the rest experienced advances. The largest increase occurred in Houston (34.9 percent); the largest decrease was in Phoenix (37.0 percent).

In the share of employment in transportation, there were decreases in eighteen cities, especially Baltimore (17.2 percent), Boston (15.0 percent), and Phoenix (13.0 percent). The largest increases in this sector occurred in San Diego (25.9 percent) and St. Louis (16.7 percent). Again, no discernible pattern seems to emerge based on location, age, or size of the cities.

The wholesale sector experienced substantial declines in the share of employment in most cities. In the exceptions, Los Angeles, Baltimore, San Diego, Cincinnati, Atlanta, Indianapolis, and Newark, the gains were quite negligible—around 2 percent. The retail sector's share of employment remained fairly stable during the six years, with only New Orleans experiencing a substantial decline.

The finance, insurance, and real estate sector had a slight increase in its share of total employment in every city except New York, Chicago, Houston, New Orleans, and Phoenix, where the decreases were negligible.

The service sector experienced the largest increases in its share of employment, and all thirty cities had increases.

CYCLICAL FACTORS IN UNEMPLOYMENT

The stability of the local labor market is determined in part by the structure of the local economy. Cyclical forces affecting the national economy tend to affect different industries with different degrees of severity. Industries thus differ considerably in their sensitivity to business fluctuations and in the severity of unemployment among the workers attached to them. Given the large variations in industrial structure among the local labor markets of the thirty largest cities, we can expect to find greater or lesser stability. Table 2-5 shows for the nation the number of workers with some unemployment in various industries for the year 1964, a representative year for the period studied. As expected, unemployment varied widely by industry, from a low of 10.2 percent of all workers in finance, insurance, and real estate to a high rate of 36.1 percent in contract construction.

TABLE 2.4

Percentage Change in Industrial Mix: Cities, 1960-66

City	Contract Construction	Manufacturing	Transportation and Public Utilities	Wholesale	Retail	Finance, Insurance, and Real Estate	Services
New York	-10.8	-6.8	14.1	-5.6	-2.8	-1.6	17.6
Chicago	-2.3	-3.4	-7.8	-1.1	3.2	-2.7	14.6
Los Angeles	-14.8	-8.7	6.3	2.7	4.2	12.1	15.3
Philadelphia	4.5	-8.0	2.8	-7.9	-1.9	7.1	24.8
Detroit	19.4	-5.8	-4.5	-4.2	-0.6	5.8	18.9
Baltimore	-1.7	-1.3	-17.2	2.5	-9.2	7.7	26.2
Houston	34.9	-8.1	-5.7	-9.2	-7.4	-3.1	20.4
Cleveland	14.6	-9.0	6.8	-2.4	4.7	10.0	19.1
Minneapolis-St. Paul	-7.1	1.9	-12.2	-15.3	0	1.3	15.5
Washington, D.C.	-4.9	-9.3	-6.3	-6.7	-13.3	3.7	18.9
St. Louis	20.0	-5.6	16.7	-11.0	-11.2	5.7	18.4
Milwaukee	2.3	-6.6	0.0	-8.6	3.7	7.4	24.6
San Francisco	-1.5	-9.8	-0.9	-11.8	-0.6	14.1	17.0
Boston	23.5	-9.5	-15.0	-12.8	-4.1	2.3	25.9
Dallas	-9.2	-4.9	6.6	-0.9	-1.1	5.5	17.2
New Orleans	21.6	6.3	5.6	-20.2	-14.6	-6.0	10.3
Pittsburgh	9.4	-7.4	-7.1	-15.9	8.0	3.5	20.1
San Antonio	-2.0	-0.6	-11.5	-12.1	-5.5	4.7	18.9
San Diego	-28.3	-29.2	25.9	5.9	22.8	22.6	39.4
Seattle	7.0	-6.2	5.6	-13.4	1.8	7.7	19.5
Buffalo	-10.6	-2.9	-12.3	-10.7	1.6	10.9	21.1
Cincinnati	4.5	-8.3	-1.5	1.3	-2.4	7.1	28.8
Memphis	8.5	-2.8	-2.8	-7.6	-7.7	19.7	10.2
Denver	-8.7	-6.9	-2.7	-7.2	1.6	2.2	13.2
Atlanta	34.5	-13.4	2.7	2.2	-10.2	7.6	15.0
Indianapolis	29.2	-0.7	-6.1	2.4	-13.8	1.3	15.0
Kansas City	-3.4	-4.2	-5.1	-3.8	5.6	4.1	11.0
Columbus	-4.9	-6.6	-3.1	-2.6	3.0	5.5	13.7
Phoenix	-37.0	22.7	-13.0	-20.4	-0.5	-4.9	14.5
Newark	25.0	-11.4	6.5	1.4	0.7	2.0	19.3

Source: 1960: County Business Patterns, U.S. Bureau of the Census, U.S. Bureau of Old Age and Survivors Insurance, cooperative report, First Quarter, 1959, Parts 2, 3, 4, 5, 6, 7, 8, 9, and 10 (Washington, D.C., 1961); 1966: County Business Patterns, U.S. Bureau of the Census, CBP-66, 4, 5, 6, 7, 10, 12, 15, 16, 18, 19, 22, 23, 24, 25, 27, 32, 34, 37, 40, 44, 45, 49, and 51 (Washington, D.C., 1967).

TABLE 2.5

Unemployment by Industry, 1964

Industry	Total Wage and Salary Workers (thousands)	Number of Workers with Unemployment (thousands)	Percent Total Workers
Agriculture	2,695	589	21.9
Mining	587	112	19.1
Contract Construction	4,501	1,624	36.1
Manufacturing	20,364	3,739	18.4
Transportation	4,843	593	12.2
Wholesale	2,388	291	12.2
Retail	11,624	1,984	17.1
Finance, Insurance and Real Estate	3,331	340	10.2
Services	18,541	2,297	12.4

Source: Samuel Saben, "Work Experience of the Population of 1964," Special Labor Force Report No. 62 (Washington, D.C., 1966), Table C-2.

We can assume, then, that cities in which the contract-construction, manufacturing, or retail sectors of the local labor market dominate are likely to have relatively less employment stability. (In 1966 the national share of employment in these three most unstable employment sectors was over 60 percent.) Cities with employment concentration in these three sectors in excess of the national share were Detroit, Cleveland, Milwaukee, Buffalo, Cincinnati, and Indianapolis. The two cities that most closely resembled the nation in employment shares in these sectors were Columbus and Pittsburgh. This fact illustrates the tremendous diversity of American cities and the complexity of the forces determining the local industrial structure. The absence of any discernible pattern in this tremendous variation is the most significant feature of the data.

Given the variation in unemployment by industry, it seems reasonable to expect that the industrial structure of cities should explain a significant amount of their differences in unemployment rates. The larger the proportion of jobs in the unstable, high-unemployment sectors, such as construction and manufacturing, the higher the unemployment rate in the local labor market. Table 2-6 depicts the

TABLE 2.6

Cyclical Industrial Mix: Cities, 1960 and 1966

City	1960	1966
New York	48.78	45.86
Chicago	60.97	59.96
Los Angeles	62.06	58.53
Philadelphia	61.42	58.05
Detroit	67.51	65.44
Baltimore	56.99	54.73
Houston	53.31	52.70
Cleveland	66.67	63.75
Minneapolis-St. Paul	56.18	56.41
Washington, D.C.,	40.83	36.36
St. Louis	58.63	55.54
Milwaukee	70.69	68.05
San Francisco	48.63	46.02
Boston	43.88	41.73
Dallas	56.03	53.70
New Orleans	43.89	43.47
Pittsburgh	62.13	61.06
San Antonio	54.18	52.26
San Diego	66.66	57.56
Seattle	62.24	60.37
Buffalo	67.39	65.92
Cincinnati	67.07	63.10
Memphis	56.32	54.57
Denver	46.59	44.86
Atlanta	50.03	46.80
Indianapolis	64.47	62.92
Kansas City	56.68	56.09
Columbus	62.49	60.38
Phoenix	56.44	57.22
Newark	58.88	55.25

Source: 1960: County Business Patterns, U. S. Bureau of the Census, U.S. Bureau of Old Age and Survivors Insurance, cooperative report, First Quarter, 1959, Parts 2, 3, 4, 5, 6, 7, 8, 9, and 10 (Washington, D.C., 1961); 1966: County Business Patterns, U.S. Bureau of the Census, CBP-66, 4, 5, 6, 7, 10, 12, 15, 16, 18, 19, 22, 23, 24, 25, 27, 32, 34, 37, 40, 44, 45, 49, and 51 (Washington, D.C., 1967).

cyclical industrial-mix measure by city,* with the measure defined as
the proportion of total employment in the manufacturing, construction,
and retail sectors. Although this measure will be referred to as the
cyclical industrial mix, it is actually a measure of the proportion of
employment in industries with unstable employment patterns due to
both cyclical and seasonal factors.

The share of employment in the cyclical sectors was not uni-
formly related to differences in unemployment rates. In 1960 the
higher the cyclical industrial mix, the higher the unemployment rate;
in 1966 the opposite relationship was observed. However, these findings are inclusive because in some cases the relationships were not
statistically significant.** This finding is important because it runs
counter to expectations. Between 1960 and 1966 every city except
Minneapolis-St. Paul and Phoenix experienced a decline in the share
of cyclical and seasonal industries. The change is even more dramatic
when we consider that the 1960 period was a recession, in which we
could expect a smaller amount of employment in these sectors than
during prosperous times. One explanation for this unusual result is
that the variations in unemployment in these different sectors are reduced substantially in times of deep recessions and high national unemployment. Thus, in 1960 some of the cities with heavy concentrations of manufacturing, construction, and retail had higher rates of
unemployment.

The labor markets of 1966, in contrast, experienced substantial
employment growth, and the sectors exhibiting the largest increases
were those most heavily affected by the economic downturn in the
early 1960's. Thus, the labor markets dominated by these sectors
benefited the most and had the lowest unemployment rates.

A new scenario is emerging from these results. The cyclically
sensitive industries are like the little girl with the curl in the nursery
rhyme: in serious recession these industries are more harmful to the

---

*The cyclical industrial mix of each city is derived by cumu-
lating the percentage share of total employment of the contract-construction, manufacturing, and retail sectors of each labor market.

**The results are far from certain; for 1960 the cyclical indus-
trial mix is positive and not statistically significant, while in the same
equation for 1966, a negative and statistically significant relationship
emerges. In another equation the 1960 relationship was positive and
significant, while the 1966 relationship was negative and insignificant.
The statistical results of the multiple regressions are presented in
the appendix. The lack of consistency supports the view that the structure is less important than we anticipated.

local economy and inflict more hardship on workers by causing more unemployment; when the economy is booming and rapid economic growth is occurring, these sectors provide the most employment opportunities.

The policy implications of this inconclusive finding are that if the workers and the municipal officials of cities want stability and minimal unemployment, then they should strive to develop a diversi- fied employment structure and, specifically, to reduce the share of manufacturing employment and increase the share of more stable sectors, such as finance, insurance, and real estate, transportation, and government. However, if the workers and officials are confident of the federal government's ability to maintain a high-level, full-em- ployment, rapid-growth economy, then a local economy dominated by heavy manufacturing industries can ride the crest of prosperity and reap the benefits of steady employment, high wages, overtime oppor- tunities, and moonlighting. An illustration of the highs and lows ex- perienced by such a labor market is provided by Detroit, Michigan. For marked contrast is the labor market of great stability, low wages, and limited growth opportunities, as illustrated by Washington, D.C. Of course, a proper balance between the two extremes can be a useful target for local officials. It is not employment growth per se but the composition of the industrial structure with regard to wages and em- ployment that will be the critical determinant of a labor market that provides maximum economic welfare for the participants. Providing diversification and stimulation to selected sectors may be as impor- tant as generating increased employment in local urban labor markets.

However, policy makers should bear in mind that the alleged benefits of diversification and the adverse effects of dependency on cyclically sensitive industries need to be weighed carefully. In local labor markets the industrial structure, in broad terms, was not con- sistently significant in explaining why cities have different unemploy- ment rates. To expect to lower unemployment rates significantly by altering the structure—a most difficult, long, and ardous task—with- out changing other characteristics or activities is a limited, narrow, and probably futile goal. In conclusion, the relationship between the industrial structure of the local labor market and heavy unemploy- ment is not strong and varies considerably with the state of the na- tional economy—harmful during recession and helpful during re- coveries.

SPATIAL BARRIERS TO EMPLOYMENT

A significant argument influencing policy makers recently has been the notion that in the past fifteen years, and especially in the last five years, the movement of jobs and industries out of the central

cities and into the suburban areas has been a major factor contributing
to high levels of city unemployment, high levels of nonwhite and slum
unemployment, and a host of related problems, such as the breakdown
of municipal services and the declining tax base. If public transportation is not available to take the residents of the city to industrial
parks and employment centers in suburbia and if they cannot afford
private transportation, the growing decentralization of jobs should have
the effect of raising unemployment and poverty in the city, especially
in the slums and among nonwhites, who are prevented from moving
their residences closer to suburbia by lack of income and by discrimination.

An index of the spatial distribution of employment by industry
was developed, measuring the share of employment in the suburban-
ring counties of an SMSA against the total employment of that SMSA*
For example, in the Chicago SMSA the suburban ring consists of
DuPage, Kane, Lake, McHenry, and Will counties, with a total employment of 292,516 in 1966. In the same year Cook County, which is
used to approximate the labor market of Chicago, had a total employment of 2,098,034. The index of spatial distribution is 12.2, that is,
12.2 percent of the total employment of 2,390,550 of the Chicago SMSA
is located in the suburban ring counties.

This measure is the best available indicator of the impact of
suburbanization on central city labor markets, but it is not an ideal
measure. It cannot take into account the relationship between the
geographic distribution of jobs and the place of residence of the total
metropolitan population and does not indicate the adequacy of the employment base relative to the total labor force.

The hypothesis is that the greater the percentage of jobs located
in the suburban ring, the higher the unemployment rate of the city and
of the nonwhite ghetto population. This hypothesis was modified to
focus on the important manufacturing sector, and the measure used
was the ratio of manufacturing in the suburban rings to total manufacturing employment in the SMSA. It has been said that the greatest
changes in the geographical location of jobs have occurred in manufacturing because of the high costs of operating in crowded, high-wage,
high-unionized central cities with limited space for expansion. As a
result the most suitable jobs have been moving away from the central
cities' labor supply. Thus, the higher the percentage of manufacturing

---

*In three cities the definition of the SMSA excluded the possibility
of having a measure of spatial distribution because the SMSA was coterminous with the central city county. These SMSA's are Los
Angeles, San Diego, and Phoenix.

jobs in suburban rings, the higher the unemployment rates of cities
and their slums.

Two other crude measures of spatial barriers to employment
for central city residents are the size of the city and population density.
If the city is large, commuting problems may be especially difficult
for a residentially segregated population. If the city is very dense in
population, this may indicate a shortage of space, making employment
expansion more difficult and expensive than in outlying areas. Thus,
high population density should be positively related to the unemployment rate, and large city size may also be positively related to the
unemployment rate, especially if public transportation is not adequate.

Another measure of the spatial barrier to employment is the
extent of residential segregation.* A high degree of residential segregation of nonwhites in a given city means that less suburban job information is available. If the nonwhite community is isolated from
the normal channels of labor market information and from personal
contacts with stable employment opportunities in the labor market,
the city unemployment rate may be higher. In addition, geographical
concentration of nonwhites in a segregated area may pose transportation
problems if employment opportunities are widely dispersed throughout the city or if the nonwhite ghetto is a considerable distance from
the major employment centers of the city.

Job Dispersal

The physical deterioration of the cities and the decline in the
quality of government services during the past fifteen years are often

---

*The index of residential segregation used in this study was de-
vised by Karl and Alma Tauber in Negroes in Cities (Aldine Publishing
Co., Chicago, 1965) and is defined by them as follows:

The value of the index may be interpreted as showing the
minimum percentage of nonwhites who would have to change
the block on which they live in order to produce an unseg-
regated distribution—one in which the percentage of nonwhites living on each block is the same throughout the city.

Data for 1960 for each city were used for both 1960 and 1966 to analyze
the impact of residential segregation on urban unemployment. Since
comparable data for 1966 were unavailable, we assumed that the measure of residential segregation in each city remained constant over the
six-year period.

thought to be in part the result of the decentralization of jobs. But
analysis of the job location shows considerable variation among the
cities. (See Table 2-7.) In 1960 jobs located in suburban rings ranged
from a high of 60.6 percent of the total jobs in Boston to a negligible
2.7 percent in Memphis, and below 5 percent for suburban rings around
Columbus, Kansas City, and Dallas. Again, there is no clear pattern
of relationship between the age, size, or location of a city and the
spatial distribution of employment. The older eastern seaboard cities
had a wide range of spatial distribution, from Boston's high of 60.6
percent to New York, with only 14.9 percent. Many of the midwestern
cities had job dispersal rates of less than 10 percent.

In all three cities in Texas, almost all the employment was concentrated in the central city county, with only a small share in the
suburban ring. Cities on the West Coast varied considerably, from
a low suburban share of 7.2 percent in Seattle to a high share of 23.3
percent in San Francisco.

Not all cities experienced an increase in job dispersal. San
Antonio, Buffalo, and Houston experienced slight decreases in the
share of suburban employment, and Dallas' and Pittsburgh's shares
remained nearly constant. However, the general trend was an increase in job dispersal from 1960 to 1966.

By 1966 Boston had nearly two-thirds of its employment located
outside the central city.* St. Louis and Washington, D. C., had substantial increases (18.2 percent and 27.2 percent, respectively), with
the result that in both cities nearly half the jobs were located outside
the central city.

Both Chicago and New York experienced an increase of approximately 25 percent in job dispersal but remained fairly low on indexes
of spatial distribution.

To summarize, during the rapid expansion of the economy between 1960 and 1966, there was considerable movement of jobs into
suburban rings around the largest cities. Employment growth was positive and substantial in almost all of the thirty largest cities, but in
most cases the growth in employment was substantially greater in the

----

*Boston's geographical boundaries are quite unusual. Suffolk
County is quite small, and a large number of independent townships
surround the city of Boston. Moreover, there is no labor market
barrier, but only a political boundary that has resulted in many jobs
being located outside the city itself. However, the Route 128 complex
of electronics firms has grown enormously, increasing job dispersal and a spatial barrier not easily bridged for residents of Boston,
particularly residents of the Roxbury slum.

TABLE 2.7

Spatial Distribution of Jobs: Share of SMSA
Employment in Suburban Ring, 1960 and 1966
(percent)

City	1960	1966	Rate of Change
New York	14.9	18.8	26.2
Chicago	9.8	12.2	24.5
Los Angeles	N.A.*	N.A.*	N.A.*
Philadelphia	31.8	37.2	17.0
Detroit	19.9	26.2	31.7
Baltimore	28.7	34.2	19.2
Houston	7.3	6.7	-8.2
Cleveland	5.8	7.4	27.6
Minneapolis-St. Paul	6.8	7.3	7.4
Washington, D.C.	37.8	48.1	27.2
St. Louis	41.1	48.6	18.2
Milwaukee	7.6	10.9	43.4
San Francisco	23.3	27.0	15.9
Boston	60.6	63.4	4.6
Dallas	4.8	4.7	-2.1
New Orleans	17.9	23.4	30.7
Pittsburgh	26.9	26.8	-0.4
San Antonio	6.4	2.7	-57.8
San Deigo	N.A.*	N.A.*	N.A.*
Seattle	7.2	8.0	11.1
Buffalo	18.3	16.9	-7.7
Cincinnati	4.8	6.9	43.8
Memphis	2.7	2.8	3.7
Denver	22.2	28.8	29.7
Atlanta	22.0	26.2	19.1
Indianapolis	8.6	10.1	17.4
Kansas City	4.8	7.9	64.6
Columbus	4.6	4.8	4.3
Phoenix	N.A.*	N.A.*	N.A.*
Newark	39.1	44.2	13.0

*Not available.

Source: 1960: County Business Patterns, U.S. Bureau of the
Census, U.S. Bureau of Old Age and Survivors Insurance, cooperative
report, First Quarter, 1959, Parts 2, 3, 4, 5, 6, 7, 8, 9, and 10 (Washington, D.C., 1961); 1966: County Business Patterns, U. S. Bureau of
the Census, CBP-66, 4, 5, 6, 7, 10, 12, 15, 16, 18, 19, 22, 23, 24, 25,
27, 32, 34, 37, 40, 44, 45, 49, and 51 (Washington, D.C., 1967).

suburban rings. The result was an increase in the share of employment located outside the central city county, or an increase in the
spatial-distribution-of-employment index. In 1960 the average index
of spatial distribution was 22.6 percent, and 1966 it rose to 26.2
percent. However, considerable variation continues to exist among
the cities.

Although the growth of employment in suburbs has been spectac-
ular and greatly exceeds the growth of employment in central cities,
the cities have not experienced decreases in their employment base.
In fact, as we have seen, employment gains were recorded in every
one of the thirty cities in the sample. In short, the unemployment
problems of the poor have not been due to a lack of aggregate demand
in the local labor markets of metropolitan areas but to factors operating in the market that prevent the efficient and equitable allocation
of people and jobs.

SPECIAL DISTRIBUTION BY INDUSTRIAL MIX

Table 2-8, which contains the spatial distribution of employment
by industrial classification for 1966,* shows that employment in the
contract-construction sector was heavily concentrated in the county
containing the central city in all but three of the cities in the sample.
The index is puzzling in view of the rapid suburbanization of American
cities. However, the home-building industry in most suburbs is not
classified as contract-construction because it is built by developers
without a contract, and then sold privately.** As a result, the employment pattern of construction work in suburbs may be greatly
underestimated.

----

*In Table 2-8 spatial distribution by industrial classification
is a measure of the percentage of jobs in each industry of the respective
SMSA's that is located outside the county or counties containing each
city. See also the explanation of spatial distribution in this chapter
under the heading "Spatial Barriers to Employment." Categories for
Los Angeles, San Diego, and Phoenix are omitted: the SMSA's for these
cities are coterminous with the central city county. Therefore, no
measures for suburban ring spatial distributions can be calculated.

**This is probably also the result of the source of data, which
are recorded by location of the business establishment. Although a
great deal of the construction activity is located in the suburbs, the
contractors themselves may still be located in the central city.

A great deal of attention has been focused on the flight of manufacturing employment to the suburban areas. Since manufacturing offers higher wages and unionization and requires limited educational attainment to perform most jobs, it is highly valued as a source of job opportunities, particularly for members of minority groups and migrants with limited skills and education. And in the suburbs, in part because of the costs of operating and the barriers to expanding in central cities, it is believed that job dispersal in the manufacturing sector will have an especially severe impact on the employment of city workers, particularly those belonging to minority groups. Thus, metropolitan areas characterized by a high proportion of manufacturing jobs in suburban areas should have a more serious unemployment problem in their central cities than areas with a large manufacturing sector within the city.

The spatial distribution of employment in the manufacturing sector was found to be quite varied and with no consistent trend. The index for manufacturing was extremely high—over 40 percent in St. Louis, Boston, Baltimore, Washington, Denver, Atlanta, Newark, and Philadelphia. The cities with the greatest concentration of manufacturing located inside the county labor market (approximately 60 percent to 80 percent inside the city) were New York, Chicago, San Francisco, Pittsburgh, Houston, Minneapolis-St. Paul, Dallas, New Orleans, Cleveland, Detroit, Milwaukee, Buffalo, Cincinnati, Columbus, Indianapolis, San Antonio, Kansas City, Seattle, and Memphis.

The highest percentage of manufacturing jobs located inside the central city was found in Columbus, Cincinnati, Dallas, San Antonio, Kansas City, Seattle, and Memphis. The only clear pattern that emerges is that cities with the greatest share of total employment in manufacturing had the greatest job decentralization in the manufacturing sector. Apparently, in these cities land for expansion of facilities was no longer available in the central city or was too expensive, and the other determinants of location, natural resources and transportation, dictated remaining in the same metropolitan location but outside the central city.

In cities that can be classified as regional service-oriented centers rather than export manufacturing centers, employment in manufacturing was still concentrated in the central city. The cities with the lowest index of spatial distribution in manufacturing are characterized by relatively small population size. Employment in the transportation and public utility sector of the city was heavily concentrated in the central city. The index for job dispersal never exceeded 42 percent. The wholesale sector is closely linked to transportation. In every city at least 52 percent of wholesale employment is located in central cities. The highest percentages of jobs located outside the city were in Boston and Newark.

TABLE 2.8

Share of SMSA Employment in Suburban Ring
by Industrial Classification, 1966
(percent)

City	Contract Con-struction	Manufac-turing	Transpor-tation and Public Utilities	Whole-sale	Retail	Finance, Insurance, and Real Estate	Services
New York	33.3	20.3	11.8	12.9	27.7	9.7	17.4
Chicago	16.0	13.3	8.5	6.6	15.2	6.6	12.3
Philadelphia	42.0	41.9	29.3	26.1	42.0	22.6	31.4
Detroit	31.0	29.8	16.0	18.1	29.4	13.7	20.2
Baltimore	39.4	44.2	18.2	18.1	39.1	14.7	24.7
Houston	7.2	9.5	4.9	2.5	8.2	4.0	4.3
Cleveland	7.6	9.0	4.7	2.4	9.1	5.1	5.1
Minneapolis-St. Paul	8.0	10.6	5.5	4.2	7.8	2.4	4.5
Washington, D.C.	65.5	54.4	39.7	38.3	56.2	41.7	37.6
St. Louis	59.2	52.6	33.2	30.6	58.0	39.1	41.7
Milwaukee	18.7	10.9	11.1	8.4	12.2	5.4	9.2
San Francisco	37.0	31.3	26.3	17.8	32.1	13.8	23.7
Boston	62.8	76.9	42.0	47.5	65.9	29.4	53.8
Dallas	4.4	7.3	2.6	1.5	6.7	2.4	3.8
New Orleans	32.7	33.8	10.3	16.8	29.1	10.2	15.0
Pittsburgh	21.4	34.3	24.9	13.7	25.4	13.7	17.1
San Antonio	1.2	4.5	2.1	1.4	3.4	1.4	2.2
Seattle	10.5	7.8	7.9	4.7	10.3	5.9	7.4
Buffalo	14.4	23.0	8.0	6.6	13.8	9.2	12.2
Cincinnati	7.2	5.0	6.6	5.0	9.4	4.3	4.1
Memphis	4.7	2.0	2.6	1.4	4.5	2.5	2.5
Denver	39.5	40.3	8.8	10.3	36.2	14.8	27.1
Atlanta	33.5	40.9	11.8	16.8	27.3	11.4	19.2
Indianapolis	8.4	9.5	9.2	4.4	17.1	5.7	8.6
Kansas City	12.3	6.0	5.2	4.2	12.0	7.7	8.4
Columbus	3.4	7.0	2.8	1.8	4.8	2.0	4.1
Newark	47.0	51.8	32.6	45.9	44.3	22.6	37.3

Source: 1960: County Business Patterns, U.S. Bureau of the Census, U.S. Bureau of Old Age and Survivors In-surance, cooperative report, First Quarter, 1959, Parts 2, 3, 4, 5, 6, 7, 8, 9, and 10 (Washington, D.C., 1961); 1966: County Business Patterns, U.S. Bureau of the Census, CBP-66, 4, 5, 6, 7, 10, 12, 15, 16, 18, 19, 22, 23, 24, 25, 27, 32, 34, 37, 40, 44, 45, 49, and 51 (Washington, D.C., 1967).

In most cities 15 percent to 20 percent of the jobs in the retail sector were located outside the central city. Notable exceptions were St. Louis (57.9 percent), Boston (65.8 percent), and Washington, D.C. (56.1 percent). The least decentralization was found in Columbus (4.8 percent), San Antonio (3.4 percent), and Memphis (4.5 percent).

The finance, insurance, and real estate service sector was heavily concentrated in the central city. Those cities that had more than 15 percent located outside the central city were Philadelphia, St. Louis, Boston, Washington, D.C., and Newark.

The service sector's index varies from 2.2 percent in San Antonio to 53.8 percent in Boston. However, most of the cities had indexes of spatial distribution indicating 15 percent to 20 percent of employment in the service sector outside the central city.

In summary, manufacturing, retail, and services were the sectors experiencing the greatest job dispersal and, thus, had higher concentrations of employment in suburban rings than the other sectors. The high dispersal in manufacturing apparently was a result of the need for land for expansion; the high indexes for services and retail employment reflect the rapid population growth in the suburban rings. The other sectors were more dependent for business success on offering services, external economies, face-to-face relations, direct contact, and so forth, thus making a central city location necessary.

From 1960 to 1966 the over-all index of job dispersal increased for all cities but three. One clear and compelling feature of the data is that the spatial distribution of jobs is accelerating. Again, the impact will be more critical for minority workers who are not in a position to follow the jobs because of financial limitations or housing and employment discrimination.

Spatial distribution of jobs was not statistically significant in explaining the differences in urban unemployment in either 1960 or 1966. Contrary to our expectations a higher share of employment located in the suburbs did not adversely affect the unemployment rate in the city.

Also in direct contrast to our expectations, the higher the degree of residential segregation, the lower the unemployment rate. This surprising but statistically significant result can be interpreted in the following way. Residential segregation of nonwhites close to the heart of the central city business district may have reduced information about suburban job opportunities for these workers, but it may have operated to improve information about city jobs. Thus, the movement of whites out of the city in pursuit of suburban jobs and of other whites on the borders of the suburbs who commute to suburban jobs permitted residentially segregated nonwhites to obtain employment in the city with less competition from the white labor force. However, it is possible that, while residential segregation helps central city residents secure employment, it also limits the range of jobs about which they are informed and thereby pressures them into less-desirable positions. This trend may be re-enforced by the movement of desirable jobs to the suburbs, even though dispersal does not affect unemployment rates.

A factor that may have an indirect effect on the unemployment rate is the capacity of the city to expand the physical space for employment growth, which allows employers to locate new firms and plants within the geographical boundaries of the city or prevents them from doing so. This capacity is a function of the availability and cost of land, the transportation facilities, and the general infrastructure, including a skilled labor force relative to the alternative locations in the suburban rings. The competition between cities and suburbs to attract new firms is intense, and the development of the federal highway program, Federal Housing Administration (FHA) and other housing programs, and improved communication methods has tilted the balance in favor of the suburbs. A crude estimate of the capacity of a city to expand can be derived by observing population density and its change over time. We can assume that the more dense the population of the city, the less land there is for expansion and, thus, the more costly property would be and the less likely employment growth in a city. The result would be more job dispersal and more unemployment in the city.

Table 2-9 shows the population density in the thirty cities in our sample for 1960 and 1966. Almost all of the cities with the greatest concentration of population, in excess of 10,000 per square mile, were primarily in the East or in the heavy manufacturing centers of the Midwest, such as St. Louis, Pittsburgh, and Chicago. Cities in the South and in Texas had the lowest population density—under 4,000 persons per square mile.

Population density increased in two-thirds of the cities between 1960 and 1966, with Memphis, Houston, and Dallas increasing at the fastest rate. In contrast, Boston, Cleveland, St. Louis, Pittsburgh, and Buffalo had decreases in population density. New York City, the largest and most densely populated city, experienced a slow increase in density.

The concept that operating costs are substantially higher in cities than in suburbs is important to analyze. More research is needed to determine the role of land values and labor supplies as costs of production influencing plant location. Planning agencies in local and state government would find such analysis extremely valuable.

The population density representing space costs was found to be significantly related to the unemployment rates of the cities. This finding tends to support the view that cities without the capacity to expand physically or cities in which the cost of plant location are

TABLE 2.9

Population Density Per Square Mile:
Cities, 1960 and 1966

City	1960	1966	Percent Change
New York	25,940	26,752	3.1
Chicago	15,993	15,960	-0.2
Los Angeles	5,635	6,342	12.5
Philadelphia	15,523	15,905	2.5
Detroit	12,102	11,682	-3.5
Baltimore	12,039	11,878	-1.3
Houston	2,923	3,574	22.3
Cleveland	11,527	10,747	-6.8
Minneapolis-St. Paul	7,584	7,572	-0.2
Washington, D.C.	12,524	13,266	5.9
St. Louis	12,296	11,413	-7.2
Milwaukee	8,237	8,380	1.7
San Francisco	11,421	11,509	0.8
Boston	15,156	13,378	-11.7
Dallas	2,676	3,261	21.9
New Orleans	3,061	3,239	5.8
Pittsburg	10,988	10,102	-8.1
San Antonio	3,971	4,728	19.1
San Diego	2,940	3,479	18.3
Seattle	6,794	7,005	3.1
Buffalo	12,994	11,729	-9.7
Cincinnati	6,527	6,475	-0.8
Memphis	3,857	4,763	23.5
Denver	7,263	7,385	1.7
Atlanta	3,584	3,780	5.5
Indianapolis	6,804	7,417	9.0
Kansas City	3,983	4,486	12.6
Columbus	5,417	6,418	18.5
Phoenix	2,349	2,741	16.7
Newark	16,884	16,133	-4.5

Note: The population is reported by city for 1960 and 1966 and includes the city of Long Beach with Los Angeles, the city of Oakland with San Francisco, and the city of Kansas City, Kansas, with Kansas City, Missouri. The geographic area utilized for 1966 was the same as that used for 1960.

Source: 1960: U.S. Bureau of the Census, Statistical Abstract of the United States 1963, Washington, D.C., 1963; 1966: Ibid. Bill Publications, Sales Management: Survey of Buying Power, (New York, June 10, 1967).

relatively high will have less employment growth and fewer employment opportunities for their labor force. Two other interpretations
are worth discussing in this context. First, high population density
may indicate an area with many poor people, some of whom may be
recent migrants. These people may have a more difficult time finding
jobs because of their limited skills, education, and experience. Sec-
ondly, densely populated areas may not have had the opportunity or
the inclination to engage in land-use planning. These cities will tend
to become predominantly residential. As Table 2-9 indicates the older
eastern seaboard cities have relatively high densities, probably have
less land set aside or used for commercial and industrial purposes
and, thus, have high land values and less room for expansion. In contrast, the southwestern, western, and south central cities and labor
markets are expanding rapidly.

The implications of this finding are of great significance. Cities
should consider limiting their size by restricting migration. Concomitantly, they should plan more industrial and commercial land
areas close to transportation and to residential centers within the
city limits. Subsidies and taxes should be used to reduce the influx
of new migrants and to stimulate out-migration into smaller cities
and suburbs. The complex relationship between population, land, and
employment needs careful study. Identification of the optimal size
population for a city with fixed land resources is important for an
entire range of social and economic policies. The measurement of
economies and diseconomies of scale from concentrated population
is a major area of needed urban research.

EMPLOYMENT GROWTH
AND THE SUPPLY OF LABOR

A classical model of the labor market views unemployment as
a temporary state of disequilibrium. As the unemployed workers
offer their services at lower wages, the wage rate would adjust downward. Employers would subsequently hire more workers at lower
wages, and the labor market would be in equilibrium once again. All
workers offering their services at the market wage would be employed.
If wages did not adjust in a downward direction, unemployment would
persist. Similarly, the model of the labor market applied to labor
shortages: If employers were unable to find workers at the market
wage, they would be compelled to raise wages to induce more workers
to enter the labor force, thus eliminating the shortage of labor. However, this competitive model is based on several assumptions that
violate the reality of the labor market. Workers are not all substitutable for one another. Movement between firms and locations is

not costless. Information regarding wages and working conditions is not universally known. And finally, numerous barriers and institutions interfere with the process of allocating workers and jobs.

The conventional view holds that factors affecting the supply of, and demand for, labor, such as migration and employment growth, should partially account for the level of unemployment in the city. However, such factors as the industrial structure of the labor market, the skill level of the labor force, and the level of minimum wages also affect the operation of the urban labor market. And, finally, labor markets may be significantly affected by the ethnic composition of the labor force, by the location of jobs, by discrimination against ethnic minority groups, and by the legal transfer of income from federal, state, and local governments and the incomes derived from participation in the illegal labor market of our cities.

For the past decade government officials and economists have debated the importance of rapid economic growth in reducing unemployment. The national problem of unemployment in the early 1960's polarized the issue along the following lines. The aggregate-demand school believed that stimulating the growth of the economy would be sufficient to bring about full employment, a target temporarily set at 4 percent unemployment by the President's Council of Economic Advisers in 1962. The structuralist school argued that too much stimulation of the economy would contribute to strong inflationary pressures, without reducing unemployment sufficiently. Labor bottlenecks in production would develop, and excess demand would force prices up. Moreover, the serious unemployment problem of the 1958-63 period had its origins in the structural changes of the economy and the labor force. The structuralists believe that educational deficiencies and immobility in the labor force, technological change, and discrimination all contributed to growing structural unemployment. This new phenomenon was not susceptible to fiscal and monetary stimulation and required new manpower strategy and training programs.

As events turned out, both schools of thought claimed partial victory when the unemployment rate dropped from 6.7 percent in 1961 to 3.8 percent in 1966.[2] The Revenue Act of 1964 and the Manpower Development Training Act of 1962 were both hailed as major factors in reducing national unemployment.

However, the largest labor markets did not follow a uniform pattern of reduction in unemployment. As we have seen, the labor market experiences of these cities varied considerably in both 1960 and 1966. Analysis of these experiences can shed light on the impact of economic growth on reducing unemployment in the cities.

The demand for labor, measured by the rate of change of employment, is usually considered to be a prime determinant of the level of national unemployment. Similarly, rapid growth in employment in

major local labor markets should have a significant impact on the level
of unemployment in the cities. However, growth of employment may
not result in lower unemployment if it induces changes in other factors
in the labor market that offset the benefits of employment growth.

If employment growth occurs in a labor market and the supply
of labor does not change, then obviously the level of unemployment
will fall. However, employment growth often leads to expansion of
the labor supply. Higher wages and job openings attract new workers
into the labor force, as well as workers who were previously discouraged from looking for work and, thus, not counted as unemployed.
If the response of the labor supply more than proportionally exceeds
the growth in employment, by definition, unemployment will rise in
the local labor market. Moreover, movement of workers between
local labor markets can contribute to substantial increases in the
labor supply of some markets, which may exceed the growth in employment.

If employment grows faster than the growth of labor supply due
to increased migration and higher labor force participation, unemployment will diminish; conversely, if supply responses exceed the demand for labor, unemployment will rise.

If employment growth is to result in lower unemployment, the
growth in job opportunities must occur in areas accessible to the
work force. The skill requirements of new jobs must match the skills
possessed by the labor force. Employers seeking workers must not
discriminate against workers who are qualified. In short, structural
factors must not offset the benefits of economic growth in local labor
markets.

The relationship of employment growth and unemployment in
local labor markets was studied for our two time periods, 1960 and
1966. The expected relationship is that the greater the increase in
demand for labor, as measured by rate of change in employment for
the preceding three or four years,* the lower the unemployment rate

----

*A three-year lag between 1956 and 1959 and a four-year lag
between 1962 and 1966 were arbitrarily selected because of the availability of data and the view that the interaction of the labor supply and
labor demand would have adjusted to a new level of unemployment
during this time. One problem in using employment change as a
measure of demand for labor is that it ignores the number of jobs
that remain unfilled because of labor market rigidities (information
flows, geographical barriers, discrimination, and so forth) and un-
qualified labor supply. A measure of job vacancies added to the
change in employment would provide a more accurate measure of the

in the city, standardizing for various other responses by the labor supply.

The growth of employment between 1962 and 1966 had a significant impact on reducing unemployment rates in the thirty largest cities in 1966. Differences in employment growth were significant in accounting for the variation in unemployment rates among the cities in 1966. Cities with the largest increases in the demand for labor tended to have the lowest unemployment rates, and cities with negligible or limited employment growth manifested higher levels of unemployment. However, the differences in the demand for labor among the thirty labor markets were not significant in explaining differences in unemployment rates in 1960. Even in cities that experienced some growth in employment, the growth was not sufficient to offset the structural barriers and changes in labor supply.

The limited growth of national employment between 1956 and 1959 had a depressing effect on all thirty major labor markets. Conversely, the rapid expansion of the national economy between 1963 and 1966 resulted in employment gains in most cities, and these gains were significantly larger in those cities with the greatest declines in unemployment. But despite the impressive growth in national employment, not all major labor markets experienced decreases in measured unemployment, nor did all cities reach the national average unemployment rate. In short, increased demand for labor is still a prerequisite for reducing unemployment, but employment growth must reach a sufficient magnitude to offset the other factors operating in the urban labor market.

The larger the growth of the labor supply, the more difficult it will be to provide sufficient employment opportunities to reduce the level of unemployment. By definition, if employment is constant and the labor force increases, the unemployment rate will rise in the local labor market. Under conditions of excess demand for labor, wages may rise substantially and may affect the amount of labor offered by the high wage earners and/or the family members in the local labor market. On balance, the net effect of rapid economic growth is usually to stimulate expansion of the labor supply.

Under conditions of a recession, with unemployment rates at high levels and employment stagnating or declining, workers unable to find jobs may cease to look for employment; thus they will no longer be counted in the labor force as unemployed. This phenomenon, known as the "discouraged worker effect," operates to reduce the measured

---

demand for labor. Unfortunately, specific data for central city job vacancies are not available for all the cities.

rate of unemployment and tends to be concentrated among the long-term, hard-core unemployed. Offsetting this response is the "additional worker effect," where members of the family of the unemployed prime wage earner enter the labor market in order to help maintain family income levels.

Obviously, in recession or prosperity, the larger the labor force, the higher the level of unemployment, all other things being equal. Both measures used to represent the labor supply factor—the labor force participation rate and the net-migration rate—are crude, reflecting levels rather than actual changes in labor supply in each of the local labor markets.* The dynamic interaction of supply and demand for labor may result in the emergence of some strange conditions in these labor markets. A labor market may be characterized by a high labor force participation rate due to past growth of the local economy, no employment growth in recent years, and very low levels of unemployment. In short, it appears to be in a favorable state of equilibrium. All potential new entrants into the labor force tend to migrate to other expanding local areas. On the other hand, a local economy could experience rapid economic growth and employment growth, along with high labor force participation rates and rapid increases in net migration and, therefore, have high levels of unemployment. Although these polar cases may exist, the more realistic view, if we can standardize for changes in employment, is that the larger the two measures of labor supply are, the higher the unemployment level in the local labor market.

Table 2-10 shows the labor force participation rates for 1960 and 1966. Variation was great in both years, but especially in the latter. In 1960 the participation rate ranged from a low of 52.5 percent in San Antonio to a high of 62.9 percent in Washington, D.C. By 1966 seven cities experienced decreases and twenty-two had increases. Except for Newark, the declines were nominal, but the increases were significant. The largest gain was registered in Memphis, from 57.3 percent in 1960 to 67.8 percent in 1966. The largest decrease was

------

*The labor force participation rate represents the proportion of the population that is either presently working or looking for work. However, it does not reflect changes in labor supply over time in response to changes in demand for labor in each city. Unfortunately, data on labor force participation rates by cities were not available on an annual basis. The other measure, net migration into the city, merely represents a crude attempt to observe what cities might have had an expansion of the labor force and population due to migration. Data on the age and education of the migrants were not available.

TABLE 2.10

Labor Force Participation Rates:
Cities, 1960 and 1966

City	1960 1960	1966
New York	58.0	57.6
Chicago	60.4	61.1
Los Angeles	58.3	59.8
Philadelphia	56.6	59.3
Detroit	55.8	57.2
Baltimore	57.3	60.4
Houston	59.5	67.0
Cleveland	57.8	55.2
Minneapolis-St. Paul	59.3	59.0
Washington, D.C.	62.9	67.1
St. Louis	56.0	60.4
Milwaukee	59.6	62.5
San Francisco	59.8	63.8
Boston	57.7	57.4
Dallas	62.3	65.8
New Orleans	53.6	54.6
Pittsburg	53.4	55.9
San Antonio	52.5	56.7
San Diego	54.8	54.7
Seattle	58.8	57.7
Buffalo	54.6	57.8
Cincinnati	55.0	60.3
Memphis	57.3	67.8
Denver	57.8	57.8
Atlanta	58.3	68.5
Indianapolis	60.0	62.9
Kansas City	59.0	62.3
Columbus	57.2	64.0
Phoenix	55.8	63.7
Newark	59.2	52.8

Note: Unemployment rates are for cities and include the city of Long Beach with Los Angeles and the city of Oakland with San Francisco for both 1960 and 1966. In 1960 the unemployment rate for Kansas City includes the cities of Kansas City, Kansas, and Kansas City, Missouri, while in 1966 the unemployment rate includes only the city of Kansas City, Missouri. Unemployment rates for 1960 are for all persons aged fourteen and over, while data for 1966 are for all persons aged sixteen and over.

Source: 1960: Census Tracts, U.S. Bureau of the Census, U.S. Census of Population, Final Reports PCH (1)—8, 13, 18, 21, 26, 27, 28, 32, 34, 38, 40, 63, 64, 70, 82, 89, 92, 93, 103, 104, 105, 116, 117, 118, 131, 134, 136, 137, 142, and 166. 1966: Paul O. Flaim, "Jobless Trends in 20 Large Metropolitan Areas," Monthly Labor Review (U.S. Department of Labor, Bureau of Labor Statistics), Vol. XCI, No. 5 (May 1968); U.S. Department of Labor, Bureau of Labor Statistics, unpublished data supplied by the Bureau of Labor Statistics, 1968; and U.S. Bureau of the Census, special tabulations prepared by the Bureau of the Census, 1969, based on annual averages form the "Current Population Survey of 1967."

found in Newark, leaving the city with the lowest participation rate
(52.8 percent).

The analysis indicates that the higher the labor force participation rates, the lower the unemployment rate in the cities. The relationship is significant in both time periods.

Apparently, when unemployment is high, workers become discouraged and drop out of the labor force. Limited employment opportunities tend to reduce the flow of new entrants and secondary
workers into the labor force. This result contradicts the additional
worker hypothesis, which states that unemployment among primary
male workers would stimulate an influx of secondary workers, females
and youngsters, in order to maintain family income levels.

A more direct test of the additional worker hypothesis is obtained
by substituting the female labor force participation rate for the total
labor force participation rate. This relationship is also inverse, providing no support for the additional worker hypothesis. Apparently,
poor employment prospects in the labor market results in the domination of the discouraged worker effect over any additional worker
response that may occur. In 1966, with better employment opportunities in general, the relationship was weaker, perhaps indicating that
more secondary workers entered the market than in 1960. The reduction in the significance of the relationship may be due to the possibility that labor markets with low unemployment rates have attracted
most of their potential labor force members and, thus, have high but
stagnant participation rates. Such a labor market would experience
a decline in unemployment in a period of economic growth. (Unfortunately we do not have data on annual rates of change in participation
rates with which to test this interpretation.)

It also appears (Table 2-11) that migrants contributed to the
level of unemployment in the cities' labor markets during the period
of rapid economic growth. One of two factors may be in operation:
(a) either the migrants are less skilled, educated, and experienced
than the residents of the city; or (b) the migrants are better skilled,
educated, and experienced. If the former is true, migrants remain
unemployed and raise the unemployment rate of the city. If the latter
is dominant, then competition from migrant labor contributes to higher
rates of unemployment among the residents.

Further, if migration rates are measured by place of origin,
we would expect that migrants from the South, or nonwhite migrants,
would have more difficulty finding employment and would thus contribute to a higher unemployment rate because of the following: (a) inferior or inadequate education, compared to other members of the
urban labor force; (b) lack of specific skills; (c) ignorance of transportation patterns; (d) unfamiliarity with the city; (e) inadequate job
information; (f) poor or different work habits, particularly for rural

TABLE 2.11

Net Migration: Cities, 1960 and 1966

City	1960	1966
New York	-10.5	- 2.4
Chicago	- 0.7	- 2.7
Los Angeles	28.2	3.6
Philadelphia	-13.7	- 3.1
Detroit	- 8.9	- 5.4
Baltimore	-14.5	- 8.8
Houston	26.3	11.1
Cleveland	2.9	- 1.3
Minneapolis-St. Paul	3.0	- 5.1
Washington, D.C.	-19.7	- 3.4
St. Louis	-24.9	-13.5
Milwaukee	1.7	- 7.9
San Francisco	-11.9	- 7.6
Boston	-20.4	-14.7
Dallas	29.7	10.0
New Orleans	- 7.2	- 4.3
Pittsburg	- 5.7	- 6.3
San Antonio	8.5	2.7
San Diego	58.5	3.6
Seattle	11.3	2.0
Buffalo	3.1	- 4.5
Cincinnati	2.7	- 2.3
Memphis	7.3	1.0
Denver	1.3	- 8.1
Atlanta	- 1.0	2.0
Indianapolis	6.6	- 2.3
Kansas City	- 0.1	- 4.7
Columbus	15.0	3.7
Phoenix	70.6	15.1
Newark	- 8.3	0.3

Note: The net migration is derived by calculating the percentage of the change in total population from 1950 to 1960 and from 1960 to 1966 that is due to net migration. The population and the net migration for 1960 and 1966 are reported for the county or counties containing each city. For example, Los Angeles' population increased by 717,200 persons from 1960 to 1966, of which 217,700 was due to net migration and 499,500 was due to natural increase. Net migration, therefore, represents 3.6 percent growth in population.

Source: 1960: County and City Data Book 1967, A Statistical Abstract Supplement, U.S. Bureau of the Census (Washington, D.C., 1967); 1966: Current Population Reports, U.S. Bureau of the Census, Series p-25, No. 427, "Estimates of the Population of Counties and Metropolitan areas, July 2, 1966: A Summary Report" (Washington, D.C., 1969).

farm workers; (g) availability of adequate welfare funds; (h) high expectations regarding the natureof the job and wage level; and (i) other
sources of income in time of crisis, i.e., relatives. Poor health and
discrimination also may affect migrants more than other members of
the urban labor force. In short, the hypothesis is that the greater the
rate of southern, or nonwhite, migration, the higher the unemployment
rate.

As shown in Table 2-11 in 1960 the southwestern and western
cities had the greatest in-migration, while many of the eastern cities
experienced substantial out-migration. Phoenix, with a rate of in-
migration of 70.6, and New York and Boston, with out-migration rates
of 10.5 and 20.4, respectively, suggest the migration flows. About a
half of the cities experienced in-migration and about a half had out-
migration in 1960. By 1966 almost two-thirds of the cities were losing
population. Moreover, the size of the migration flows to the cities
experiencing in-migration was reduced sharply. For example, Phoenix's rate declined from 70.6 to 15.1. Similarly, San Diego went from
58.5 in 1960 to 3.6.

Seven cities switched from net in-migration to net out-migration
in the course of six years. Only fourteen cities were losing population
in 1960; only eleven were gaining by 1966. A number of cities reduced
their outflow of population substantially, such as New York, Philadelphia, Washington, D.C., and St. Louis. It is not possible to tell which
component of the net-migration figures accounts for the decline in net
(out-) migration. However, the figures on nonwhite and white adult
populations indicate that whites are continuing to move into the suburbs
but more nonwhites are moving into the cities. Cities are still losing
population but less so than in an earlier period.

It should be noted that migrants have by and large not moved into
the cities with the lowest unemployment rates. This raises an interesting question about the forces influencing migration. Perhaps, when
employment and economic growth were at a standstill, as in 1960, the
type of migration was different from the mid-1960's, a period of expansion. The migrants in the earlier period may have been the most
skilled and educated, many of whom had secured a job before moving,
while in the latter period, the general employment opportunities seemed
in abundance and stimulated many unskilled and uneducated migrants,
made optimistic by the rapid growth of the economy, to move from
rural areas. Under such conditions, the migration of the 1960 period
did have a strong relationship with the unemployment rate, unlike the
migration of the 1966 period.

Further support of the argument that the differential impact is
rooted in the composition of the migrant stream comes from examination of the shares of total migrants that are from the South, that
are foreign-born, and that are nonwhite. The findings reveal that

of the three measures, only nonwhite migration was significantly related to the unemployment rate.* Most of the nonwhite migrants went to northeastern cities, which experienced the greatest rise in unemployment. A large proportion of the net migration into cities in the West, on the other hand, was apparently of a quality not likely to contribute to unemployment problems.

Thus, direct measures of the demand for, and supply of, labor appear to be fairly important factors in contributing to labor market disequilibrium but were substantially less important than had been anticipated.

EFFECT OF THE WAGE LEVEL

Another important factor influencing urban unemployment is the prevailing wage level in the city. Theoretically, the wage rate is a product of the interaction of the supply and demand for labor, as is the unemployment rate; however, empirically, the wage rate may make an independent contribution in explaining differences in unemployment rates. Employers may be reluctant to hire additional workers in labor markets with high wage rates. Moreover, it may have the adverse effect of driving out old employers and discouraging prospective employers from entering the labor market, thus retarding the rate of employment growth or causing a decrease in employment. In either case, high wage-rate areas would tend to have higher rates of unemployment. This relationship would be stronger in a labor market that requires complex and difficult skills, high education, and sophisticated information; the disadvantaged group would be worse off in such a market with high wages than in one with low wages, because high wages imply higher levels of productivity and education. Thus, members of the unskilled labor force would not be able to compete for these jobs, and greater unemployment would prevail among this group. If no substantial skill differences exist and wage rates do not adjust in a downward direction, then we would expect higher rates of unemployment—that is, a more severe market disequilibrium.

Unionization, which contributes to higher wage rates and offers substantial resistance to wage reductions, should lead to high-wage labor markets with wage rigidity. In this circumstance we should

---

*In contrast to these findings, we observe that cities with a large migration from another country in 1960 had lower unemployment rates. The relationship was statistically significant. The quality of the migrants and not the quantity affect the unemployment problem.

expect a higher level of unemployment among certain groups of the labor force and for the city as a whole, particularly during sluggish economic activity and recession. The inability of portions of the labor force to qualify for jobs will be higher, the higher the prevailing wage level, regardless of whether the high wages are due solely to skill and productivity or in part to unionization.

An alternative view of the relationship between prevailing wage levels and local unemployment claims that artificial floors on wages interfere with the forces of supply and demand and cause increased unemployment. Evidence of the impact of federal minimum wages on national and industry unemployment is inconclusive. However, the recent increase in youth unemployment, despite a drop in national unemployment, has been blamed on the minimum-wage law, raising wages to $1.60 an hour and broadening the base of employment coverage. If the minimum-wage law is to have a substantial disemployment effect, we would expect it to emerge in those labor markets that have the lowest average wage rates and among the lowest-paid, least-skilled, and least-educated marginal workers.

Thus the impact of minimum-wage laws on employment for non-whites, slum residents, and young workers is expected to be greater because they are employed in greater numbers in the low-wage sector of the urban labor market.

The data* show that high-wage labor markets in fact have higher unemployment rates than low-wage markets and that the relationship is more significant in times of recession than prosperity. Differences in the wage factor did contribute to the explanation of variations in unemployment rates among the cities. The results suggest that high-wage labor markets dominated by unionized manufacturing industries probably have greater wage rigidity and consequently higher levels of unemployment, particularly during recession, than low-wage labor markets. Unionized sectors characterized by high wage rates, fixed by contractual collective-bargaining relationships, strongly resist wage reduction, despite the existence of excess supplies of labor. In contrast, low-wage areas with less unionization find it easier to absorb a labor force with a wide range of skills and education, particularly those workers at the low end of the distribution of skills and education.

---

*Obviously, it would have been preferable to use the relevant minimum-wage laws applicable to each city; unfortunately, we were unable to obtain such data. The measure used was the hourly wage for production or nonsupervisory workers in the manufacturing sector. This was reported by SMSA in Employment and Earnings Statistics for States and Areas 1939-66, U.S. Bureau of Labor Statistics (Washington, D.C., 1968).

Moreover, sectors of the local economy that are especially subject to employment instability tend to have higher wage rates in partial
compensation for less annual employment. Cyclical and seasonally
sensitive industries thus have higher wages and more unemployment.
This relationship emerges clearly during a period of national economic
recession.

The evidence provides no support for the disemployment effects
of minimum wages on the city's labor force. Low-wage labor markets
tended to have less, not more, unemployment than high-wage markets
in both 1960 and 1966. Although a direct test of the minimum wages
prevailing in the sample cities was not undertaken, the federal minimum-wage law did not have an adverse impact on the major low-wage
urban labor markets. Two qualifications are necessary: First,
even these labor markets may have sufficiently high market wages
that the minimum was not important for the majority of the labor
force, but this does not mean that it did not have an adverse employment effect on smaller and lower wage subsectors of the urban
labor markets. Second, the minimum wage may have had an impact
on the employment of certain groups of the labor force in the cities
but the impact may not have been sufficiently large or significantly
different among these groups between the low and high-wage labor
markets in the sample. It does suggest that the impact of the federal
minimum wage on low-wage labor markets was not sufficient to produce increased rates of unemployment in the cities. In contrast and
perhaps offsetting the minimum-wage impact, high-wage areas have
more unemployment than low-wage areas, providing support for the
wage-rigidity view of urban unemployment.

In summary, we have observed that cities possess substantially
different industrial structures and an equally varied spatial distribution of jobs. While employment growth has occurred in practically
every city, the suburbs have had even faster growth. As a result there
has been an increase in job dispersal in these metropolitan areas.

The industrial structure of the urban economy, as measured
by the share of employment in manufacturing, construction, and retail, was unfairly related to urban unemployment. Inconclusive evidence indicates that a higher share of employment in unstable industries
is associated with higher rates of unemployment in periods of recession
and lower rates in periods of prosperity.

Some types of migration were significantly related to unemployment rates in 1960. The larger the migration rate from a different
county, the lower the unemployment rate; however, if the migration
was nonwhite, it resulted in higher unemployment.

A significant relationship emerged between wage level and unemployment: the higher the average level of wages, the higher the unemployment rate. An opposite but significant relationship was observed

between the labor force participation rate and unemployment: the
higher the labor force participation rate, the lower the unemployment
rate.

Employment change itself was not found to be significantly related to unemployment in either period.

In conclusion, these economic factors were not sufficient to explain differences of unemployment rates among cities. The unemployment problems of these cities have not been due solely to a lack of
aggregate demand and employment growth in the local labor markets
but to structural factors operating in the market that prevent the efficient and equitable allocation of people and jobs.

3

**STRUCTURAL
FACTORS
IN URBAN
UNEMPLOYMENT**

The industrial structure, the location of employment, changes in the supply and demand for labor in the urban market, and the impact of wage rigidities have been examined as the major factors accounting for differences in urban unemployment. The findings do not provide a complete or satisfactory explanation of unemployment differences among the thirty largest cities. It is appropriate to explore other factors that can supplement analysis of these economic factors. In this chapter we shall analyze the skill quality of the labor force and its relationship to the educational requirements of employers, the health of the labor force, the role of discrimination in employment, and the relationship of factors operating outside the conventional labor market (e.g., welfare and criminal activities) on the operation of the labor market and on the level of unemployment.

EDUCATIONAL BARRIERS

The rapid growth of employment between 1963 and 1966 and the rising number of job vacancies advertised in the newspapers and by placement services throughout the country led many to believe that there was an excess demand for labor and serious labor shortages in many labor markets. Yet alongside this high vacancy rate was substantial unemployment among certain groups in the labor force. In 1966, at a time when the national rate was 3.8 percent, nonwhite workers and young workers (whites plus nonwhites aged sixteen to twenty-four had an unemployment rate of 8.7 percent. Young non-white workers aged sixteen to nineteen were the most seriously hurt, with unemployment reaching 26.5 percent.[1] One explanation for this serious disequilibrium in the national labor market and its subsystem of local labor markets was the mismatch of workers and jobs.

Employers had vacancies for jobs requiring high levels of education, skill, and experience, while the workers without jobs were new entrants into the labor force or migrants attracted into the labor markets—and both groups lacked the education and skills that were in demand.

The existence of a heterogeneous labor force with substantial variations in educational attainment and skills and many employers who demand a wide variety of skills and education may create an educational gap that can offset the numerical balance between the supply and demand of labor, causing a serious disequilibrium in the labor market. The number of job vacancies may equal the number of unemployed workers in the labor market, but the skill gap prevents an effective matching of men and jobs. The larger the gap, the greater the unemployment in the city's labor market.

It is realistic to expect lower unemployment rates in labor markets with a more educated supply of labor. As a matter of record this relationship seems to be firmly established. However, we can hypothesize that such a condition reaches its full impact only when a tight labor market exists and, in fact, that the opposite relationship may prevail in a recession. The concept is analogous to the wage-rigidity argument, that is, better-educated workers tend to be less adaptable. Skilled workers have a propensity to remain unemployed longer rather than accept employment at lower wages than they expect or less satisfying work. Moreover, their financial assets are greater and, therefore, they can afford to stay out of work longer in search of suitable employment. On the other side, employers may be reluctant to hire overqualified workers at high wages for fear that they will be less productive because of low morale, increased frustration, and higher turnover. In short, an educational rigidity may operate in the local market, resulting in higher rates of unemployment during recessions in areas possessing a more skilled and educated labor force.

It is plausible to expect that the higher the demands of employers for an educated labor force, the more unemployed people there will probably be. Of course, if employers' demands adjusted rapidly and realistically to the available supply, we could expect that the demand for labor quality would not be related to unemployment rates prevailing in the local labor market.

Another important hypothesis to be examined is the relative importance of the demand and supply of labor adjusted by quality as a determinant of the unemployment rate. In certain industries and jobs a specified level of education or skills is required for hiring. Thus, in an area characterized by a high level of education required for employment, we should expect to find higher rates of unemployment. The difficulty with this interpretation is that it focuses only on the demand side neglecting the educational attainment of the prospective labor force. In addition, the quality of employed workers may reflect not the skills and education needed to perform their jobs but the fact that employers have a preference for a highly educated work force, whether or not it is related to performance and productivity, and are willing to pay for this preference.

In order to minimize the problem of the interaction of supply and demand, we include a variable that allows us to observe the independent relationship of high quality of labor demanded and the unemployment rate in a given area. This variable, which is the educational demand for labor as measured by the number of years of school completed by the employed work force, is presented in Table 3-1.* There was remarkably little variation among the thirty cities in either time period.** The lowest level of educational attainment of employed workers in 1960 was 11.42, in Milwaukee, and the high was 11.81, in Washington, D.C. Between 1960 and 1966 the educational attainment of employed workers in the thirty urban labor markets rose between 4.6 percent and 5.8 percent. By 1966 every city had a

------

*In Table 3-1 the educational demand of labor measures the average number of years of education demanded of the labor force by the local labor market. The measure is derived from a national industry-occupation matrix and national data on the median years of school completed by the employed civilian labor force. For each of nine industries the percentage of total employment in each occupation is multiplied by the median years of education completed for that occupation. The results are cumulated and divided by 100, producing a coefficient of demand for education in each industry. The coefficient for each industry is then multiplied by its respective absolute employment in a given labor market and the results aggregated to obtain the total years of education demanded of the labor force for all nine industries. When divided by total employment the result is an index of educational demand of labor for each city. The industry-occupation matrix used for 1960 is for persons aged fourteen and over, while the matrix used for 1966 is for persons aged sixteen and over. The median years of school completed by the employed civilian labor force for 1960 and 1966 is for persons aged eighteen and over.

**One reason for this is that the educational demand of labor for each city is calculated using a national industry by occupation matrix and national figures for median years of education completed by occupation. Therefore, the measure is a reflection of each city's industrial structure expressed in years of education.

TABLE 3.1

Educational Demand of Labor: Cities,
1960 and 1966

City	1960	1966	Percent Change
New York	11.64	12.19	4.7
Chicago	11.50	12.08	5.0
Los Angeles	11.51	12.11	5.2
Philadelphia	11.51	12.11	5.2
Detroit	11.44	12.05	5.3
Baltimore	11.53	12.13	5.2
Houston	11.51	12.09	5.0
Cleveland	11.45	12.06	5.3
Minneapolis-St. Paul	11.56	12.13	4.9
Washington, D.C.	11.81	12.38	4.8
St. Louis	11.53	12.11	5.0
Milwaukee	11.42	12.04	5.4
San Francisco	11.60	12.17	4.9
Boston	11.68	12.25	4.9
Dallas	11.53	12.10	4.9
New Orleans	11.62	12.15	4.6
Pittsburg	11.49	12.11	5.4
San Antonio	11.64	12.20	4.8
San Diego	11.47	12.13	5.8
Seattle	11.48	12.07	5.1
Buffalo	11.44	12.05	5.3
Cincinnati	11.45	12.06	5.3
Memphis	11.56	12.12	4.8
Denver	11.63	12.19	4.8
Atlanta	11.59	12.14	4.7
Indianapolis	11.48	12.05	5.0
Kansas City	11.52	12.09	4.9
Columbus	11.52	12.10	5.0
Phoenix	11.57	12.12	4.8
Newark	11.52	12.11	5.1

Source: 1960: U.S. Bureau of the Census, U. S. Census of Population: 1960, Subject Reports, Occupation by Industry, Final Report PC (2)-7C (Washington, D.C., 1963), Table 1; Handbook of Labor Statistics 1967, U.S. Department of Labor, Bureau of Labor Statistics, Bulletin No. 1555 (Washington, D.C., 1967), Table 28; and County Business Patterns, U.S. Bureau of the Census, U.S. Bureau of Old Age and Survivors Insurance, cooperative report, First Quarter, 1959, Parts 2, 3, 4, 5, 6, 7, 8, 9, and 10 (Washington, D.C., 1961); 1966: Handbook of Labor Statistics 1967, Tables 15 and 28; County Business Patterns, U.S. Bureau of the Census, CBP-66, 4, 5, 6, 7, 10, 12, 15, 16, 18, 19, 22, 23, 24, 25, 27, 32, 34, 40, 44, 45, 49, and 51 (Washington, D.C., 1967).

level of attainment of over 12 years of schooling. The lowest level was still in Milwaukee (12.04) and the highest was still in Washington, D.C. (12.38). New Orleans had the smallest improvement and San Diego the greatest.

In contrast to the demand for labor quality, the educational attainment of the population* varies considerably, as seen in Table 3-2. San Diego and Seattle had populations with the greatest number of years of education, followed closely by Denver, Los Angeles, San Francisco, Dallas, Phoenix, Washington, D.C., and Minneapolis-St. Paul. The populations possessing the lowest educational attainment were found in Newark, San Antonio, New Orleans, St. Louis, and Baltimore.

By 1966 only Newark, St. Louis, and Baltimore had an average number of school years completed below 9.5. Seattle had the highest educational attainment (11.9). One-third of the cities had populations with over 11 years of education, while only eight cities had under 10 years of school.

EDUCATIONAL GAP

A measure of the educational mismatch in the labor market consists of the difference between the education possessed by the population and that required by the employers. Clearly, the larger the educational gap, the higher the unemployment rate in a given area. Ideally, educational gap should be measured by quality of job vacancies against quality of unemployed labor, plus potential labor force entrants. However, data limitations force us to use employers' demand, as measured by the educational attainments of the employed and the education possessed by the population in a given locality.

The educational gap is presented in Table 3-3. ** Since the variations are found primarily in the supply measure, there is a considerable similarity in the variations, although they are not identical. In 1960 the most serious imbalances were in Newark, St. Louis, Baltimore, San Antonio, and New Orleans. Eight other

---

*It would have been desirable to utilize data for the educational attainment of the labor force in each city. Since they were unavailable the educational attainment of the population for persons aged twenty-five years and over for each city was used in their place. (See Note to Table 3-2.)

**The educational gap is derived by subtracting the educational supply of labor from the educational demand of labor for each city.

TABLE 3.2

Educational Supply of Labor: Cities,
1960 and 1966

City	1960	1966
New York	9.50	10.30
Chicago	9.49	10.30
Los Angeles	10.81	11.40
Philadelphia	9.12	10.10
Detroit	9.38	9.90
Baltimore	8.82	9.30
Houston	10.16	11.20
Cleveland	9.06	9.50
Minneapolis-St. Paul	10.55	11.10
Washington, D.C.	10.53	10.80
St. Louis	8.84	9.30
Milwaukee	9.83	10.40
San Francisco	10.44	11.20
Boston	10.01	10.30
Dallas	10.39	11.40
New Orleans	8.95	9.60
Pittsburg	9.48	10.50
San Antonio	8.73	9.70
San Diego	11.08	11.60
Seattle	11.14	11.90
Buffalo	9.25	9.90
Cincinnati	9.53	10.60
Memphis	9.59	10.40
Denver	10.94	11.10
Atlanta	9.58	10.50
Indianapolis	10.10	10.90
Kansas City	10.14	10.80
Columbus	10.27	11.40
Phoenix	10.48	11.30
Newark	8.68	8.80

Note: The educational supply of labor is a weighted average of the years of school completed by the population aged twenty-five and over. In 1960 the measure was derived by using subgroups of educational attainment—e.g., persons who completed one to four years of school, five to seven years, and so forth. The mean years of each subgroup was weighted by the number of persons contained within it, and a simple average was then computed. The only difference in the computations for 1966 was that data were available for each year of educational attainment—e.g., one, two, three, four, and so forth.

Unemployment rates are for cities and include the city of Long Beach with Los Angeles and the city of Oakland with San Francisco for both 1960 and 1966. In 1960 t the unemployment rate for Kansas City includes the cities of Kansas City, Kansas, and Kansas City, Missouri, while in 1966 the unemployment rate includes only the city of Kansas City, Missouri. Unemployment rates for 1960 are for all persons aged fourteen and over, while data for 1966 are for all persons aged sixteen and over.

Source: 1960: Census Tracts, U.S. Bureau of the Census, U.S. Census of Population, Final Reports PCH (1)—8, 13, 18, 21, 26, 27, 28, 32, 34, 38, 40, 63, 64, 70, 82, 89, 92, 93, 103, 104, 105, 116, 117, 118, 131, 134, 136, 137, 142, and 166; 1966: U.S. Bureau of the Census, special tabulations prepared by the Bureau of the Census, 1969, based on annual averages from the Current Population Survey of 1967.

TABLE 3.3

Educational Gap: Cities, 1960 and 1966

City	1960	1966
New York	2.14	1.89
Chicago	2.01	1.78
Los Angeles	0.70	0.71
Philadelphia	2.39	2.01
Detroit	2.06	2.15
Baltimore	2.71	2.83
Houston	1.35	0.89
Cleveland	2.39	2.56
Minneapolis-St. Paul	1.01	1.03
Washington, D.C.	1.28	1.58
St. Louis	2.69	2.81
Milwaukee	1.59	1.64
San Francisco	1.16	0.97
Boston	1.67	1.95
Dallas	1.14	0.70
New Orleans	2.67	2.55
Pittsburg	2.01	1.61
San Antonio	2.91	2.50
San Diego	0.39	0.53
Seattle	0.34	0.17
Buffalo	2.19	2.15
Cincinnati	1.92	1.46
Memphis	1.97	1.72
Denver	0.69	1.09
Atlanta	2.01	1.64
Indianapolis	1.38	1.15
Kansas City	1.38	1.29
Columbus	1.25	0.70
Phoenix	1.09	0.82
Newark	2.84	3.31

Source: 1960: Census Tracts, U.S. Bureau of the Census, U.S. Bureau of Population, Final Reports PCH (1)—8, 13, 21, 26, 27, 28, 32, 34, 38, 40, 63, 64, 70, 82, 89, 92, 93, 103, 104, 105, 116, 117, 118, 131, 134, 136, 137, 142, and 166; U.S. Census of Population: 1960, Subject Reports, Occupation by Industry, Final Report PC (2)-7C (Washington, D.C., 1963); Handbook of Labor Statistics 1967, U.S. Bureau of Labor Statistics, Bulletin No. 1555 (Washington, D.C., 1967); and County Business Patterns, U.S. Bureau of the Census, U.S. Bureau of Old Age and Survivors Insurance, cooperative report, First Quarter, 1959, Parts 2, 3, 4, 5, 6, 7, 8, 9, and 10 (Washington, D.C., 1961)

1966: U.S. Bureau of the Census, special tabulations prepared by the Bureau of the Census, 1969, based on annual averages from the current population survey of 1967; Handbook of Labor Statistics 1967, Tables 15 and 28; and County Business Patterns, CBP-66, 4, 5, 6, 7, 10, 12, 15, 16, 18, 19, 22, 23, 24, 25, 27, 32, 34, 37, 40, 44, 45, 49, and 51 (Washington, D.C., 1967).

cities had gaps in excess of two years. The smallest gaps, less than one year, were found in the labor markets of San Diego, Seattle, Denver, and Los Angeles.

By 1966 the educational imbalance had worsened in Los Angeles, Detroit, Baltimore, Cleveland, Washington, D.C., Minneapolis-St. Paul, St. Louis, Milwaukee, Boston, San Diego, Denver, and Newark. Newark again earned the distinction of having the greatest imbalance, and Seattle again had the smallest educational gap. In only nine cities was the gap over two years.

The virtually universal response to this education gap has been to attack the deficiencies in the labor supply by providing more education and training for the unskilled and disadvantaged, particularly among minority groups. Amendments to the Manpower Development Training Act in 1963, 1966, and 1968 reflect this emphasis on training and educating disadvantaged workers, but neither differences in the quality of the urban labor force, as measured by educational attainment levels of the population, nor deficiencies in the quality of labor supply compared to employer requirements, also measured by educational attainment, were significant in explaining urban unemployment differences in the thirty largest cities.

The relationship of the educational gap and the unemployment rate was directly opposite in 1960 and 1966. During the 1960 recession the larger the educational gap, the lower the unemployment rate in the cities; this relationship was statistically significant. In prosperous 1966 the larger the educational gap, the higher the unemployment rate. However, the relationship was not significant in 1966, indicating that the educational gap concept was less important in accounting for high rates of unemployment than we would expect it to be. In fact, in some circumstances the educational gap contributed to less unemployment.

One possible interpretation of this unexpected inverse relationship for 1960 runs along the following lines: under conditions of high unemployment, a labor market characterized by a small educational gap may find that its skilled and educated workers who have been recently laid off have more difficulty finding employment. Workers whose skills approximate what the employers want and need may not be willing to work in lower-skilled jobs. In short, an education or skill rigidity exists in labor markets that are close to equilibrium with respect to educational quality of labor supplied and demanded. Workers resist underemployment for psychological and economic reasons. Moreover, such labor markets tend to have workers who have had more favorable employment experiences— better jobs, high wages, and less unemployment—and, thus, have the financial ability to remain unemployed and prolong the job search rather than accept a low-wage, low-status job. This argument is similar to the wage-rigidity concept, which was also supported by our findings. Thus, we find that the labor markets with the least disparity between worker quality and job requirements have a more difficult adjustment to a declining economy and loose labor market. The result is higher rates of unemployment in these cities. In contrast, labor forces of cities with the largest educational gaps experienced less unemployment in 1960. One other explanation may be the discouraged worker phenomenon. If the gap is very large, it may cause workers to become discouraged and drop out of the labor force. The result would be lower unemployment rates where workers are waiting out the temporary slowdown or lay-off to return to the labor force.

The skill-rigidity concept is reinforced by the unexpected relationship between the educational attainment of the population and the unemployment rate in 1960. The more educated the population in a labor market, the higher the unemployment rate. The relationship is highly significant and is consistent with the education-rigidity concept. Educated and skilled workers remain unemployed, partly because of their psychological resistance to taking poorer jobs and their financial capacity to cater to their disposition. Unskilled and semiskilled workers would tend to accept a much greater range of jobs and, thus, have lower rates of unemployment. Perhaps jobs requiring education and skills are more sensitive to cyclical fluctuations. The data on unemployment by industry indicate that construction and manufacturing have much more instability than other sectors. The large numbers of skilled workers in such industries may account for the higher rates of unemployment in cities dominated by these sectors.

Merely providing more education for the population, therefore, will not automatically ensure a lower rate of unemployment, unless we pay attention to other strategic factors, such as the rate of growth of employment. Moreover, under no-growth or limited-growth conditions, a highly educated labor force will have a more difficult adjustment and higher unemployment rates in the short run, although it is likely that eventually they displace less-skilled workers.

In a tight labor market such as existed in 1966, there was an insignificant relationship between education of the urban population and the unemployment rate. Again, the cautious conclusion is that education per se, and even the educational gap, are not so important as we had expected in explaining the differences among these cities in the rates of unemployment. Redirection toward other strategic factors is necessary to reduce urban unemployment. Even when substantial employment growth occurred, the education of the population was not a powerful contributor toward lower unemployment.

In 1960 there was no significant relationship between the educational demand of employers and the unemployment rate.* In 1966 a significant relationship emerged: the higher the educational demand, the lower the unemployment rate. This could be due to the rapid growth of the manufacturing and construction sectors in 1966. It is also possible that, in labor markets characterized by high education and skill requirements, the unskilled workers are more likely to become discouraged and drop out of the labor force, thus lowering the unemployment rate. Discrimination can have a similar effect.

In sum, our analysis does not support the idea that higher levels of education are necessarily associated with lower unemployment rates. In 1960 a higher level of education among the population of a city was significantly related to higher unemployment rates, and in 1966 there was no significant relationship between these two variables. Higher educational demands by employers were not significantly related to unemployment rates in 1960 and were, in fact, associated with lower rates in 1966. The gap between educational demand and supply in a city was not significantly related to unemployment rates in 1966, and in 1960 the greater the gap, the lower the unemployment rate.

The implications of these findings are that a large investment intended to increase the average educational level of the labor force in cities may not be the most effective allocation of scarce public resources if the objective is to reduce unemployment in the major cities. The results suggest that other measures would be more effective in reducing the urban unemployment problems faced by the most disadvantaged members of the labor force.

HEALTH

Health is often regarded as an important factor influencing both the quantity and the quality of the supply of labor. A healthier labor force is often more productive and is obviously preferred by employers. Poor health operates as a significant labor market barrier, preventing a worker from finding and holding a job. Absenteeism and lateness are related to poor health, as well as reduced work effort and lower productivity. In the surveys undertaken by the Bureau of Labor Statistics, poor health was frequently cited as a major factor contributing to unemployment, particularly among hard-core slum unemployed. The wide divergence between the white and

---

*In one case, the labor market barriers model, the relationship was statistically significant.

nonwhite populations in the incidence of such diseases as tuberculosis and venereal disease may be a major reason for the differences in white/nonwhite unemployment rates.

However, the relationship between unemployment and health is difficult to establish empirically. Poor health may force workers out of the labor force, thus reducing the measured rate of unemployment, or it may stimulate additional family members to enter the labor force to maintain the family income. If these secondary workers cannot find employment, the measured rate of unemployment will rise. Moreover, if a labor force is unhealthy, but not to the point of incapacitation, then poor health may result in lower productivity, lateness, absenteeism, and poor morale and ultimately will be transmitted into higher rates of unemployment. In short, there is no simple relationship between measures of poor health and measured rates of unemployment in a local labor market.

The tuberculosis rate per 100,000 people, shown in Table 3-4, may not be the best indicator of the over-all health of a community compared to hospital days per population. However, because of the disproportionate incidence of tuberculosis among the nonwhite population, it may account in part for the higher unemployment rate among nonwhites. Moreover, tuberculosis is highly correlated to other respiratory diseases and illness and, thus, may reflect poor health that will interfere with the workers' decision to work and the employers' decision to hire.

The rate of tuberculosis varies substantially by city, from a low of 17.8 per 100,000 persons in San Diego to a high of 84.3 in Baltimore in 1960. By 1966 San Diego was still the healthiest city, with a decline to 15.2, while Newark, with a rate of 79.6, had the unhealthiest population. The general trend has been downward for the incidence of tuberculosis in these major population centers; every city, except Newark, Atlanta, Pittsburgh, Houston, and Washington, D.C., had substantial decreases in the tuberculosis index. In Seattle, Cleveland, Milwaukee, San Antonio, Memphis, and Columbus, the index fell by more than 40 percent in the six years between 1960 and 1966.

Poor health was significantly related to high unemployment rates in the cities during the recession of 1960, but was not significantly related in 1966. The explanation for these relationships may be as follows. Workers with health problems tend either to experience more unemployment or to become incapacitated and drop out of the labor force. Under the latter condition the size of the labor force does not decrease because the entrance of secondary workers from the sick individual's family more than offsets the drop-off of primary workers. During recessions the secondary workers are more likely to be unable to find jobs, and unemployment rates rise. However,

TABLE 3.4

Incidence of Tuberculosis Per 100,000
Persons: Cities, 1960 and 1966

City	1960	1966	Percent Change
New York	60.4	45.6	-24.5
Chicago	79.3	54.9	-30.8
Los Angeles	45.0	33.2	-26.2
Philadelphia	70.0	46.4	-33.7
Detroit	70.2	66.4	- 5.4
Baltimore	84.3	75.4	-10.6
Houston	39.1	40.2	2.8
Cleveland	61.6	34.1	-44.7
Minneapolis-St. Paul	21.0	16.3	-19.2
Washington, D.C.	67.1	68.6	2.2
St. Louis	56.2	46.8	-16.7
Milwaukee	37.4	21.0	-43.9
San Francisco	66.3	56.6	-14.6
Boston	62.4	45.9	-26.5
Dallas	29.7	22.3	-24.9
New Orleans	40.2	38.5	- 4.2
Pittsburg	49.3	49.7	0.8
San Antonio	57.1	31.8	-44.3
San Diego	17.8	15.2	-14.6
Seattle	50.3	22.2	-55.9
Buffalo	56.8	46.9	-17.4
Cincinnati	43.5	30.0	-31.0
Memphis	34.2	19.9	-41.8
Denver	22.0	18.7	-15.0
Atlanta	41.7	47.2	13.2
Indianapolis	42.4	40.2	- 5.2
Kansas City	39.0	33.1	-15.1
Columbus	39.5	20.0	-49.4
Phoenix	39.1	25.2	-35.6
Newark	73.9	79.6	7.7

Note: The incidence of tuberculosis is reported by city for 1960 and 1966. Data for the cities of Minneapolis-St. Paul, Memphis, Denver, Atlanta, Indianapolis, Kansas City, Columbus, Phoenix, and Newark were not available for 1960. The figures used for these cities were those recorded in 1962.

Source: 1960: Reported Tuberculosis Data, U.S. Department of Health, Education and Welfare, Public Health Service (1962 ed.; Washington, D.C., 1962), Table C; and Reported Tuberculosis Data, U.S. Department of Health, Education and Welfare, Public Health Service (1964 ed.; Washington, D.C., 1964), Table 34: 1966: Reported Tuberculosis Data, U.S. Department of Health, Education and Welfare, Public Health Service (1968 ed.; Washington, D.C., 1968), Table 29.

during prosperous years the secondary workers are more likely to find employment and consequently unemployment rates may not rise significantly. Health and its impact on income and unemployment need further study, but preliminary evidence indicates that health improvement may be a strategic policy area in improving the economic status of the disadvantaged, as well as the efficiency of the labor market.

DISCRIMINATION

The effects of racial discrimination on the unemployment experienced by the residents of a city are complex. One hypothesis simply states that employment discrimination against nonwhites would tend to raise nonwhite unemployment rates and lower the white rates, leaving the total rate unchanged. Racial discrimination will allow less-skilled whites to find employment and, thus, will lower the white unemployment rate, but nonwhites will have higher unemployment rates, offsetting white gains and leaving the over-all unemployment rate unchanged.

However, more subtle forces may be at work in discriminatory labor markets. If nonwhites who are discriminated against have a greater propensity to drop out of the labor force, the result will be lower nonwhite unemployment rates. On the other hand, if the nonwhite labor force is very large and discrimination against nonwhites is so pervasive that white employers will not hire them except for specified jobs, even though all whites are employed, the city would have a higher unemployment rate. The elimination of competition for jobs between nonwhites and whites in a white-dominated labor market may raise the over-all unemployment rate. The result would be particularly evident when examining nonwhite and slum unemployment rates.

A labor market containing employers who practice racial discrimination and job exclusion or one in a community with prejudiced attitudes, revealed in restricted education, housing, and employment opportunities, will probably have a higher rate of unemployment for nonwhites. To the extent that nonwhites comprise a significant portion of the population and the labor force, the city—and particularly nonwhites and slum residents—will have a higher unemployment rate compared to communities where the practice of racial discrimination is less pronounced.

It would be desirable to have an accurate measure of employment discrimination by city, but unfortunately none is available. One crude measure of racial discrimination is the prevalence of nonwhite workers in low-status, low-wage occupations. Using data collected by the Equal Employment Opportunity Commission (EEOC), we have

constructed an index reflecting the disproportionate percentage of
nonwhites in these low-wage occupations, relative to whites.*

One weakness of this measure should be apparent: it does not
take into account differences between white and nonwhite workers in
skill, training, experience, and especially educational attainment and
achievement. Thus, differences in the distribution of the white and
nonwhite population among occupations may not reflect direct employment discrimination. Nevertheless, the measure can be used as
a reflection of all types of discrimination against nonwhites, present
and past. If nonwhites had had equal opportunities for education and
training, employment experience of similar quality, and family
structures maintained on a level comparable to the white majority,
we would expect, in the absence of employment discrimination, to
observe similar proportions of nonwhites and whites in each broad
occupational group. The discrepancy is a measure of total discrimination. The higher the city's index of discrimination, the more unemployment we should expect among the nonwhite and slum population
(adversely affecting the city's over-all unemployment rate).

The occupational distribution of whites relative to nonwhites is
found in Table 3-5.** An index of 1.00 would indicate that the percent

------

*The EEOC data contain information submitted by employers
subject to Title VII of the Civil Rights Act of 1964 with 100 or more employees and by employers holding federal government contracts, or first-
tier subcontracts, or purchase orders of $50,000 or more with 50 or
more employees. Small firms and government workers are excluded
from the sample. The data are reported separately for Orientals,
American Indians, Spanish-surnamed Americans, blacks, and total
employees. In order to make this data comparable to that used for 1960
from the U.S. census, Orientals, American Indians, and black employees
were grouped to form a nonwhite category. Spanish-surnamed Americans were grouped with whites because, according to the census definition, most Spanish-surnamed Americans are classified as white.

**In Table 3-5 the occupational distribution measures the dif-
ference in the occupational structure of whites and nonwhites. The
variable is derived from a percentage distribution of employed white
and nonwhite members of eight major occupational categories (farmers,
farm managers, farm laborers, and foremen being excluded). A ratio
of the percentage of whites to nonwhites in each category is calculated.
These ratios are multiplied by the total (white plus nonwhite) employed
in their respective occupational categories, which are then cumulated
and divided by the total (white plus nonwhite) employed in all the categories. The result is an index whose value reflects the degree to which

of nonwhites in each occupation is equivalent to the whites. First, we notice a sharp variation in the index among the thirty cities. In 1960 the lowest indexes were found in Cleveland (1.31), New York (1.36), Seattle (1.39), and Chicago (1.41). The southern cities had the highest index of occupational discrimination, with Atlanta (3.72) and Dallas (3.15) at the top. However, there were two nonsouthern cities with an index above 2.0 (Milwaukee and Kansas City). An interesting feature of the index was the significant variation found among the southern cities, particularly among Texas cities. San Antonio's index was quite low (1.85) compared to Houston's (2.54), which in turn was substantially lower than Dallas' (3.15). Perhaps a key to this variation is the impact of the sizable government employment in San Antonio compared with that of Dallas and Houston.

We find, upon examining the two different sets of data on occupational status, a substantial difference in the position of nonwhites and a higher index of discrimination in twenty-eight of the thirty largest cities between 1960 and 1966. Despite the significant economic progress of the country as a whole and pioneering civil rights legislation, the index of the occupational discrimination against nonwhites was higher in every city but San Diego and Phoenix in 1966 than 1960. In the most extreme case, Memphis, the index was more than double, 2.94 to 6.19. The number of cities with an index in excess of 2.0 jumped from seven, mostly in the South, to twenty-one.

Based upon these data the record is clear and disturbing: the labor market opportunities for nonwhites residing in our central cities may have worsened substantially relative to whites, despite economic progress, record lows of unemployment, and higher educational levels of nonwhites, particularly in central cities. However, two important caveats must be presented. First, more recent national figures lead to an opposite conclusion. From 1960 to 1970 the percent of employed whites in the preferred white collar occupations went from 46.6 percent to 50.8 percent, while the figure for nonwhites went from 16.1 percent to 27.9 percent. At the same time the percent of employed whites that were in the nonpreferred occupations of farm

---

white and nonwhite occupational distributions differ. A value of 1.00 signifies two equal distributions. The more this value differs from 1.00, the more unequal the distributions become. The occupational distribution for 1960 is reported by city for employed persons aged fourteen and over and includes figures for the city of Long Beach with the city of Los Angeles, the city of Oakland with the city of San Francisco, and the city of Kansas City, Kansas, with the city of Kansas City, Missouri. The occupational distribution for 1966 is reported for the employees of firms listed in the single asterisked footnote on p. 70 and for the SMSA that contains each city.

TABLE 3.5

Occupational Distribution of Whites Relative to
Nonwhites: Cities, 1960 and 1966

City	1960	1966	Percent Change
New York	1.36	1.81	33.1
Chicago	1.41	2.28	61.7
Los Angeles	1.43	1.61	12.6
Philadelphia	1.48	2.09	41.2
Detroit	1.48	2.85	92.6
Baltimore	1.68	3.09	83.9
Houston	2.54	3.61	42.1
Cleveland	1.31	2.49	90.1
Minneapolis-St. Paul	1.69	1.83	8.3
Washington D.C.	1.59	2.30	44.7
St. Louis	1.56	2.56	64.1
Milwaukee	2.16	2.41	11.6
San Francisco	1.46	1.70	16.4
Boston	1.44	1.67	16.0
Dallas	3.15	4.62	46.7
New Orleans	2.38	4.42	85.7
Pittsburgh	1.79	2.33	30.2
San Antonio	1.85	2.15	16.2
San Diego	1.70	1.54	-9.4
Seattle	1.39	1.73	24.5
Buffalo	1.83	2.33	27.3
Cincinnati	1.91	2.34	22.5
Memphis	2.94	6.19	110.5
Denver	1.67	1.84	10.2
Atlanta	3.72	4.69	26.1
Indianapolis	1.90	2.70	42.1
Kansas City	2.11	2.84	34.6
Columbus	1.65	2.24	35.8
Phoenix	1.83	1.76	-3.8
Newark	1.43	2.14	49.7

Source: 1960: Census Tracts, U.S. Bureau of the Census, U.S. Census of Population, Final Reports PCH (1)—8, 13, 18, 21, 26, 27, 28, 32, 34, 38, 40, 63, 64, 70, 82, 89, 92, 93, 103, 104, 105, 116, 117, 118, 131, 134, 136, 137, 142, and 166; 1966: Job Patterns for Minorities and Women in Private Industry 1966, U.S. Equal Opportunity Commission Equal Employment Opportunity Report No. 1, Part I (Washington, D.C., 1968).

laborers and foremen went from 3.0 percent to 1.6 percent, while the share of nonwhites in the same occupations decreased from 9.0 percent to 2.9 percent.2 These data indicate that nonwhites have been making occupational gains at a faster rate than whites. Second, the data in Table 3-5 were drawn from different sources for 1960 and 1966, and the sources are not directly comparable in certain respects.* The shortcomings of the available data for the years studied may have some effect on our rather striking finding.

A more direct measure of racial discrimination in employment is the occupational-distribution index, adjusted for relative educational attainment of whites and nonwhites. Table 3-6** contains such an index for 1960 and 1966. (A measure that approaches zero reflects the absence of employment discrimination, for example, if a city had an occupational index of 1.5 and an educational index of whites over nonwhites of 1.5, then the occupational difference is due to education and not to discrimination in employment. The result would be a figure of zero.) In 1960 Atlanta had an unusually high rate of employment discrimination measured by this concept, a rate of 2.31. The other southern cities followed a similar pattern: even after adjusting for

---

*Since the data utilized to calculate the measure of discrimination in 1960 and 1966 were not directly comparable, the measures do not definitively show that racial discrimination in employment increased during that period. However, the data for 1966 from the EEOC indicate the severity of employment discrimination in the larger companies of the urban labor market, while the data for 1960 from the U.S. Census of Population reveal the level of discrimination in the entire urban labor market. There is no a priori reason to assume that larger companies discriminate more than smaller firms. If any bias exists it would probably be that smaller companies discriminate more than larger ones. If this is the case the comparison of changes in the index probably understates the increase in the index of discrimination. However, the changes can be due to substantial demographic shifts in the urban population. If more unskilled nonwhites have migrated into the city, while unskilled whites have either retired or migrated to suburban locations and jobs, the index would increase. (For further explanation see Table 3-5 and footnote on p. 70)

**In Table 3-6 the occupational distribution adjusted for educational attainment is derived by subtracting the ratio of the white to nonwhite educational supply of labor from the index of occupational distribution. The result is an index which reflects the difference in the occupational distribution of whites and nonwhites after the educational backgrounds of their respective population groups have been discounted. Also, see Table 3-2, Table 3-5, and footnote on p. 70)

TABLE 3.6

Occupational Distribution, Adjusted for Educational
Attainment: Cities, 1960 and 1966

City	1960	1966	Percent Change
New York	0.29	0.71	144.8
Chicago	0.26	1.14	338.5
Los Angeles	0.33	0.51	54.5
Philadelphia	0.37	0.94	154.1
Detroit	0.38	1.71	350.0
Baltimore	0.51	1.83	258.8
Houston	1.27	2.48	95.3
Cleveland	0.27	1.28	374.1
Minneapolis-St. Paul	0.64	0.83	29.7
Washington, D.C.	0.32	0.99	209.4
St. Louis	0.47	1.34	185.1
Milwaukee	1.02	1.28	25.5
San Francisco	0.26	0.51	96.2
Boston	0.36	0.46	27.8
Dallas	1.84	3.34	81.5
New Orleans	1.00	3.21	221.0
Pittsburgh	0.64	1.26	96.9
San Antonio	0.85	1.06	24.7
San Diego	0.55	0.37	-32.7
Seattle	0.25	0.63	152.0
Buffalo	0.69	1.09	58.0
Cincinnati	0.66	1.14	72.7
Memphis	1.41	4.64	229.1
Denver	0.58	0.79	36.2
Atlanta	2.31	3.39	46.8
Indianapolis	0.71	1.54	116.9
Kansas City	0.97	1.59	63.9
Columbus	0.48	1.27	164.6
Phoenix	0.52	0.65	25.0
Newark	0.36	1.08	200.0

Source: 1960: Census Tracts, U.S. Bureau of the Census, U.S.
Census of Population, Final Reports PCH (1)—8, 13, 18, 21, 26, 27, 28,
32, 34, 38, 40, 63, 64, 70, 82, 89, 92, 93, 103, 104, 105, 116, 117, 118,
131, 134, 136, 137, 142, and 166, (Washington, D.C., 1962); 1966: Job
Patterns for Minorities and Women and Private Industries, U.S. Equal
Opportunity Commission, Equal Employment Opportunity Report No. 1,
Part I (Washington, D.C., 1968); U.S. Bureau of the Census, special
tabulations prepared by the Bureau of the Census, 1969, based on
annual averages from the "Current Population Survey of 1967."

education, employment discrimination was strong in Memphis (1.41), Dallas (1.84), Houston (1.27), and New Orleans (1.00). However some nonsouthern cities also had high employment discrimination—Indianapolis, Pittsburgh, Minneapolis-St. Paul, Cincinnati, Milwaukee, Buffalo, and Kansas City, with rates ranging from .64 to 1.02 in 1960. Nonwhites experienced the least employment discrimination in New York, Chicago, San Francisco, Cleveland, and Seattle, all with indexes under .30.

The EEOC data used for 1966 indicated more employment discrimination against nonwhites, with a sharp rise in every city except San Diego. Differences of more than 300 percent were registered in Chicago, Detroit, and Cleveland. In Baltimore, Washington, D.C., New Orleans, Memphis, and Newark, the index was more than 200 percent higher than the 1960 index. It appears that employment discrimination may have been more widespread and more marked in 1966 than 1960; despite gains in education, nonwhites had inferior jobs to 1960 relative to the white labor force in the cities.

Another way to examine employment discrimination is to take a ratio rather than a difference between the occupational and the educational measure of the position of nonwhites and whites in each city. The discrimination ratio is derived by dividing the index of occupational distribution of whites and nonwhites by the ratio of white to nonwhite average years of school completed. The result is an index that reflects the ratio of white and nonwhite occupational distribution with respect to the ratio of white and nonwhite years of school completed. Table 3-7* contains the results of this calculation, which is less sensitive to absolute differences.

The southern cities still had the highest indexes of employment discrimination, but the range diminished sharply, from 2.64 in Atlanta to 1.22 in San Francisco and Seattle. (A ratio of 1.00 indicates the absence of employment discrimination.) San Francisco, New York, Chicago, Los Angeles, Washington, D.C., and Seattle had indexes of less than 1.3, while Houston, Dallas, and Atlanta were over 2.0.

Nevertheless, in 1966 the EEOC employment discrimination index measured as a ratio was substantially higher than 1960 everywhere but San Diego. New Orleans had the largest difference (112 percent) and its index reached 3.65, the second highest of all the cities. (Memphis had 3.99.) The index of employment discrimination

---

*In Table 3-7 the discrimination ratio is derived by dividing the index of occupational distribution by the ratio of the white to nonwhite educational supply of labor. The result is another index that reflects the difference in the occupational distribution of whites and nonwhites after the educational backgrounds of their respective population groups have been discounted. Also, see Table 3-2, Table 3-5, and the single asterisked footnote on p. 70.

was over 3.0 for all southern cities except San Antonio. But nonwhites
did not fare well in the North either. Substantially higher indexes were
found in Chicago, Detroit, Kansas City, Baltimore, Cleveland, St. Louis,
Pittsburgh, Columbus, Indianapolis, and Newark; in 1966 all these cities
had an index of over 2.0, indicating significant employment discrimination. Only Boston and the western cities had rates under 1.6, with
modest differences in the index of employment discrimination between
1960 and 1966.

In summary, using two different and rather crude measures, it
appears as if the relative economic status of nonwhites compared to
whites in the largest cities of the United States in terms of occupational
distribution did not improve. Even worse, despite the fact that the
educational levels of nonwhites improved substantially between 1960
and 1966, they appear to have experienced a more severe problem,
intensification of employment discrimination, in 1966 than in the
earlier period. The practice of employment discrimination, measured
by these indexes, was greater in southern cities, but took place and
may have increased in all the largest cities in the United States. Moreover, the degree of employment discrimination in 1966 compared to
1960 was alarming, especially in light of the conditions of full employment, rapid economic growth, rising levels of education, and progres-
sive civil rights legislation, as well as a host of efforts by civic
groups struggling for economic equality and equity.

The measures developed—the occupational distribution of whites
and nonwhites, the discrimination ratio, and the index of residential
segregation described in Chapter 2—were used to test the relationship
between discrimination and a city's total unemployment rate.

The impact of discrimination on the city's unemployment rate
was negligible in both 1960 and 1966. Neither the employment discrimination ratio nor the occupational distribution index of whites relative
to nonwhites had a significant relationship to the unemployment rate.

In direct contrast to the employment discrimination finding,
residential segregation exhibited a highly significant relationship to
the unemployment rate (See Chapter 2.) In communities with a high
degree of residential segregation between whites and nonwhites, there
were considerably lower over-all rates of unemployment. Again, this
may reflect either strong discrimination against nonwhites, which
may mean a clearer definition of jobs and occupations for nonwhites
and whites, thus helping both groups to find their "own" jobs, or it
may reflect better job information networks among workers of each
race in their segregated communities. Better job information through
informal channels can ease the search for employment and reduce
unemployment, even if the information is limited to highly segregated
and less desirable jobs. Residential segregation, contrary to other
findings, may not in and of itself lead to increased unemployment for
a city. However, it may result in an employment problem for a portion

TABLE 3.7

Discrimination Ratio: Cities, 1960 and 1966

City	1960	1966	Percent Change
New York	1.27	1.65	29.9
Chicago	1.25	2.00	60.0
Los Angeles	1.30	1.46	12.3
Philadelphia	1.33	1.82	36.8
Detroit	1.35	2.50	85.2
Baltimore	1.44	2.45	70.1
Houston	2.00	3.19	59.5
Cleveland	1.26	2.06	63.5
Minneapolis-St. Paul	1.61	1.83	13.7
Washington, D.C.	1.25	1.76	40.8
St. Louis	1.43	2.10	46.9
Milwaukee	1.89	2.13	12.7
San Francisco	1.22	1.43	17.2
Boston	1.33	1.38	3.8
Dallas	2.40	3.61	50.4
New Orleans	1.72	3.65	112.2
Pittsburg	1.56	2.18	39.7
San Antonio	1.85	1.97	6.5
San Diego	1.48	1.32	-10.8
Seattle	1.22	1.57	28.7
Buffalo	1.61	1.88	16.8
Cincinnati	1.53	1.95	27.5
Memphis	1.92	3.99	107.8
Denver	1.53	1.75	14.4
Atlanta	2.64	3.61	36.7
Indianapolis	1.60	2.33	45.6
Kansas City	1.85	2.27	22.7
Columbus	1.41	2.31	63.8
Phoenix	1.40	1.59	13.6
Newark	1.34	2.02	50.7

Source: 1960: Census Tracts, U.S. Bureau of the Census, U.S. Census of Population, Final Reports PCH (1)—8, 13, 18, 21, 26, 27, 28, 32, 34, 38, 40, 63, 64, 70, 82, 89, 92, 93, 103, 104, 105, 116, 117, 118, 131, 134, 136, 137, 142, and 166 (Washington, D.C., 1962); 1966: Job Patterns for Minorities and Women in Private Industry, U.S. Equal Opportunity Commission, Equal Employment Opportunity Report No. 1, Part I (Washington, D.C., 1968); and U.S. Bureau of the Census, special tabulations prepared by the Bureau of the Census, 1969, based on annual averages from the "Current Population Survey of 1967."

of the minority labor force who are trapped in low-wage or otherwise undesirable jobs. Thus, the reason for using public policy to
decrease residential segregation is not necessarily to reduce over-all
unemployment rates, but to help a portion of the labor force gain access
to a wider range of employment opportunities.

WELFARE

For many observers the critical aspect of the urban crisis is
not racial conflict or black domination of cities but the overloaded
welfare system and its draining of the scarce resources of municipal
government. But is the welfare crisis the inevitable and deplorable
result of demographic changes in the population of the cities, or is
it a mitigating factor in urban unemployment? An examination of the
welfare case rates and payment levels for the thirty largest cities
will provide a partial answer.

Table 3-8 shows the welfare case rates per 1,000 persons for
the thirty largest cities in the United States. For 1960 the range
was from a low rate of 1.2 to a high of 11.0 per 1,000 persons. The
most interesting feature of the table is the rapid rise in welfare case
rates in most of the cities, despite competition for tax dollars from
such other vital social services as education, sanitation, and public
protection. This has aggravated the financial condition of municipal
governments and exacerbated racial and ethnic tensions between
welfare-dependent populations and the working classes. At a time
of national prosperity, full employment, and a rapidly growing gross
national product, all but four of the largest cities (Indianapolis,
Houston, Kansas City, and Washington, D.C.) had increases in the
welfare case rate. Baltimore earned the distinction of having the
greatest percentage growth in this measure of the welfare population—
191 percent between 1960 and 1966—followed by Newark, with an
increase of 161 percent; Cleveland, 134 percent; Boston, 131 percent;
Los Angeles, 116 percent; and New York and San Francisco, slightly
over 100 percent each.

The size and the variation of the welfare case rates in these
cities also increased substantially. The city with the heaviest incidence
was Baltimore (16.3), followed by Boston (14.8), St. Louis (13.5),
New York (12.4), Newark (11.5), and San Francisco (11.1). In contrast to these high rates, we find Dallas, Houston, and Indianapolis
with the lowest case-rate populations of 1.7, 1.1, and 2.3, respectively.
It should be noted that the welfare case rate may not accurately reflect
the eligible dependent population in a dynamic labor market. There
is a growing body of evidence revealing that the local administrative
practices of welfare agencies in the cities can have an impact on who

TABLE 3.8

Welfare Cases per 1,000 Population:
Cities, 1960 and 1966
(percent)

City	1960	1966	Percent Change
New York	6.1	12.4	103.3
Chicago	4.8	6.9	43.8
Los Angeles	3.7	8.0	116.2
Philadelphia	6.5	8.8	35.4
Detroit	4.9	6.9	40.8
Baltimore	5.6	16.3	191.1
Houston	1.2	1.1	-8.3
Cleveland	2.9	6.8	134.5
Minneapolis-St. Paul	3.5	5.8	65.7
Washington, D.C.	6.0	5.9	-1.7
St. Louis	11.0	13.5	22.7
Milwaukee	3.1	4.0	29.0
San Francisco	5.5	11.1	101.8
Boston	6.4	14.8	131.3
Dallas	1.4	1.7	21.4
New Orleans	6.3	7.4	17.5
Pittsburgh	5.3	7.5	41.5
San Antonio	2.9	3.7	27.6
San Diego	3.7	5.7	54.1
Seattle	2.9	4.2	44.8
Buffalo	4.0	6.8	70.0
Cincinnati	4.0	6.4	60.0
Memphis	5.0	6.0	20.0
Denver	5.7	10.9	91.2
Atlanta	3.6	5.9	63.9
Indianapolis	3.2	2.3	-28.1
Kansas City	5.0	5.0	0.0
Columbus	3.7	6.9	86.5
Phoenix	5.0	5.7	14.0
Newark	4.4	11.5	161.4

Note: The welfare case rate is derived by dividing the total number of welfare cases of Aid to Families with Dependent Children in a city by that city's population. The population and the number of cases for 1960 and 1966 are reported for the county or counties containing each city.

Source: 1960: "Recipients of Public Assistance and Total Assistance Payments, by Program, State, and County, June 1960," U.S. Department of Health, Education and Welfare, Welfare Administration, National Center for Social Statistics, Report No. A-8 (Washington, D.C., 1960); and "Estimates of the Population of Counties and Metropolitan Areas, July 1, 1966: A Summary Report," Current Population Reports, U.S. Bureau of the Census, Series P-25, No. 427 (Washington, D.C., 1969); 1966: "Recipients of Public Assistance and Total Assistance Payments, by Program, State, and County, June 1966," U.S. Department of Health, Education and Welfare, Welfare Administration, National Center for Social Statistics, Report No. A-8 and Current Population Reports (Washington, D.C., 1960).

and how many persons receive welfare.* Moreover, the large increase in welfare population observed between 1960 and 1966 is due
in part to the militant efforts of the welfare rights movement to
educate the eligible population to their rights and encourage them to
demand their legal benefits. A trend toward more liberal interpretation
of the welfare laws, as well as more liberal administration, may have
also contributed to the growth in the welfare case rate.

Table 3-9 reveals a dramatic difference among the thirty largest
cities in the level of payments to welfare recipients. Again, the three
major cities of Texas had the lowest rates in the sample, between
$16.00 and $18.00 per welfare recipient per month in 1960. The highest
payments were in Minneapolis-St. Paul ($51.89) and Newark ($47.27).
The cities in California also had welfare payments over $45.00 per
month, as did Boston and Seattle.

The other southern cities had rates above the cities in Texas but
were still the lowest in the sample, ranging from $18.25 in Memphis
to $23.93 in New Orleans. One surprising feature was the extremely
low payment rate ($22.26) in St. Louis, a city with an extremely high
case rate. It is possible that when more people are sharing a limited
welfare budget, all get less. An interesting area for further research
is the relationship between payment levels and case rates, but we were
not able to fully explore the issue in this study.

Despite rising costs of living and increased real wages, the
level of welfare payments did not increase proportionally. In Detroit,
Washington, D.C., San Diego, Seattle, Buffalo, and Phoenix, the payment rate declined. And in Chicago, Los Angeles, Minneapolis-St. Paul,
Milwaukee, and Pittsburgh, the increase in payments was negligible,
less than 1 percent.

The largest increases were registered in Baltimore (43.9
percent), Cincinnati (29.2 percent), Dallas, San Antonio, Houston,
and Memphis (approximately 26 percent each). However, even these

------

*The unusually low rates prevailing in Texas tend to support
this view of the importance of local administrative attitudes and
pictures. It has been reported that the Houston welfare agency and
the state welfare agency are extremely stringent and conservative
and have made serious attempts to minimize their case rate by
eliminating or discouraging eligible families. See a preliminary
draft of a study of the Houston labor market by Vernon M. Briggs,
Jr. entitled Black Employment in a Tight Labor Market: The Houston
Experience for the U.S. Department of Labor and the Equal Employment Opportunity Commission.

TABLE 3.9

Welfare Payment Rates: Cities, 1960 and 1966

City	1960	1966	Percent Change
New York	43.29	51.37	18.7
Chicago	41.07	41.26	0.5
Los Angeles	45.59	45.64	0.1
Philadelphia	32.34	33.93	4.9
Detroit	39.68	36.62	-7.7
Baltimore	27.98	40.26	43.9
Houston	16.60	20.85	25.6
Cleveland	33.76	38.11	12.9
Minneapolis-St. Paul	51.89	52.43	1.0
Washington, D.C.	33.66	33.34	-1.0
St. Louis	22.26	25.90	16.4
Milwaukee	44.40	44.68	0.6
San Francisco	45.91	47.66	3.8
Boston	46.01	53.48	16.2
Dallas	15.96	20.11	26.0
New Orleans	23.93	24.52	2.5
Pittsburgh	34.77	34.99	0.6
San Antonio	17.41	21.95	26.1
San Diego	46.71	43.10	-7.7
Seattle	45.04	35.87	-20.4
Buffalo	41.08	38.83	-5.5
Cincinnati	27.08	34.99	29.2
Memphis	18.25	23.08	26.5
Denver	34.48	41.84	21.3
Atlanta	23.18	24.33	5.0
Indianapolis	25.92	29.64	14.4
Kansas City	23.16	25.31	9.3
Columbus	29.86	35.08	17.5
Phoenix	30.12	28.76	-4.5
Newark	47.27	53.50	13.2

Note: The welfare payment rate is derived by dividing the total payments for welfare cases of Aid to Families with Dependent Children by the total number of recipients receiving those payments. The population and the number of cases for 1960 and 1966 are reported for the county or counties containing each city.

Source: 1960: "Recipients of Public Assistance and Total Assistance Payments, By Program, State, and City, June 1960," Report No. A-8 (Washington, D.C.), U.S. Department of Health, Education and Welfare, Welfare Administration, National Center for Social Statistics; 1966: "Recipients of Public Assistance and Total Assistance Payments, By Program, State, and City, June 1966,' Report No. A-8 (Washington, D.C.), U.S. Department of Health, Education and Welfare, Welfare Administration, National Center for Social Statistics.

increases (most occurring in cities with extremely low absolute levels
in 1960), represent for all but Baltimore less than a 5 percent annual
rise. In times of rapid inflation such increases would tend to worsen
the real standard of living of the publicly supported population. Their
economic condition is aggravated by the fact that most of their expenditures are on items that have had the greatest price increases: rent,
food, and public transportation.

In 1966 welfare payments in excess of $50 per recipient were
made in Minneapolis, Boston, Newark, and New York. The midwestern
cities of St. Louis, Kansas City, and Indianapolis and the southern
and southwestern cities of Dallas, Houston, New Orleans, San Antonio,
Memphis, Atlanta, and Phoenix had the lowest rates.

The argument has been advanced that a high welfare case rate
and welfare payment rate or a combination of the two measures, reflecting both size and payment level available to the dependent population, would have an impact on the labor force decisions of workers,
particularly females. High case rates and payments rates would
raise the opportunity cost of working relative to receiving welfare
and would tend to have a depressing effect on the supply of labor. If
there were fewer people in the labor force and if the people who
dropped out were less skilled and educated than those who stayed in
the labor force (as we suspect is the case among the welfare population), then we would expect to find less unemployment in such a labor
market.

During the recession of 1960 we found a weak and insignificant
relationship: the incidence of welfare in a city had no relationship to
the unemployment rate. This result is interesting because it runs
counter to the conventional notion that high unemployment rates in a
labor market result in higher welfare case rates. There may be
stronger forces than economic factors and the unemployment rate
dictating the number of people receiving public support from Aid to
Families with Dependent Children. The administrative decisions of
state and local welfare officials could be more significant determinants
in a loose, sluggish economy.

In 1966 the relationship was completely different: the larger
the case rate, the higher the unemployment rate. (The relationship
approached the level of significance and in some equations was
significant.) This result is more in accordance with conventional
wisdom and our a priori expectations that high rates of unemployment
drive more people onto the welfare rolls. Apparently, being on welfare
has not led people to drop out of the labor force and not be counted as
unemployed workers. This may be because of the greater abundance
of job opportunities in 1966 and attempts by welfare administrators
to reduce the welfare rolls by encouraging recipients to seek employ-

ment. Moreover, the impact of the welfare rights movement and the increased militancy of welfare mothers may have put a larger percentage of people on welfare rolls than in 1960.

The welfare payment rate was significantly related to the unemployment rate only in 1966. However, the result was not consistent with our expectation. We found that high payment rates were related to high unemployment rates. This does not support the view that if opportunity costs of working are high, people will drop out of the labor force and, thus, lower the unemployment rate. High payment rates have not led to lower unemployment rates. However, the welfare population may be only a small fraction of the total labor force and, thus, may have a negligible impact on the unemployment rate.

CRIME AND DRUG ADDICTION

Fear is often cited as the strongest force pushing middle-class people out of the city and aggravating the conditions of urban decay. The fear of robbery, rape, assault, and murder has pervaded the thoughts of urban dwellers, and the mass media have contributed to their belief in constantly increasing urban crime waves. The crime problem has been worsened by the increase in the number of narcotics addicts, who need to obtain money to satisfy their habit and often must resort to criminal activities. Drug addicts in New York City have been estimated to number as many as 125,000 in 1971,[3] and approximately 10,000 people are said to be working in the industry as pushers, importers, and so forth. And both crime rates and drug addiction are increasing rapidly.

Police protection is inadequate, because of limited personnel, inefficient use of resources, and collusion and corruption. People are afraid to leave their homes at night. Activities, socialization, and entertainment decrease. The urban dweller is a prisoner in his own home. He cannot leave after dark; the human contacts and socialization and other benefits of the city are beyond reach. It is this atmosphere that contributes to the view of an urban crisis. Table 3-10 measures property crime in the thirty largest cities, with an index combining crime rates per 100,000 population for robbery, larceny, auto theft, and burglary.

The crime index varies substantially among cities, with Los Angeles having the highest rate and Buffalo the lowest. Almost every city experienced a rapid rise in crime, with Kansas City, New York, Baltimore, Washington, Boston, and Buffalo all more than doubling. In sharp contrast, Chicago and St.Louis had relatively stable crime problems.

TABLE 3.10

Property Crime Index: Cities, 1960 and 1966

City	1960	1966	Percent Change
New York	1271	2971	133.8
Chicago	1772	1926	8.7
Los Angeles	2446	3494	42.8
Philadelphia	813	1133	39.4
Detroit	1437	2744	91.0
Baltimore	1046	2398	129.3
Houston	1506	2204	46.3
Cleveland	669	1256	87.7
Minneapolis-St. Paul	1251	2080	66.3
Washington, D.C.	986	2192	122.3
St. Louis	1570	1820	15.9
Milwaukee	740	1162	57.0
San Francisco	1500	2628	75.2
Boston	809	1727	113.5
Dallas	1144	1631	42.6
New Orleans	1903	2710	42.4
Pittsburgh	877	1239	41.3
San Antonio	1564	1979	26.5
San Diego	1242	1594	28.3
Seattle	1344	1949	45.0
Buffalo	650	1303	100.5
Cincinnati	655	953	45.5
Memphis	1101	1878	70.6
Denver	1586	1931	21.8
Atlanta	1228	1801	46.7
Indianapolis	1255	2008	60.0
Kansas City	886	2082	135.0
Columbus	1250	1702	36.2
Phoenix	1905	2649	39.1
Newark	1504	2113	40.5

Note: The property crime index is derived from a total index of reported crimes per 100,000 population. The total index includes seven categories: forcible rape, robbery, aggravated assault, larceny of $50 and over, auto theft, murder and nonneglect manslaughter, and burglary. The property crime index we used is for the SMSA containing each city and includes only the categories of robbery, larceny of $50 and over, auto theft, and burglary.

Source: 1960: Uniform Crime Reports for the United States 1960, U.S. Department of Justice, Federal Bureau of Investigation. (Washington, D.C., 1960), Table 4; 1966: Uniform Crime Reports for the United States, 1966, U.S. Department of Justice, Federal Bureau of Investigation, (Washington, D.C., 1966), Table 5.

The relationship between crime and unemployment in a city was not significant in either 1960 or 1966. Apparently, the size of the total labor force in these areas is great enough so that the relatively small number of people engaged in illegal activities does not influence over-all unemployment rates.

MODELS OF URBAN UNEMPLOYMENT

The interdependent relationships of the strategic factors discussed in this and the preceding chapter and the unemployment rates of the cities was established in a series of models. A methodological and a substantive consideration dictated the use of three basic models. While it would have been desirable to analyze all of the factors in one complete model, the limited number of cities (thirty) and slums (sixteen) studied made this impractical. Moreover, there has been considerable debate over whether economic forces or structural labor market barriers were more important determinants of national and urban unemployment. In order to examine the weight of each of these arguments, it was useful to construct clusters of factors representing these views. The three basic models are the following: (a) an economic model, consisting of such factors as employment change, labor force participation rates, migration rates, wage level, welfare payment rates; (b) a structural labor market barriers model, consisting of educational deficiencies, health, discrimination, spatial distribution of jobs, residential segregation; and (c) an industrial structure model, consisting of the shares of employment in each major industrial sector. In some cases a joint model was developed to combine key factors in each of the models. Moreover, the clustering of the independent factors into three basic models facilitates the comparison of these factors with the cities, nonwhites, slum and slum youth unemployment. The models and the regression results are discussed in the order in which they appear in the appendix.*

We have examined the impact and relationship of several factors believed to contribute to the extreme variations in urban unemployment in 1960 and 1966. The model that combines economic and structural factors with no demographic traits explained 67 percent of the variation in unemployment rates among the cities in 1960 and almost 57 percent in 1966. The health, participation rate, and education of the labor force

---

*It was not possible to include all the regression results; in a few cases the actual coefficients are not presented, such as population density, property crime per addict, expenditures per pupil, spatial distribution, and residential segregation index.

were the most significant factors in 1960, while net migration, the participation rate, and the demand for labor quality were critical in 1966.

Substituting the educational gap in the same model did not change the explanatory power in 1960, but reduced it in 1966 to only 40 percent. Moreover, the significance of all the factors was reduced. In 1960 the cyclical industrial mix was significant, along with the educational gap and the health and the employment change variable.

When the demographic characteristics of the labor market are included, the explanatory power of the model changes negligibly in most respects. This model accounts for three-fourths of the variation in unemployment rates in the city in both 1960 and 1966. The nonwhite unemployment rate is the major factor accounting for the variation in each period. In 1960 health and the participation rate are still the most significant of the remaining factors. However, in 1966 the demand for labor quality, employment change, net migration, and the cyclical industrial mix all take on added importance and are significant factors in accounting for the variation in city unemployment rates.

An attempt was made to explore separately the impact of the factors closely related to supply of labor and demand for labor. The demand factors include cyclical industrial mix, employment change, quality of labor demanded, and spatial distribution of jobs. This demand model accounts for a very small amount of the variation in unemployment rates in both periods (38 percent and 33 percent, respectively). Moreover, the only factor that was significant in both periods was the spatial distribution of jobs. The greater the job dispersal in the metropolitan labor market, the greater the unemployment rate. In 1966 the growth in employment and the quality of labor demanded by employers were found to be significant. The higher the quality demanded by employers and the greater the employment growth, the lower the unemployment rate in an urban labor market. The cyclical mix approached a significant level only in 1960, and no other demand factors were related in a critical way to the level of unemployment in the cities.

The supply model was slightly more successful in accounting for the variations (43 percent and 42 percent in 1960 and 1966, respectively). In both years the poorer the health of the labor force, the higher the unemployment rate. The participation rate was also significant: the higher the participation rate, the lower the unemployment rate. Education and net migration were found to be relatively unrelated to the level of unemployment in both periods.

An economic model, consisting of the wage rate, employment change, net migration, and labor force participation rate, explained the largest amount of the variation in 1960 (60 percent) but the lowest amount in 1966 (only 27 percent). This seems to indicate that economic forces are more important in explaining differences in unemployment in a recession than in a period of near-full employment. The inclusion of the welfare payment rate did not alter the explanatory power of the economic model in either period. However, the welfare case rate did contribute to explaining differences in 1966 but not in 1960. The higher the welfare case rate, the higher the rate of unemployment in the city in 1960. The wage rate was significant in 1960 only, but was significant in 1966 when the welfare case rate was included.

The impact of the type of migration was also explored, with 1960 data on migration from different counties, from the South, and for nonwhites. First, the explanatory power of the model using migration from a different county rises from 60 percent to 65 percent. The greater the migration from a different county, the lower the unemployment rate. This supports the notion that those migrating across counties in a sluggish economy were able to find employment without displacing residents. Net-migration data reveal that the cities with the greatest employment growth attracted most of the migrants.

Second, although southern migration was associated with higher unemployment, the relationship was weak. Southern migrants apparently were of sufficiently different quality and went to so wide a variety of cities as not to have the expected adverse impact in 1960.

The nonwhite migration did have a serious adverse impact on the labor markets. The higher the nonwhite migration, the more unemployment in the city. The model accounted for 69 percent of the variation, the highest of all the separate models. The cities that had the largest share of nonwhite migrants in relation to the total population also had the most serious unemployment problems.

In summary, migration in a recession did not contribute to higher unemployment in the cities receiving the new migrants. However, high rates of nonwhite migration did contribute to higher rates of unemployment and a more serious imbalance.

Finally, no significant relationship was established between the ratio of nonwhite to white unemployment and the unemployment rate of the city for either time period. There is no tendency for cities with high unemployment rates to have a higher ratio of nonwhite to white unemployment rates. The evidence is contrary to the view that if unemployment rates fall, nonwhites will do proportionately better and the ratio will fall.

The larger the nonwhite labor force, the higher the unemployment rate in the cities both in 1960 and 1966, but in neither period was the relationship statistically significant. Domination of a labor market by nonwhites in itself should not cause market disequilibrium in the form of higher rates of unemployment. In fact, a large nonwhite labor force may make it extremely difficult for employers to practice racial discrimination in hiring and promotions.

The Structural Model

The basic structural model contains demand for, and supply of, labor quality, health, spatial distribution, residential segregation, discrimination, and the educational gap. This model accounts for a significant amount of variation in both periods (69 percent and 56 percent, respectively) and appears to be more important than the economic models presented earlier.

The model indicates that labor markets in which employers demand a high quality of labor, complemented by a high quality supplied by the workers and with a high degree of residential segregation, will have low unemployment rates. These relationships are in operation in both 1960 and 1966 and are significant. In contrast, discrimination (measured by the occupational distribution of jobs between whites and nonwhites), health, and spatial distribution do not emerge in this model as significant factors. However, poor health has an adverse impact on unemployment in the cities.

Finally, the property-crime measure was not significant in explaining differences in urban unemployment. The significance may be greater in analyzing unemployment for slums than for the city. However, the finding is contrary to the conventional view that unemployment causes crime. Here, we can view crime as an alternative to work, which thus lowers the measured rate of unemployment in a labor market.

In summary, the joint model combining the economic, structural, and demographic characteristics best explains differences in urban unemployment in both 1960 and 1966, accounting for approximately 75 percent of the variation.

Under conditions of a national economic recession, a serious imbalance in the urban labor market will be associated with

1. A very high rate of nonwhite unemployment.
2. A large nonwhite labor force.
3. An unhealthy labor force.
4. Low labor force participation.
5. High educational attainment of the work force.
6. A high degree of job dispersal into the suburbs.
7. High prevailing wage levels.
8. A low rate of migration from other countries.
9. A high rate of nonwhite migrants.
10. A low degree of residential segregation.

11. A low quality of labor demanded by employers.
12. An industrial mix dominated by manufacturing and construction.
13. A small educational gap.

Under conditions of national prosperity and rapid economic growth, labor markets in our major cities will tend to have high unemployment if they possess the following characteristics:

1. A high nonwhite unemployment rate.
2. An unhealthy labor force.
3. A low quality of labor demanded by employees.
4. A high net-migration rate.
5. A small employment increase.
6. A small share of the industrial structure in construction, manufacturing, and retail.
7. High spatial distribution of jobs.
8. A low participation rate.
9. Low wages.
10. Low index of residential segregation.
11. A large educational gap.

The most striking differences in the relationship of these strategic factors in the two periods were the following:

1. An educated labor force had an adverse effect in a recession and a favorable impact during a period of rapid economic growth.
2. Employment growth did not have a favorable impact on the rate of unemployment in 1960, but it did in 1966.
3. Net migration contributed to high unemployment in 1966, but migration from different counties had a favorable impact in 1960.
4. The cyclical industrial mix was undesirable in 1960 but favorable in 1966.
5. Health was significant in both periods but was more important in 1960.
6. A high welfare case rate was closely related to the high unemployment rate in 1960 but had the opposite relationship in 1966.
7. A large educational gap was related to lower unemployment in 1960 but to higher unemployment rates in 1966.
8. Quality of labor demanded by employers was much more significant in 1966 than in 1960, while the wage rate seemed to be more significant in 1960 than in 1966.

DETERMINANTS OF NONWHITE UNEMPLOYMENT
RATES IN MAJOR CITIES

The model that best explained the variations in unemployment
rates among the cities in 1960 and 1966 incorporated economic and
structural factors with the nonwhite unemployment rate. The nonwhite unemployment rate explains a major proportion of the differences among the cities' unemployment rates. The higher the nonwhite rate, the higher the city unemployment rate. In 1960 almost 70
percent of the variation in the unemployment rate was due to this factor,
while in 1966 it accounted for about 63 percent. The cities with low
unemployment rates have very few nonwhites unemployed. The implication is clear: in order to reduce the disequilibrium in the labor
market of a city, substantial reductions must be made in the nonwhite
unemployment rate.

It seems imperative, therefore, to try to explain why these cities
have different nonwhite unemployment rates.

Two basic models containing many of the factors related to the
hypotheses presented earlier are applied to the nonwhite unemployment
rates in 1960 and 1966 for the thirty cities. The models are structural
and economic, with some modification of variables more relevant to
nonwhites. For example, the economic model consists of the wage
rate, the nonwhite labor force participation rate, the cyclical industrial
mix, employment change, nonwhite migration, and the spatial distribution of jobs.

These factors accounted for 77 percent of the variation in the
nonwhite unemployment rates in 1960 but 51 percent in 1966. In the
earlier recessed period the wage rate, the cyclical industrial mix,
and the nonwhite labor force participation rates were extremely
significant factors. The higher the wage rate and the cyclical industrial
mix, the worse off nonwhite workers were in the urban labor markets
in 1960. However, high nonwhite participation rates were related to
low unemployment rates. Although the other factors were not significant, they did reveal some interesting relationships: high nonwhite
migration rates contributed to more nonwhite unemployment—the
more job dispersal into the suburbs, the more nonwhite unemployment
in the cities. Employment change was the least important factor in
accounting for nonwhite unemployment rates in 1960.

In 1966 a similar set of factors emerged as significant determinants or correlates of nonwhite unemployment. Nonwhite participation rates and cyclical industrial mix remained important, but the
wage rate was insignificant. One interesting finding is the difference
in the effect of the cyclical mix on the city's unemployment rate compared to the nonwhite rate in 1966. The rapid growth of these cyclical

sectors during the boom helped to reduce the city's unemployment rate, but it did not help the nonwhites and, in fact, contributed to higher rates of unemployment. This seems to indicate that the growth of employment and the domination of employment by construction, manufacturing, and retail will help the white labor force and harm the nonwhite labor force. Apparently, nonwhites have difficulty in finding employment in these sectors. Discrimination and lack of education may be the cause of the inequality of opportunity in these cyclical sectors of the labor market.

Another significant finding is the adverse effect of job dispersal on nonwhite unemployment rates. Spatial distribution of jobs was not significant in 1960 but, with the rapid acceleration in job dispersal between 1960 and 1966, accompanied by large nonwhite migration into the cities, the nonwhite unemployment rate rose in 1966 in cities with the greatest job dispersal.

And finally, the growth of employment had a negative impact on the nonwhite workers residing in the cities. Rapid employment growth apparently stimulated more nonwhites to enter the labor force and migrate into the cities, where they failed to find jobs. Meanwhile, housing discrimination prevented nonwhites from moving to the suburbs to obtain jobs. Employment growth, particularly in labor markets dominated by construction and manufacturing, thus was associated with higher unemployment among nonwhites.

Further support for this employment discrimination concept is found in the favorable relationship between the size of the service sector and nonwhite unemployment. The larger the service sector, the lower the unemployment rate for nonwhites; the result is much more significant in 1966 than in 1960. Moreover, when we include the government sector,* we also observe a favorable relationship for nonwhite workers. The service sector has many job opportunities for nonwhites, and government is one of the least discriminating sectors; thus, we observe a lower unemployment rate for nonwhites in labor markets that have large government sectors and service employment.

The structural model is much less significant than the economic model, explaining only 24 percent of the variation in unemployment in 1960 and 35 percent in 1966. Nevertheless, the individual relationships

---

*In the multiple regression analysis employment data for the government sector were taken from the U.S. Department of Labor publication Employment and Earnings Statistics for States and Areas, 1939-1966 (Government Printing Office, Washington, D.C., 1967). The data were reported for the SMSA that contained each central city.

identify other significant factors influencing the nonwhite unemployment rate. This puzzling result may be due to the existence of a tight dual labor market, where jobs are clearly defined for whites and nonwhites in cities. The southern cities illustrate this rigid dual labor market historically. Under such conditions nonwhites and whites do not compete. If the nonwhite labor force is large, nonwhites will obtain control over all available nonwhite jobs, and the rest may become discouraged and drop out of the labor force. The result is a lower rate of unemployment among nonwhites. In a very sluggish economy nonwhite workers may do better in a rigid, dual labor market than by competing with whites for the same scarce jobs. In other words, it is better to have two queues, nonwhite and white, than one in which all the nonwhites are concentrated at the end of the line. During a recession, some whites and nonwhites will work under the two queues of a dual labor market, but under one queue in a recession, only whites work. Thus, southern labor markets take better care of nonwhites than northern labor markets during recessions and slow economic growth, a condition that has prevailed in the South for many years. A dual labor market is unjust and inequitable if it prevents workers from obtaining the best jobs by relegating positions by race, but it is equally unjust to place workers at the end of a single queue and then generate an inadequate amount of employment growth, which never reaches a large number of workers at the end of the queue. In a tight labor market in a time of rapid growth, we observe that the more discrimination, the higher the unemployment rate of nonwhites. When all or most of the whites are employed in single- and double-queue labor markets that do not hire nonwhites (despite their improved education) for the better jobs that are growing faster in a booming economy, discrimination will result in more nonwhite unemployment. The result is barely significant in 1966, indicating that more and more nonwhites are breaking the discrimination barriers.

The higher education of nonwhites was related to lower unemployment rates in 1960 and 1966. The same was not true for the labor force as a whole in 1960. An educational rigidity existed: the labor force with a high level of education had higher rates of unemployment. The educational rigidity was not operable among nonwhites. Because of the historic difficulty of securing jobs commensurate with their education and their limited financial assets to ride out temporary recessions and layoffs, educated nonwhites were more willing than comparably educated whites to take less desirable employment and lower wages; thus they experienced less unemployment than whites of comparable education.

The size of the nonwhite labor force was significantly related to the nonwhite unemployment rate but not in the way we anticipated. The larger the relative size of the nonwhite labor force, the lower the nonwhite unemployment rate. In contrast, a large percent of nonwhites in the labor force tends to contribute to higher unemployment rates in the city as a whole. Apparently, discrimination against nonwhites may be less in areas where nonwhites are well represented, perhaps because more and better job information is available. Domination of the labor force will be useful to nonwhites who are trained and educated. Less discrimination and more information will lead to better jobs, higher incomes, and lower unemployment.

Residential segregation had a favorable impact on nonwhite unemployment in 1966 but not in 1960. Apparently, being locked into a limited residential area away from jobs in suburbs did not have a sufficiently strong negative effect to offset the benefits of better job information and closer proximity to the central business district, especially during times of business expansion. Residential segregation had a more significant favorable effect on the city's over-all unemployment rate than on the nonwhite, particularly in 1960. This seems to indicate that residential segregation operated to help ethnic groups but was much more meaningful to white workers. Moreover, it may lessen job competition and reduce information between groups but improve information within each ethnic labor force. Thus, in dual labor markets, residential segregation during a recession would reinforce the discrimination effect, helping both groups to experience less unemployment.

The health of the labor force was less important for nonwhites than for the total labor force, particularly in 1960. Poor health did contribute to the higher nonwhite unemployment rates, but only in 1966 was it a significant factor. Again, the dual labor market concept may be a useful interpretation. If male nonwhite workers fall ill and drop out of the labor force, the rate would decline unless secondary workers entered the force, but jobs for nonwhite males are well defined in a dual labor market, and so secondary female workers become discouraged by the limited openings and do not seek work. In 1966 this system seemed to be breaking down, either because of the civil rights legislation and the militant feminist movement or more likely because more job opportunities were opening up for nonwhite secondary workers in an expanding economy. Nevertheless, enough workers remained without work to make the relationship between poor health and high nonwhite unemployment rate significant in 1966.

Surprisingly, the indexes of welfare did not have a significant relationship with the nonwhite unemployment rate. The size of the case load and the welfare payment levels had no bearing on the labor force decisions of nonwhites and, thus, no impact on the rate of unemployment. Moreover, high unemployment rates did not result in a higher welfare index in a city.

The most interesting result, with perhaps the greatest impact on future policy in the manpower area, is the significant impact on the unemployment rate of the availability of alternative unearned income. Contrary to the literature, the more property crimes in a city, the lower the unemployment rate for nonwhites in both time periods. People engaged in crime and people supported by criminal activity had means of support that allowed them not to work and not to be counted in the labor force. The dramatic result is less unemployment in cities with high property crime rates.

In summary, we find the following characteristics associated with, and contributing to, high nonwhite unemployment rates in both periods:

1. High-wage areas provide fewer job opportunities for nonwhites, who tend to have less skill and education.
2. Nonwhite participation rates reflect a sensitive labor force response to expanding employment opportunities—more participation when unemployment is low and less participation when unemployment is high.
3. The cyclical industrial mix sectors are associated with high nonwhite unemployment, indicating employment discrimination.
4. The larger the services and government sector, the lower the nonwhite unemployment.
5. The higher the educational attainment of the nonwhites, the lower their unemployment rate.

The factors that were significant in the tight labor market of 1966 and not in the recession of 1960 were as follows:

1. The more spatial distribution of jobs, the higher the nonwhite unemployment rate.
2. The worse the health of the labor force, the higher the nonwhite unemployment rate.
3. The more property crime, the lower the nonwhite unemployment rate.
4. The larger the nonwhite labor force, the lower the nonwhite unemployment rate.
5. The more the discrimination by occupational distribution, the higher the nonwhite unemployment rate.

Finally, only with regard to discrimination did 1960 data indicate a significant relationship: the more employment discrimination, the lower the nonwhite unemployment rate.

The most striking finding was the absence of any relationship between the white/nonwhite educational gap and the nonwhite unemployment rate. The queue hypothesis based on educational differences does not seem to be significant in explaining why nonwhites have high unemployment rates. Perhaps it may explain the high rates of nonwhite to white unemployment, but it does not help to explain high levels of nonwhite unemployment in the urban labor market.

4

THE SEGMENTATION OF THE URBAN
LABOR MARKET[1]

The paradox of life in America during the past decade can be seen in the startling differences in life-styles, income levels, attitudes, and opportunities between life in affluent suburbia and in its geographical neighbor, the inner city slum.

In 1966 the nation's unemployment rate was down to 3.8 percent,[2] while the thirty largest cities averaged 4.3 percent. The average rate of unemployment for sixteen slum areas was 9.4 percent. And this figure, bad as it is, masks the fact that in some slums the rate was substantially higher. For the poverty areas of our largest cities differ not only in style and character but also in the operation and structure of the local economy and the local labor market. It is true that slums have some common elements: poverty and unemployment, substandard and deteriorated housing, abandoned hopes and great frustration. However, Harlem is as different from Watts as it is from Forest Hills. The slums of San Antonio are vastly different from those of Boston. All slums do not have rows of broken down wooden shacks. All ghettos are not inhabited by blacks. All slums are not located close to the central business district. All poverty areas are not affected with the same degree of poverty and unemployment. Moreover, the forces contributing to these conditions also vary from slum to slum.

Table 1-2, which shows the unemployment rates for the sixteen slum areas in 1960 and 1966 illustrates this diversity. (Data for 1960 were obtained by reconstructing the slum areas, using census tract data for the same physical boundaries specified in the 1966 survey.) The extremely large range indicates that there were wide differences in the economic conditions afflicting these areas of the urban labor

market. In 1960 the rate averaged 10.3 percent; Philadelphia's slum
had the highest rate, 15.0 percent; and the lowest unemployment rate,
found in Bedford-Stuyvesant, 7.0 percent, was still higher than the
national rate of 5.5 percent. In 1966 Chicago's South Side had the
lowest rate, 5.3 percent, and Phoenix the highest, 13.2 percent.

In both periods of economic activity, there was a wide variation
in slum unemployment rates. In fact, national economic growth did
not have a favorable effect on the unemployment rate in some slum
areas. For example, Oakland had an unemployment rate of 13.1 percent
in 1960 and 13.0 percent in 1966, and South Los Angeles had a rate of
11.0 percent in 1960 and 10.7 percent in 1966. In other slums unemployment rates actually increased, while the national rate fell to 3.8
percent. The slum areas of St. Louis and Phoenix experienced the
most serious problems, with unemployment rates rising from 9.8
percent to 12.9 percent and from 9.7 percent to 13.2 percent, respectively, between 1960 and 1966.

The slums of Chicago experienced the largest declines, but the
accuracy of these figures has been disputed. Bedford-Stuyvesant,
Philadelphia, San Antonio, San Francisco, Boston, East Los Angeles,
South Los Angeles, and Oakland also experienced decreases in unemployment, but most of these decreases were quite small compared to
the dramatic declines in the unemployment rates of the cities and the
nation. The result was a deterioration in the employment status of
slum residents relative to the rest of the city population. All but four
of the thirty cities (St. Louis, Los Angeles, Atlanta, and Newark) experienced decreases in unemployment, and the magnitude of these
decreases exceeded the declines in the slum areas. For example,
the rate fell from 5.2 percent to 4.1 percent in New York City as a
whole but decreased in Bedford-Stuyvesant from 7.0 percent to 6.2
percent. In the same period the rate increased from 7.7 percent to
8.1 percent in Harlem and from 8.2 percent to 9.0 percent in East
Harlem.

Most of the slum areas had unemployment rates twice as high
as their cities, and in some cases the unemployment rates were three
times higher than the national rate. Nevertheless, the unemployment
rate of the slums understates the severity of the employment problem.
A new measure developed by the Department of Labor takes account
of underemployment, as well as unemployment, by calculating, in
addition to the measured rate of unemployment, the number of workers
only employed part-time for economic reasons, workers earning less
than $60 per week, an estimate of the nonparticipants who normally
would be available for employment, and an estimate of those who are
missing from the sample statistics because of errors in counting.
The results for 1966, presented in Table 4.1, indicate that an average
of one-third of the population of ten slums is facing a serious

TABLE 4.1

Components of the Subemployment Rate:
Slum Areas, 1966

Slum Area	Unem-ployment Rate	Em-ployed Part-Time	Earnings under $60 per Week	One-Half the Male Nonparti-cipants	One-Half the Under-Count	Total
Harlem	7.0	3.6	8.1	2.4	7.5	28.6
East Harlem	7.6	7.0	8.9	2.9	6.7	33.1
Brooklyn	5.2	6.4	6.8	1.8	7.4	27.6
Philadelphia	8.7	2.1	11.3	3.2	8.9	34.2
St. Louis	10.4	4.2	13.5	2.1	8.7	38.9
San Antonio	7.1	5.7	27.7	2.3	4.6	47.4
Phoenix	10.7	6.1	13.6	3.8	7.5	41.7
New Orleans	8.1	7.0	19.6	3.0	7.6	45.3
San Francisco	10.7	5.6	4.6	—	3.7	24.6
Boston	6.0	5.8	4.7	2.6	5.1	24.2
Total	7.7	5.2	11.5	2.5	7.0	33.9

Source: "Urban Employment Survey of 1966, "unpublished data
prepared by the U.S. Department of Labor, Bureau of Labor Statistics.

employment problem.* The variation among the slums is striking.
Even Boston and San Francisco, with low rates of 24.2 percent and 24.6
percent, respectively, still have almost one out of every four people in
the poverty area affected. San Antonio and New Orleans had the worst
problem, reflected in a subemployment rate of 47.4 percent and 45.3
percent, respectively, nearly twice the rate of Boston and San Francisco. The two components of the subemployment rate that have the
largest variation are the poverty rate and the unemployment rate.

BARRIERS TO THE EMPLOYMENT OF
SLUM DWELLERS

A number of theoretical models have been advanced to explain
why ghetto labor markets differ from one another and from the larger

*Data were only available for the ten slum areas of the "Urban
Employment Survey of 1966."

urban labor markets. We will test the validity of several of these models in order to discover what factors can lead to a reduction of unemployment and poverty among ghetto dwellers.

There are five major structural barriers alleged to contribute to unemployment among slum dwellers. Each diagnosis has led to appropriations or legislation designed to eliminate it. The deficiencies in skills and educational attainment of the slum population are considered a major determinant of high unemployment. This view underlies the large-scale expenditures made in manpower training and education for slum dwellers.

Another critical employment barrier facing slum dwellers is racial discrimination in urban labor markets, which prevents many black and Spanish-speaking people from obtaining employment, regardless of their skills and education. A conviction that discrimination is a major factor in slum unemployment has resulted in such legislation and programs as the 1964 Civil Rights Act and the creation of the EEOC.

Recent changes in the distribution of jobs in urban centers have stimulated the view that spatial barriers are an important factor reducing employment opportunities for slum dwellers. This concept has led to such programs and legislation as scatter-site open housing in suburbs and experimental transportation programs designed to make jobs in the suburbs more accessible to urban slum dwellers.

Attention has also focused on the industrial structure of the local economy. It has been contended that a dual labor market exists, consisting of a primary sector with high wages and relatively stable employment, and a secondary sector, with low wages, high turnover, and unstable employment. In general, slum workers cannot cross over from the segregated secondary labor market into the primary elite labor market. The federal government does not yet have any major programs directed at changing the demand side of the private urban labor market.* Minimum-wage legislation has been the only legislation that does have such an impact, although not intentionally. Recent efforts to raise minimum wages and expand the coverage, introduce large-scale public employment programs and wage subsidies, and organize workers in the low-wage, casual, secondary labor markets have as an objective the restructuring of the demand side of the urban labor market.

---

*A recently enacted public employment program, the Emergency Employment Act of 1971, is the first recent effort of the government to create jobs.

Finally, the labor market behavior of slum dwellers, as opposed to that of the nonslum city labor force, is influenced by the income received from transfer payments, particularly from the welfare system and from participation in the illegal economy. The availability of income from sources outside the regular channels of work can have a definite impact on the labor force behavior and the unemployment level among slum dwellers.

Implicit in all these theories is the belief that large increases in jobs in cities, which is a necessary condition, would not be sufficient to achieve substantially lower unemployment rates for the slum population.

But what would be the most efficient way to solve the employment problems of the slums? In what areas should funds be allocated? What programs should be dissolved or expanded? Would more money spent on education yield better results than encouraging unionization, wage subsidies, or antidiscrimination laws?

Education

The predominant assumption of manpower and poverty programs aimed at improving the skills and education of disadvantaged minority groups was that their low levels of skills and education were a prime cause of slum dwellers' unemployment and poverty. Although employment opportunities were growing rapidly, most of the new jobs required higher levels of skills and education than ghetto dwellers possessed.

As Table 4-2 shows, in fifteen of the sixteen slum areas, educational attainment of residents increased substantially between 1960 and 1966, from an average of 8.0 grades to 8.8. However, there were considerable differences among the slums in the two periods. In 1960 the slum population of San Antonio had the lowest educational attainment, only 5.8 grades, and that of San Francisco, with 9.4 grades, had the highest. In 1966 San Francisco's slum residents still had the highest educational attainment at 9.9 grades and San Antonio the lowest, 6.1 grades. However increases in excess of 10 percent had occurred among slum residents of Harlem, Bedford-Stuyvesant, Philadelphia, New Orleans, and South and West Chicago. Within the same city Harlem had a high educational attainment of 9.6 grades, while East Harlem had 7.9 grades; East Los Angeles had an educational level of 7.6 grades compared to South Los Angeles, with 9.3 grades. It appears that slums dominated by Spanish-speaking minorities, whether Mexican-Americans or Puerto Ricans, have lower levels of educational attainment than the black-dominated slums.

Presumably, the more education possessed by the residents of a slum area, the less unemployment they should experience. However, a comparison of the educational attainments of slum residents and the

TABLE 4.2

Educational Supply of Labor:
Slum Areas, 1966

Slum Area	1960	1966	Percent Change
Harlem	8.57	9.56	11.55
East Harlem	7.34	7.89	7.49
Brooklyn	8.52	9.63	13.03
Philadelphia	7.62	8.77	15.09
St. Louis	8.11	8.74	7.77
San Antonio	5.79	6.12	5.70
Phoenix	7.08	7.58	7.06
New Orleans	7.20	8.08	12.22
San Francisco	9.35	9.87	5.56
Boston	8.94	9.70	8.50
South Chicago	8.13	9.24	13.65
West Chicago	7.50	8.36	11.47
Cleveland	8.63	8.98	4.06
East Los Angeles	7.83	7.60	-2.94
South Los Angeles	8.88	9.25	4.17
Oakland	8.88	9.43	6.19

Note: Unemployment rates are for the same geographic areas in 1960 and 1966, as defined by census tracts. The unemployment rates were recorded in the years as listed, except for Cleveland, which was recorded in April 1965; South and East Los Angeles, which were recorded in November 1965; and Oakland, which was recorded during May-August 1966. All unemployment rates are for persons aged fourteen years and over. The educational supply of labor is a weighted average of the years of school completed by the population aged twenty-five and over. In 1960 the measure was derived by using subgroups of educational attainment—e.g., persons who completed one to four years of school, five to seven years, and so forth. The mean years of each subgroup was weighted by the number of persons contained within it, and a simple average was then computed. The only difference in the computations for 1966 was that data were available for each year of educational attainment—e.g., one, two, three, four, and so forth.

Source: 1960: Census Tracts, U.S. Bureau of the Census, U.S. Census of Population, Final Reports PCH (1)—8, 13, 18, 21, 26, 27, 28, 32, 34, 38, 40, 63, 64, 70, 82, 89, 92, 93, 103, 104, 105, 116, 117, 118, 131, 134, 136, 137, 142, and 166; 1966: "Urban Employment Survey of 1966," unpublished data prepared by the U.S. Department of Labor, Bureau of Labor Statistics; "Characteristics of Selected Neighborhoods in Cleveland, Ohio: April 1965," U.S. Bureau of the Census, Current Population Reports, Series p-23, No. 21 (Washington, D.C., 1967); "Characteristics of the South and East Los Angeles Areas: November 1965," U.S. Bureau of the Census, Current Population Reports, Series p-21, No. 18 (Washington, D.C., 1966); "Housing and Population Tabulations From the 701 Household Survey of Oakland, Revised August 1968," University of California, Berkeley, Survey Research Center (Berkeley: University of California Press, 1968).

education required by employers is a more meaningful measure. The educational gap between supply (measured by the attainment of the slum residents) and the demand for labor should be reflected in higher unemployment rates in areas where the educational barriers are greatest. Table 4-3 shows the educational gap for the sixteen slum areas. On the average the slum residents were 3.54 grades below the employer's requirements in 1960 and 3.47 grades below in 1966. Thus, despite a considerable gain in the absolute level of education of slum residents, the educational gap did not narrow significantly. Again, there was considerable variation among the slums in each period, in both absolute and relative measures. In 1960 and 1966 the slum residents of San Francisco faced the lowest educational gap, 2.25 and 2.30 grades, respectively, while San Antonio had the severest educational barrier, 5.85 to 6.08 grades, respectively. Both cities experienced slight increases in the educational gap; the absolute levels of education increased in both poverty areas, but less rapidly than the requirements of the employers.

The educational attainment appeared to have no significant relationship to the amount of unemployment experienced by slum residents, either in a period of sluggish economic activity or in a rapidly growing economy.* In a recession the amount of employment generated is not sufficient to provide jobs for all the labor force, regardless of their education and skill. In a period when employment growth was substantial, slum residents still remained at the end of the queue, even though their average educational attainment rose slightly.

Slum with small educational gaps did not have lower rates of unemployment. Conversely, areas with very large gaps between the educational attainment of the slum labor force and employers' requirements did not have significantly higher rates of unemployment. For example, although the slum residents of San Antonio faced the most severe educational barriers—more than 6 grades difference between their educational attainment and the level of education required in 1966—their unemployment rate—8.1 percent—compared favorably with that of San Francisco, with an educational gap of only 2.30 grades in 1966 but a slum unemployment rate of 11.1 percent. Furthermore, while the educational gap increased in San Antonio between 1960 and 1966, the unemployment rate dropped by 10 percent.

---

*The results show the higher the educational attainment, the higher the slum employment rate in 1966; the opposite relationship existed in 1960.

TABLE 4.3

Educational Gap: Slum Areas, 1966

Slum Area	1960	1966	Percent Change
Harlem	3.07	2.63	-14.33
East Harlem	4.30	4.30	0.00
Brooklyn	3.12	2.56	-17.95
Philadelphia	3.89	3.34	-14.14
St. Louis	3.42	3.37	- 1.46
San Antonio	5.85	6.08	3.93
Phoenix	4.49	4.54	1.11
New Orleans	4.42	4.07	- 7.92
San Francisco	2.25	2.30	2.22
Boston	2.74	2.55	- 6.93
South Chicago	3.37	2.84	-15.73
West Chicago	4.00	3.72	- 7.00
Cleveland	2.82	3.08	9.22
East Los Angeles	3.68	4.51	22.55
South Los Angeles	2.63	2.86	8.75
Oakland	2.72	2.74	0.74

Note: The educational gap measure is derived by subtracting the educational supply of labor of slum residents from the educational demand of labor of the city within which the slum area is located.

Source: 1960: Census Tracts, U.S. Bureau of the Census, U.S. Census of Population, Final Reports PCH (1)—8, 13, 18, 21, 26, 27, 28, 32, 34, 38, 40, 63, 70, 82, 89, 92, 93, 103, 104, 105, 116, 117, 118, 131, 134, 136, 137, 142, and 166 (Washington, D.C., 1962); U.S. Bureau of the Census, U.S. Census of Population: 1960, Subject Reports, Occupation by Industry, Final Report PC (2)—7C (Washington, D.C., 1963); Handbook of Labor Statistics, 1967, U.S. Department of Labor, Bureau of Labor Statistics, Bulletin No. 1555 (Washington, D.C., 1967); and County Business Patterns, U.S. Bureau of the Census, U.S. Bureau of Old Age and Survivors Insurance, cooperative report, First Quarter, 1959, Parts, 2, 3, 4, 5, 6, 7, 8, 9, and 10 (Washington, D.C., 1961); 1966: "Urban Employment Survey of 1966," unpublished data prepared by the U.S. Department of Labor, Bureau of Labor Statistics; "Characteristics of Selected Neighborhoods in Cleveland, Ohio: April 1965," U.S. Bureau of the Census, Current Population Reports, Series p-23, No. 18 (Washington, D.C., 1967); "Characteristics of the South and East Los Angeles Areas: November 1965," U.S. Bureau of the Census, Current Population Reports, Series p-23, No. 18 (Washington, D.C., 1966); "Housing and Population, Tabulations From the 701 Household Survey of Oakland, Revised August 1968," University of California at Berkeley, Survey Research Center (Berkeley: University of California Press, 1968); Handbook of Labor Statistics, 1967, and County Business Patterns, U.S. Bureau of the Census, CBP-66, 4, 5, 6, 7, 10, 12, 15, 16, 18, 19, 22, 23, 24, 25, 27, 32, 34, 37, 40, 44, 45, 49, and 51 (Washington, D.C., 1967).

An alternative concept concerns the educational deficiencies
of slum labor force members in comparison to other workers competing for jobs in the broader urban labor market. Larger differences
in educational attainment between slum residents and city residents
should be reflected in higher levels of unemployment for the former.

This measure is related to the so-called queue hypothesis,
which conceives of the work force arrayed along a continuum by a
measure of productivity reflected by their education attainment. As
employers require additional workers, they move down the queue.
According to this view, it is not what employers want but with whom
the slum residents must compete for the scarce jobs that is the
critical factor.

The relative educational differences between the slum residents
and the city labor force are presented in Table 4-4. In the slum areas
of Cleveland, Harlem, Bedford-Stuyvesant, and St. Louis, less than
one grade of school separated the slum residents from the rest of
the city in 1960. In several other areas slum residents had a relative
educational deficiency of more than two grades. In the six years
between 1960 and 1966, the educational gap between the slum and city
residents increased in eight of the sixteen slums. Residents of
Roxbury (Boston) and Bedford-Stuyvesant cut the educational gap by
more than three-tenths of a grade.

Again, we find that the educational barriers are greatest in the
slums with Spanish-speaking populations. The poverty section of
Cleveland still had the smallest gap, only five months, while East
Los Angeles and Phoenix had the highest gap, 3.8 years and 3.7 years,
respectively. Spanish Harlem was better off than the Mexican-American
slums of the southwest.

The hypothesis was that educational deficiency of the slum labor
force compared to the labor force in the city should contribute to heavy
unemployment in these poverty areas. Once again, education was
found to be unimportant in explaining the unemployment rates of slum
residents. The findings do not support the queue theory that blacks
and Spanish-speaking minorities are at the end of the line because
of their educational deficiencies and, therefore, are not given jobs
until the level of aggregate demand is so high as to force employers
to hire the educationally deficient. Moreover, the findings indicate
that improvements in the absolute levels of education (which did
occur between 1960 and 1966) will not be sufficient to provide better
employment opportunities or to lower unemployment rates in slum
areas.

Two possible interpretations may be attached to this finding.
First, it may be that the education received by slum residents is
inferior to that received by others in the city and, therefore, a uniform
measure of years of school completed is not an adequate gauge of the

TABLE 4.4

Educational Gap: City Minus Slum Areas, 1966

Slum Area	1960	1966
Harlem	0.93	0.74
East Harlem	2.16	2.41
Brooklyn	0.98	0.67
Philadelphia	1.50	1.33
St. Louis	0.73	0.56
San Antonio	2.94	3.58
Phoenix	3.40	3.72
New Orleans	1.75	1.52
San Francisco	1.09	1.33
Boston	1.07	0.60
South Chicago	1.36	1.06
West Chicago	1.99	1.94
Cleveland	0.43	0.52
East Los Angeles	2.98	3.80
South Los Angeles	1.93	2.15
Oakland	1.56	1.77

Note: The education gap measure is derived by subtracting the educational supply of labor of slum residents from the educational supply of labor of the city within which the slum area is located.

Source: 1960: Census Tracts, U.S. Bureau of the Census, U.S. Census of Population, Final Reports PCH (1)—8, 13, 18, 21, 26, 27, 28, 32, 34, 38, 40, 63, 64, 70, 82, 89, 92, 93, 103, 104, 105, 116, 117, 118, 131, 134, 136, 137, 142, and 166 (Washington, D.C., 1962); 1966: U.S. Bureau of the Census, special tabulations prepared by the Bureau of the Census, 1969, based on annual averages from the Current Population Survey of 1967; "Characteristics of Selected Neighborhoods in Cleveland, Ohio: April 1965," U.S. Bureau of the Census, Current Population Reports, Series p-23, No. 21 (Washington, D.C., 1967); "Characteristics of the South and East Los Angeles Areas: November 1965," U.S. Bureau of the Census, Current Population Reports, Series p-23, No. 18 (Washington, D.C., 1966); and "Housing and Population, Tabulations From the 701 Household Survey of Oakland, Revised August 1968," University of California, Berkeley, Survey Research Center (Berkeley: University of California Press, 1968).

actual educational achievement of the two groups. If this is the case public policy should be directed to improving the quality of education received by slum residents rather than only extending the length of time in school. Also, since our measure refers only to the education of the population over age twenty-five, the finding may not apply to younger slum residents. In fact, recent evidence compiled by the Bureau of Labor Statistics indicates that more and more younger nonwhites are going to college and are able to translate this educational attainment into higher occupational status.[3]

A second, and not necessarily contradictory, interpretation is that educational differences coexist with a segmented or dual labor market, in which there are two distinct, noncompeting groups, and educational gains alone are not sufficient to enable slum dwellers to compete with the majority group. This dual market may be the result of segregation that screens out black and Spanish-speaking minorities as undesirables. In every urban labor market, secondary jobs, nonunionized, at low wages, with high turnover, limited opportunity, and poor working conditions, may be reserved for blacks and other minorities, while the preferred jobs are the domain of the whites. When breaks in the job-segregated market occur, racial discrimination is practiced, openly or subtly. Thus, the industrial structure of the city's economy will be a measure of job segregation and the reservation system. Cities that are dominated by a casual, low-wage, low-income industrial sector will have more employment for slum residents and lower unemployment rates. There is no evidence that education and training alone will be sufficient to overcome this stiuation.

Discrimination

The more discrimination there is in a city, the higher the non-white unemployment rate and the ratio of nonwhite to white unemployment. The effects of discrimination are especially severe in the poorest elements in the community, where power and resistance are weakest, where information and knowledge are absent, and where disadvantage is greatest.

Nevertheless, an alternative view is consistent with a labor market dominated by discrimination against nonwhites. It may be that active employment discrimination occurs only against nonwhites who have the desire and the qualifications to compete for preferred occupations and jobs. In this view slum dwellers are not a real or a perceived threat to white employees and employers. They may be resigned to accepting the worst jobs in the low-wage, casual employment sectors of the urban economy. Thus, discrimination may not result in more slum unemployment.

The range of discrimination in the cities that contain the slum areas is considerable. Tables 3-5 and 3-6 show two measures of discrimination: the nonwhite/white occupational distribution index and the employment discrimination index adjusted for education. In 1960 Cleveland and New York City had the lowest occupational-distribution index, indicating the best opportunities for nonwhites vis-à-vis whites. Atlanta had the highest index. The index based on EEOC data for 1966 revealed considerably more discrimination in every city except Phoenix and San Diego, indicating that citywide opportunities in the better occupations, which may have improved for nonwhites, improved even more for whites, suggesting that the nonwhites' occupational status relative to whites may have been worse in 1966, after substantial economic progress, than in 1960.

Recent studies support the view that efforts to raise the income and improve the employment status of minorities, particularly blacks, will not be successful unless we attack the problem of racial discrimination. Moreover, the discrimination aimed at these minorities must be attacked not only in the arena of employment but in other vital areas that affect their economic status, such as housing, schools, and financial institutions.

If discrimination has such a powerful effect on the unemployment rates of nonwhites, we would expect it to have an even greater impact on nonwhite slum residents who are also handicapped by limited education and skills, poor work habits and attitudes, and so forth. Quite surprisingly, neither of our two measures of discrimination was significantly related to the unemployment rate in the sixteen slum areas.* Only in 1960 did occupational distribution emerge as a significant factor: the greater the discrimination, the higher the slum unemployment rates. Moreover, the more precise measure of employment discrimination was not significant in either period. Perhaps the slum residents were so deficient in skills and education that they offered no competition for the better employment opportunities, and discrimination, either direct or subtle, was unnecessary. An extension of this argument is that segregation places most slum residents in a clearly defined category, eligible for specific jobs in specific industrial sectors of the urban labor market and ineligible for others.

The finding illuminates the structure of the job market facing slum residents and nonwhites. Nonwhites who are not residents of slums have more qualifications to compete with white workers for

---

*The measures of discrimination used in this analysis were those reported in Tables 3-5 and 3-6 for the central city containing each slum area.

preferred jobs with higher wages, better promotional opportunities, better working conditions, more stable employment, and greater status. In order to preserve these jobs from the competition of these nonwhites, employment discrimination is practiced: employers either refuse to hire nonwhites or offer them employment at low wages and status relative to their qualifications. Slum residents are eliminated from the competition by their deficiencies in formal education and skills and are assigned to the segregated secondary wage market. If a nonwhite succeeds in obtaining the education, skills, and experience required to break through the primary market, the secondary barrier of employment discrimination is interjected into the process. The result is that an educated nonwhite is placed in a job in the more stable employment environment of the primary sector but below his training, education, and experience.

This interpretation is consistent with the significant relationship found between nonwhite unemployment and occupational discrimination in the thirty cities and with the absence of any significant relationship between employment discrimination and slum unemployment rates in either period. Furthermore, the interpretation is supported by the interesting finding that neither absolute nor relative educational levels are important factors contributing to the difference among slums in unemployment rates.

In light of the fact that educational and discrimination barriers were not strategically related to the level of unemployment in the slums, it seems plausible that the employment growth occurred mostly in the primary labor market reserved for nonminority group workers. If the labor market of the ghetto is indeed segregated, as we have argued, then rapid employment growth will not affect the unemployment of slum residents, unless the growth is in areas, jobs, and industries employing large numbers of unskilled and uneducated workers. Further support of this view comes from examination of the job-vacancy data in newspaper advertisements in the largest cities. During the expansionary period job advertisements were plentiful, while many slum residents remained unemployed. But the vacancies were for noncompetitive primary sector jobs that were clearly out of reach of slum residents.

Employment growth in the primary sectors of the urban labor market, increased absolute and relative educational levels of slum residents, and reduction of employment discrimination will not be sufficient to reduce slum unemployment. Ghetto dwellers in our largest labor markets are locked into a specific, segregated, low-wage, high-turnover, casual labor market, and the structure of this market prevents the standard economic and social improvements from affecting their economic and employment status. An approach to the employment problems of slum residents will not be successful unless there is economic growth and a simultaneously comprehensive attack on all the structural barriers, including relative educational levels.

Minimum Wage

Economic theory, under the assumption of a self-regulating competitive labor market, predicts that arbitrarily setting wage rates higher than the market-determined wage rates will result in a reduction in employment. Marginal firms will close their doors and go out of business; others will attempt to relocate in areas where lower wages prevail; and others will hire only those workers whose productivity exceeds the new arbitrary wage. Even if competitive conditions do not prevail, it is reasonable theoretically to predict displacement of labor at a high minimum-wage rate. Moreover, if the areas affected are the low-wage sectors of the urban economy, employing marginal workers with limited skills and education, an increase in the minimum-wage level may have important effects on the labor market of the ghetto dwellers.

This concept was examined using the data on the sixteen slums.* The hypothesis was that low-wage areas should be more adversely affected by the imposition of the federal minimum-wage law than high-wage areas because they were more likely to have marginal jobs that would be eliminated. This was not the case. The low-wage areas had lower unemployment rates and the high-wage areas had higher unemployment rates.

This relationship indicates some support for the segregated labor market theory. Low-wage areas would tend to have a greater number of employment opportunities for ghetto workers than high-wage areas, which are likely to require skills and education, whether or not they are in fact needed to perform the job.**

The close relationship between high-wage areas and high slum-unemployment rates provides further support for the noncompeting groups theory as well as for the dual labor market concept. Classical

---

*The wage rate used in this analysis was that reported in Chapter 2 (footnote on p. 54) for the central city containing each slum area.

**See Ivar Berg's interesting book supporting the view that requirements are arbitrary and often quite irrelevant to employment performance: Education and Jobs: The Great Training Robbery (New York: Praeger Publishers, 1970).

theory assumes that all labor is substitutable. If wage rates are high, members of the unemployed group will offer their services at lower wages, and the wage rate will adjust downward. The positive relationship between the wage rate and slum unemployment rate refutes this theoretical prediction.

It is possible to interpret this finding as a result of discrimination, as well as the existence of a dual labor market. In this case not only are there distinct sectors in which nonwhites are virtually excluded from employment (dual labor market), but there also would be sectors in which nonwhites are either paid wages or given positions below their qualifications (discrimination).[4] However, we have already noted the findings that occupational discrimination in employment was not a significant factor in slum unemployment. Again, the findings point to the structure of the labor market and the segregation of ghetto dwellers into the low-wage, casual sector as the major factors contributing to higher rates of unemployment among slum residents.

ALTERNATIVES TO EMPLOYMENT

Welfare

The operation of the welfare system in a city is bound to have a significant impact on the economic status and behavior of the ghetto population. Conventional wisdom would lead one to expect that the more people on welfare, the more unemployment there will be among the slum residents. Heavy unemployment among slum residents would stimulate more people to apply for, and receive, welfare. It is also possible to observe the opposite effect: as people receive welfare, they tend to drop out of the labor force and, thus, reduce the level of unemployment. These two forces may offset each other, leaving no apparent relationship between the size of the dependent population and the slum unemployment rate.

Furthermore, the dynamics of the welfare and unemployment relationship may be even more complex. If the residents of slum areas experience severe unemployment, this would stimulate more males who abandoned their families to look for alternative sources of income. One alternative is welfare, which in many places often requires the male to desert his family so that they are eligible to receive relief.* Meanwhile, although he may continue to search for employment

---

*In a number of states the Aid to Families with Dependent Children-Unemployed Parent program is in effect, and the desertion issue is not relevant.

he may not be counted as unemployed, since he has no legal residence.
But the female, who may have been seeking employment before receiving welfare and counted as unemployed, is now out of the labor
force. The effect of these combinations of choices on the unemployment
rate of a slum area is uncertain. Moreover, the relationship between
the welfare system and illegal activities in the urban labor market
further complicates the operation of the ghetto labor market and the
decisions of ghetto dwellers to enter the labor force and be enumerated
by census takers in measuring the rate of slum unemployment.

Analysis of the sixteen slum areas reveals that the welfare case
rate was not related to the slum unemployment rate in either period.*
In 1960 the opposite relationship emerges. This may be explained by
the rapid expansion of jobs in the preceding three years: many welfare
recipients may have remained in the labor force seeking to supplement
their welfare income. Since the welfare case-rate relationship operates
through the labor force decisions of welfare mothers, it is probably
offset by other factors influencing the labor force participation rates
and, consequently, the level of slum unemployment. However, it is
clear that increasing the welfare case rate is not a solution to lowering
the labor force participation rate and, thus, the slum unemployment
rate. Furthermore, high rates of slum unemployment are not related
to high welfare case rates in these cities. Other factors are causing
the large increase in the case-rate loads. Therefore, the converse
proposition is also true: reducing slum unemployment will not have
great impact in reducing the welfare case rates in these cities.

A more direct measure of the impact of welfare on the ghetto
labor force is the size of the payments offered by local welfare systems. The payment structure varies considerably, depending on the
locality, the labor market, and the local administration of the federally
supported system. High payments mean that the decision to enter the
labor force and earn an income from employment represents a significant sacrifice. Therefore, we would expect labor markets that
have a liberal welfare system to have lower participation rates, a
smaller supply of unskilled workers, and, therefore, lower unemployment in the slums. For females with dependent children, the welfare
payment rate represents a measure of the opportunity cost of working.
It may also indirectly represent the income available to a male attached

---

*The welfare case rate used in this analysis is derived by
dividing the total number of welfare cases of Aid to Families with
Dependent Children in a city by that city's population. The population
and the number of cases for 1960 and 1966 are reported for the county
or counties containing each city.

indirectly to a family receiving welfare. The male worker, even though officially not a member of the welfare family, may derive considerable support from the welfare mother. Moreover, under poor economic conditions and limited job opportunities, particularly for the black male worker, high welfare rates encourage him to drop out of the labor force, reducing the rate of unemployment in the slums.*
High rates of welfare payments lessen the pressure to enter the labor force and seek employment. Clearly, low payment levels put greater pressure on the adults to enter the labor force. A similar argument holds for children in a welfare family: high payments should depress their incentive to enter the labor force. The rewards of work after taxes and work-related expenses may be quite low compared to welfare payments.

Cities that had high welfare payments had relatively low rates of unemployment in the slum areas.** This tends to support the view that welfare payments have a tendency to depress participation and, thus, lower unemployment rates. However, in areas where there is very little slum unemployment and, therefore, fewer people who may be eligible for welfare, cities may be able to offer higher levels of welfare payments. That is, a fixed budget for welfare can be allocated to a few people with relatively high payments or to many people with low payments. The weight of the argument seems to be more with depressing the labor force participation effect than with the decision of welfare administrations dictated by the level of slum unemployment, particularly since the funds are primarily from federal sources.

The welfare payment rate was not significantly related to the slum unemployment rate in 1960. Apparently, the lack of job prospects in a recessed economy had a greater influence on the decision not to enter the labor force than the high opportunity costs from the welfare payments available in 1960.

––––––––––––––––––––

*This concept is supported by the result that emerges before and after standardizing the economic model with the welfare payments measure. The employment change was positively associated with unemployment in slums without the welfare payment rate in the model. After this factor was included, the employment changes had a favorable impact on slum unemployment. If high payments cause a smaller labor force, then a given change in employment should reduce slum unemployment rates.

**The welfare payment rate is derived by dividing the total payments for welfare cases of Aid to Families with Dependent Children by the total number of recipients receiving those payments.

The Illegal Market

As an alternative to the legitimate dual market, the illegal labor market offers considerable incentive to many residents of slum areas. Crime and hustling can provide higher incomes, more status and prestige, more exciting work, and better hours and working conditions than the low-wage casual sectors. Moreover, this illegal market may be of sufficient size to affect the extent to which, and the ways in which slum residents participate in the regular dual market.

Employment opportunities in the urban labor market are severely restricted for the ghetto population and labor force. Job and industrial segregation seem to dominate the operation of the ghetto labor market. Residual employment in the casual, low-wage sectors offers poor working conditions, great instability, high turnover, and disorganization. Frustration and hopelessness stimulate the ghetto dweller to seek other activities in pursuit of the better life. The illegal market of criminal activities is readily available and serves as an attractive alternative to the legitimate employment available to a slum dweller, offering high remuneration and status, flexible hours, glamorous activities, and excitement. Moreover, hustling and stealing and gambling and prostitution are alternatives to dying a slow death in the oppressive slums of the cities. If the illegal market is large and accessible, if it provides alternative job activities to ghetto dwellers, it should have a definite impact on slum unemployment. First, if people are engaged in illegal activities, they are likely to tell the enumerators that they are employed, lest their standard of living would arouse suspicion. Second, if the income generated from these activities was sufficiently large to allow them to make transfer payments to relatives, friends, and so forth, this would raise their income level and influence their employment and labor force behavior. Moreover, if friends or relatives were unemployed, it would make it easier for people already engaged in illegal activities to support them temporarily and encourage their entrance into these new and rewarding pursuits.

A property crime index for the thirty cities is presented in Table 3-10. All the cities containing the slum areas experienced sharp increases in the amount of property crime, ranging from 133.8 percent in New York City to 8.7 percent in Chicago. Moreover, the table reveals considerable variation among the cities in both time periods. In 1960 Cleveland had the lowest property-crime rate, 669 per 100,000 population, compared to 2,446 in Los Angeles. Los Angeles retained the distinction of having the worst crime record of all the major cities, with a rate of 3,494 per 100,000 in 1966. The safest city in 1966 was Philadelphia, the City of Brotherly Love, with a rate of 1,133 per 100,000.

The cities that had the greatest amount of property crime in 1966 had a significantly lower unemployment rate in the slums.* Apparently, income-earning potentials in the illegal sector offer an acceptable alternative to secondary employment and unemployment in the slums.

Another interesting relationship supports the concept of the illegal labor market for slum residents. In 1966 a measure of property crime per reported heroin addict[5] was significantly related to the slum unemployment rate. The greater the amount of property crime per heroin addict, the higher the rate of slum unemployment. Apparently, addicts engage in criminal activities to earn money to support their habit, while nonaddicts engage in these activities as an alternative to working in the casual labor market or to being unemployed. Therefore, the more property crime committed by nonaddicts, the more alternative income for ghetto dwellers and the lower the unemployment rate. Moreover, addict-related property crime does not lower slum unemployment rates, because addicts are rarely enumerated in labor force samples and those responding are likely to be nonparticipants. In either case their crimes probably reduce the potential income of other participants in the illegal economy of the cities and raises unemployment.

The importance of illegal activities in the ghetto labor market is also supported by interviews with unemployed youth in Harlem, presented in Chapter 6.

SPATIAL BARRIERS

The physical structure of the urban labor market can have an impact on the employment of residents of inner city ghettos.

We have noted that job dispersal into the suburban areas ringing the central cities has accelerated rapidly during the past decade. However, the measure of job dispersal has no significant relationship to the slum unemployment rates in either 1960 or 1966. This findings is surprising because it contradicts the findings of other studies and because job dispersal was found to be an important factor influencing nonwhite unemployment rates in the city as a whole in 1966. Slum residents in an urban labor market that had a relatively large proportion of jobs in suburban areas did not have significantly higher rates

---

*The property crime index used in this analysis was that reported in note to Table 3-10 for the central city containing each slum area.

of unemployment than residents of poor areas with jobs in closer physical proximity to their homes.*

One possible explanation may be that those areas with the greatest job dispersal also were the least segregated residentially. Thus, if housing discrimination is not practiced to any significant extent, ghetto dwellers may find it possible to relocate in suburban areas that are accessible to jobs. Other factors may account for this surprising finding. First, jobs located in the suburbs may have characteristics other than location that prohibit slum residents from securing them. Manufacturing, retail, and professional services are the activities growing most rapidly in the suburban labor market, and many of these areas require skilled labor. Second, unskilled jobs in suburban areas are usually filled by workers who live in the slum areas of the suburban communities themselves; thus, the availability of these jobs would not have much effect on the employment rates of slum residents of the central city. Third, the suburban labor market generally has the characteristics and structure of the primary labor market; therefore, it automatically excludes slum residents because of their characteristics of race, education, and skill level. Thus, the growth of jobs in the primary sector of the suburban economy has no significance for slum residents, although it does for nonwhite nonslum residents of the city; any growth in the secondary market of suburban areas is filled by nonwhites already living in the suburban slums or by importation of foreign workers.

It is not surprising that the experimental transportation programs in several major cities, such as Watts, Los Angeles, the slums of St. Louis, and the Roxbury, Boston, area, have not had great success in reducing the unemployment problems of the residents of these slums. Finding inexpensive transportation is only one of the job problems facing slum residents. Lack of skills, limited education, poor information, racial and housing discrimination, inequitable financial opportunities and motivation—all these employment barriers must be overcome, as well as the transportation problems. If the other problems were solved simultaneously so that the black slum dweller could secure a decent employment position in a suburban location, he could purchase the necessary transportation.

Housing segregation had an adverse effect on the level and distribution of nonwhite employment in Chicago and Detroit, according to John Kain,[6] who hypothesized that racial segregation in housing

---

*The measure of spatial distribution used in this analysis was that reported on p. 38 (single-asterisked footnote), re Table 2-7, for the central cities containing each slum area.

affects the distribution of black employment and reduces black job opportunities, and, further, that postwar suburbanization of employment has seriously aggravated the problem. Kain offers several reasons why housing market segregation may affect black employment:

1. The difficulty of reaching certain jobs from black residence areas may discourage blacks from seeking employment there.
2. Blacks may have less opportunity to learn about jobs distant from their place of residence.
3. Employers located outside the ghetto may discriminate against blacks out of fear of retaliation from white customers or because they feel little pressure not to discriminate.
4. Similarly, employers in or near the ghetto may discriminate in favor of blacks.

However, contrary to Kain's findings in Detroit and Chicago, our data indicate that housing segregation had a favorable impact on the unemployment problems of ghetto dwellers,* in both the recessed economy of 1960 and the prosperous economy of 1966.** Job information may be the key factor in this unexpected result. Housing segregation in areas of rapid job dispersal may cause higher unemployment rates in the slums because of the difficulty of finding out about jobs

---

*The measure of residential segregation used in this analysis was that for the city containing each slum area.

**The rigidity of the dual labor market and the institutional forces restricting ghetto dwellers to the secondary market are supported by a number of investigations made by state and local human rights and civil rights organizations. Recently, the New York State Division of Human Rights has examined many areas of employment in the city in what can be labeled "the elite sectors of the urban service economy," such as finance, insurance, real estate, advertising, communications, and so forth, The general findings are similar for example,in a recent article in The New York Times (Monday, July 13, 1970) the Human Rights Division of New York State accused the New York Stock Exchange, the symbol of the financial community, of an antiblack bias in hiring. Similar examples can be found in published and unpublished reports of the work of civil rights and human rights groups in other cities. Moreover, the record of many major employers in hiring nonwhite workers is dismal as seen from the records of the Equal Employment Opportunity Reports.

and the cost of commuting to the new job locations. However, as noted, this affects the primary and suburban labor markets chiefly. The quantity and reliability of job information among ghetto dwellers are greatly increased with increased personal contact, such as results from residential segregation. Since ghetto dwellers are virtually excluded from entering the primary market, including suburban employment, lack of information regarding these opportunities and physical distance from these jobs would have no significant impact on the rate of unemployment for slum residents. But if jobs are available, information reduces the job search time; if jobs are not available, it may reduce the labor force by causing voluntary withdrawal of discouraged but well-informed workers.

The results again support the notion of a dual labor market. The growth of jobs, their dispersal to the suburbs, the improvement of transportation to the suburbs, and the relocation of city slum residents to the suburban slums will not reduce the unemployment problem in the city's slum areas, nor will it reduce the employment barriers that face these poor, unskilled persons. Concentrated efforts are required to simultaneously open up more opportunities in the primary market, as the education and training of the unskilled slum dwellers improves, and to change the structure, characteristics, and modes of operation of the casual, low-wage, unstable sector of the urban economy.

INDUSTRIAL STRUCTURE

Rates of unemployment among industries depend on the amount of work they offer experienced workers throughout the year. Table 2-4 indicates the different rates of unemployment experienced by workers attached to the major industrial groups. To our surprise this measure of industrial structure did not explain the variation of unemployment rates in the cities. Nevertheless, we proceeded to analyze the impact of the industrial structure of the city labor market (see Table 2-2) on the ghetto labor force, expecting to observe an even weaker relationship.

The findings are startling. Rather than less impact, the industrial structure had more impact on slum unemployment rates, particularly for 1966, than any other factor or model. In 1966 the industrial mix model explained 82 percent of the variation in slum unemployment rates, and all the industrial sectors had significant relationships with the slum unemployment rate. The industrial mix was less effective in explaining the slum unemployment rates in 1960, but even then it accounted for nearly 50 percent of the variation.

An examination of the relationship of the individual sectors provides strong support for the dual labor market theory. The most interesting result is the relationship between the size of the service sector and the slum unemployment rate. In 1960 a large service sector was associated with very low levels of unemployment in the slums, while in 1966 the opposite relationship was observed. In a period of recession employment opportunities in other sectors may be very limited for slum residents; thus, a large service sector should help to reduce slum unemployment. While this explanation would not account for the seemingly adverse effect of the service sector in 1966, other dramatic changes occurred that would affect this relationship. There was an increase in the required skill level and professionalization of many occupations in the service category. The civil rights movement and the development of black pride led many young blacks to reject employment in the low-wage service sector. Alternative income sources were more readily available, either from the welfare system or from illegal activities. Better employment opportunities were available in other sectors of the growing, dynamic economy of the 1966 period. These events changed the relationship but not the importance of the service sector.

It is also worth noting that the instability of the service sector has more impact in a very tight labor market than in a very loose labor market. In the latter case any employment in any sector is better than no employment; in a tight economy all sectors have low unemployment, and the service sector, therefore, has relatively poor stability. In this circumstance a large service sector, even though it offers more opportunity to slum workers than any other sector, still contributes to higher unemployment rates among ghetto dwellers.

The significance of the industrial structure emerges even more clearly from an examination of the other sectors. The cities that had the largest shares of employment in construction, finance, and manufacturing had the largest amount of slum unemployment: a significant relationship existed in 1966. Apparently, it is the segregation of the jobs available to slum residents and their exclusion from key sectors that accounts for the high unemployment rate.

Only two industrial sectors, retail and wholesale, had a significant and favorable effect on the slum unemployment rate. The larger either of these sectors in 1966, the lower the rate of slum unemployment. Interestingly, the relationship between the size of employment in government and the slum unemployment rate shifted during the six years. In 1960 the larger the government sector, the higher the unemployment rate; by 1966 the opposite relationship was observed. Several factors can account for the change: in a recession, government jobs are highly regarded because of their security and

stability. Intense competition for these scarce and valued jobs made
it virtually impossible for uneducated workers in slum areas to secure government employment. However, recent efforts to redesign
qualifications and testing procedures and to open up new jobs in
community action agencies, New Careers, and other manpower training
and poverty programs, as well as more enforcement of antidiscrimination statutes by state and local officials made it easier for nonwhites,
particularly slum residents, to find jobs in the government sector.
Moreover, the government sector was one of the areas experiencing
substantial employment growth during this period.

To recapitulate the findings, for nonwhites in general, occupational discrimination against those possessing the requisite skills and
qualifications is a critical employment barrier. Slum residents are
confined to the low-wage, casual sectors of the economy and experience
high unemployment rates. The poor are unable to enter the primary
sector, because of limited skills, education, and information and because the doors are locked by discrimination and prejudice. The job
opportunities are only in the secondary sector. Restructuring the
casual secondary labor market and reorganizing the work force in
these sectors will be a more effective way of improving the employment status of slum residents, although it is necessary to break
down the entry barriers into the primary sector as the upgrading and
development of the people living in the slums occurs.

It is interesting to note the effect of rapid economic growth on
the economic conditions of the inner city residents. A dynamic local
economy might exhibit a large and growing manufacturing sector supplied by an active and creative financial sector and characterized by
a large-scale expansionary building program. Such a city would
naturally attract a large number of migrants, many of whom are
likely to be displaced from the agricultural sector. But the evidence
indicates that slum residents cannot obtain employment in these
growth sectors either, because of limited skills, experience, and
education, or because of discrimination or job hoarding by the elite
white labor force. The growth of the local economy does not help
slum residents directly but, in fact, attracts large numbers of would-
be workers to compete for the jobs in the more stagnant secondary
sector of the economy. Intense job competition prevents unionization,
encourages lower wages, and leads to instability. The result is higher
levels of unemployment among the slum residents, increased welfare
case rates, more illegal and criminal activities, and a growing
reluctance to work in the low-wage, service-dominated sector of the
economy.

It should be apparent that what appears to be desirable for the
white city labor force and the suburban labor force—that is, a rapidly
growing, dynamic, central city economy—often causes serious problems

for the city itself. The urban white labor force, faced with higher taxes, poorer services, closer contact with the migrant and slum residents, deteriorating schools, and limited housing is easily attracted to live in the suburbs while working in the city. The city loses further revenue from income and property taxes, and more industries move into the suburbs because of the expanded labor supply and the lower taxes and costs of space, causing even further erosion of the city's power to generate revenues. The vicious circle continues, as revenues decline and demands for supportive services skyrocket, leaving less for the other services of urban life: sanitation, recreation, schools, police, and fire protection. Less service for more money forces more people to leave. Yet, a growing number of new migrants appear, attracted by the belief that the city offers more job opportunities and better services than their current rural residences or, at least, higher welfare payments and the greater availability of public support. The secondary sector needs and wants a growing supply of workers. The primary sector either follows or leads its work force to the suburbs or attacks the municipal government for higher taxes and deteriorating services, while it cooperates with the Urban Coalition and the Urban League to improve the conditions of the poor and the minority groups entering the city.

The unemployment rate of a city has a spillover effect on the unemployment rate of slum areas in the city. The higher the unemployment in the city, the higher the rate of unemployment in the slums. Although this finding is due in part to the fact that the city unemployment rate includes the slum unemployment rate, it does indicate that, before the slum unemployment rate can be improved, it will be necessary to lower unemployment rates for the large urban labor market. However, economic and employment growth alone will be insufficient because of the operation of structural factors and, most important, the existence of a dual labor market, with slum dwellers segmented into the secondary and illegal labor markets of the urban economy.

The lack of importance of educational barriers, spatial barriers, and employment discrimination and the importance of the industrial structure, the wage level, and illegal activities point to the existence of a rigidly divided economy: a primary, elite, high-wage, stable-employment sector and a casual, secondary, low-wage unstable sector. Supplementing the secondary economy is the illegal market, providing income and employment to those who are attracted to it by the depressed conditions of the secondary market. The elimination of educational deficiencies, both absolute and relative, the growth of employment in the city, the improvement of transportation, the elimination of housing discrimination in the suburbs, the halt of job dispersal into the suburbs, the elimination of migration, and the reduction of the labor force in the slum areas—none of these events alone will have a substantial impact on the employment problems of slum residents or significantly reduce their subemployment or unemployment rates. Only if public policy is also directed toward restructuring the industrial structure, organization, modes of operation, and degree of worker organization in the secondary market and simultaneously providing training and employment opportunities for slum residents in the primary sector will we be able to move toward a solution for the economic and social problems of these slum residents.

Young nonwhite workers aged sixteen to nineteen have the highest rate of unemployment of all groups in the national labor force—29.1 percent, nearly ten times the unemployment rate of white adult workers aged twenty years and over in 1970.[1] Moreover, the unemployment rate of these severely disadvantaged members of the labor force had worsened substantially since 1960, when it was 24.4 percent, despite a rapid acceleration in the growth of the economy producing a record number of new job opportunities. From 1960 to 1970 the number of unemployed youngsters aged sixteen to nineteen rose from 713,000 to 1.106 million. Youth employment opportunities increased by over 2 million jobs, but this was not sufficient to absorb the unusual growth of the youth labor force, which increased from 4.842 million to 7.246 million between 1960 and 1970 (primarily as a result of the post-World War II baby boom).

In 1960 the unemployment rate for white workers aged sixteen to nineteen years was 13.4 percent; for nonwhites in this age group it was 24.4 percent. Between 1960 and 1970 the over-all white unemployment rate for those between sixteen and nineteen remained virtually stable, but for nonwhites it jumped dramatically, as we have seen.

For the older segment of the youth labor market, those aged twenty to twenty-four years, the over-all unemployment rate fell slightly, from 8.7 percent to 8.2 percent; however, the decrease was less than for the adult labor force. The expansion of the economy contributed to a slight decrease in unemployment among nonwhite males in the same age group, from 13.1 percent in 1960 to 12.6 percent by 1970.

Young female workers, both white and nonwhite, had more serious problems than their male counterparts, with the nonwhite females experiencing the highest rates of unemployment. By 1970 approximately one-third of the nonwhite females who were sixteen to nineteen years of age were unemployed.

122

The employment problem confronting young workers, particularly nonwhites, is considerably worse in the slum areas of our largest cities. In 1966 unemployment rates of young workers (sixteen to nineteen) living in twelve slum areas ranged from approximately 20 percent to 40 percent. (See Table 5.1.)* These figures exceed the highest rate of unemployment experienced during the Great Depression of 1929-33. Moreover, the position of these youngsters relative to either white youngsters or the labor force as a whole is steadily worsening. Youngsters in ghetto areas had at least five times the rate of unemployment experienced by all other workers in 1966 and at least one and one-half times that of their white age-peers.

These twelve slum areas vary considerably in the unemployment rates of young workers. Moreover, there are considerable differences among the various subage groups within the fourteen- to twenty-four-year range. (See Table 5.1). Boston's slum area of Roxbury had the lowest unemployment rate for fourteen to twenty-four year olds—14.8 percent—nearly five times the rate for the city itself. The slum area of St. Louis had the highest rate—30.3 percent—nearly eight times the national unemployment rate.

Statistical analysis of various factors advanced to explain to the variations in youth unemployment among slum areas does not provide a full understanding of the employment problems of these youngsters. Many factors cannot be quantified. Data are not collected for subgroups of the labor force in small geographic areas. What data are collected are often inaccurate and of limited scope. Moreover, the type of information required often cannot be obtained by census enumerators in federal surveys of poor areas. In order to obtain a more accurate view of the employment problems of young workers living in ghetto areas, we undertook a series of interviews in depth with unemployed black youth in Harlem, to complement the statistical analysis. This chapter contains the statistical analysis; Chapter 6 analyzes the material obtained from the interviews.

THE NATURE OF THE LABOR MARKET FOR YOUTH

Edward Kalachek, in an excellent monograph summarizing the literature on the youth labor market and youth unemployment, cites a number of areas of employment that have large concentrations of

---

*The data for young workers aged fourteen to twenty-four were only available for the twelve slum areas of the Urban Employment Survey of 1966.

TABLE 5.1

Unemployment Rates of Youth: Slum Areas, 1966

Slum Area	14-19	16-19	20-24	14-24
Harlem	30.6	27.8	11.8	19.5
East Harlem	27.8	25.1	8.0	16.6
Brooklyn	22.4	20.0	7.0	13.1
Philadelphia	29.6	26.6	13.6	22.0
St. Louis	40.4	39.2	18.9	30.3
San Antonio	25.9	24.6	10.3	18.7
Phoenix	28.9	27.0	13.5	21.8
New Orleans	36.4	34.7	11.6	22.2
San Francisco	39.0	35.7	14.0	20.8
Boston	25.9	21.2	7.4	14.8
South Chicago	22.1	21.9	8.2	15.1
West Chicago	20.7	18.2	5.1	12.8

Source: "Urban Employment Survey of 1966," unpublished data prepared by the U.S. Department of Labor, Bureau of Labor Statistics.

young workers. (See Table 5.2.) In a sense, there are two distinct labor markets, with a large area of overlap where adults and youth substitute for each other quite freely. However, there are sectors of the economy in which workers fourteen to nineteen years of age and adult male workers are segregated, and no substitution between them occurs. In these sectors and occupations a high degree of segregation based on age is enforced by a variety of legal and institutional factors operating on the supply and demand of labor.

The size of the youth labor force and youth labor force participation rates are affected by many factors that do not affect the adult labor market to the same extent, if at all.

1. There are school-attendance laws established by state legislatures and varying considerably by state, requiring youngsters to attend school a certain number of days per year and a certain number of hours per day until they reach a specified age.

2. State and federal legislation regarding health and safety conditions, hours of work, overtime, child labor, and so forth operate to reduce the number of employment opportunities for young workers.

3. Trade union restrictions often stipulate the age of admission into a union or into an apprenticeship program. In many places of employment covered by union shop provisions, it is impossible for

TABLE 5.2

Distribution of Employment by Major Occupations
for the United States, 1960
(percentage distribution)

Occupation	Total Work Force	Males, Ages 18-19	Males, Ages 14-17	Females, Ages 18-19	Females, Ages 14-17
Professional and Technical Workers	11.6	3.4	1.0	6.2	2.5
Managers and Officials	8.7	1.2	.5	.5	.3
Clerical Workers	15.0	11.5	6.5	49.7	20.5
Sales Workers	7.5	7.7	19.3	7.7	17.1
Craftsmen and Foremen	14.0	10.0	3.8	.5	.4
Operatives	19.2	26.6	15.2	9.4	5.9
Private Household Workers	2.8	.2	.8	5.5	21.7
Service Workers	8.8	8.4	11.0	11.8	17.6
Nonfarm Laborers	5.0	14.5	17.5	.6	1.0
Farm Laborers	2.3	9.1	16.2	1.0	3.5
Occupation Not Reported	5.1	7.4	8.3	7.1	9.6
Total*	100.0	100.0	100.0	100.0	100.0

*Components may not sum exactly to total due to rounding.

Source: Census of Population: 1960, U.S. Bureau of Census, Vol.
1, in Edward Kalachek, "The Youth Labor Market," a joint publication
of the Institute of Labor and Industrial Relations, The University of
Michigan—Wayne State University, and the National Manpower Policy
Task Force (Washington, D.C., 1969).

young workers to obtain employment. Moreover, union seniority
provisions favor older workers in terms of promotion and rehiring
after layoffs and, thus, place young workers at a further disadvantage
in keeping jobs.

4. Certification, licensing, and formal educational requirements
in many occupations and industries prevent youth from obtaining
employment.

5. Employers and personnel offices may use age and formal educational criteria as a way of screening out young employees because they believe these workers to be less stable.

6. The location of jobs is more significant to young workers than adults, since youngsters often do not have the means of commuting to and from work by private transportation. This restricts the available job opportunities to the neighborhood the young worker resides in or to one accessible to public transportation. Young workers who live at home or attend school cannot follow employment opportunities in other counties, states, or countries, as many adults can. Since youngsters in school require part-time work, the time that must be spent traveling to work is less than that spent by adults and, thus, restricts the number of job opportunities.

7. Young workers often have a higher preference for leisure and need less income than adult workers. As a result the youth labor market is characterized by higher rates of job turnover.

8. Because, as noted, part-time work characterizes a large segment of the youth labor market, the youth labor force is in direct competition with a subset of the female labor force also requiring part-time work, flexible hours, and extra secondary income.

9. The youth labor market may be favorably affected by the growth and cost of fringe benefits and overtime work but it may be unfavorably affected by the increase in minimum-wage laws affecting low-wage firms and industries and reducing employment opportunities in those sectors of the urban economy.

10. The provision of welfare payments to mothers with dependent children may reduce the need for teenage children to seek employment to support the family.

11. New entrants into the labor force are in an experimental stage, looking for a suitable job. This requires frequent job changes and a higher level of unemployment during the job-search process.

These general factors clearly have a differential impact on adult and young workers, explaining in part their different employment patterns and unemployment rates. But we are concerned with discovering why unemployment and employment experiences differ among young workers, particularly among young nonwhite workers living in various ghetto areas. In order to shed some light on this question we focused on a number of hypotheses that we believed might account for these differences:

Did any of the standard economic forces or conditions account for the variation in youth unemployment among slum areas? Did employment growth of an urban economy have any impact? Did some areas have employment growth in youth-sensitive jobs compared to others, and did this account for different unemployment rates? Did the changes in the labor supply of young workers affect the unemployment

rate of young workers in slum areas? Did the minimum wage level
have an adverse impact on youth unemployment? Or did the welfare
system, the size and/or the level of payments, have an impact on the
unemployment rate of young workers living in slums? Did female
labor force participation have an adverse effect on youth unemployment
in a slum area? Or was the difference among areas in youth unemployment due to the differences found in the local labor markets' unemployment rates?

It may well be that economic factors do not have a very significant
impact on youth unemployment and that the substantial variations that
exist are due either to the industrial structure of the urban economy,
reflecting the job opportunities available to young workers, or to the
large number of structural employment barriers in a local labor
market. For example, the differences may be due to differences in the
educational achievement of youngsters in different communities or to
gaps that exist between the educational attainments of young workers
and the employers' requirements. If education is not significant, the
differences may be due to discrimination against nonwhites by employers and trade unions. The location of jobs may be of critical
importance in some labor markets and not in others. Perhaps the
income and activities in the illegal sector of the urban economy affect
youngsters in slum areas and their level of unemployment. And,
finally, health may be a vital factor affecting youth unemployment,
either directly, if they are not able to work, or indirectly, by forcing
youngsters into the labor force to aid their ailing parents.*

Unfortunately, research and policy making are seriously ham-
pered by the paucity of data for local areas, particularly central cities.
The collection of data by SMSA ignores the political realities of government decision making, as well as the important differences between
the central city and the surrounding suburban communities. Regional
data often hide glaring trends that in the aggregate portray a picture
of prosperity and growth, but in the disaggregate reveal rapid decay
and deterioration in the central city, offset by great affluence and
growth in the surrounding counties.

---

*Although there were other factors worth analyzing, we were
unable to obtain the necessary data. For example, it would be useful
to examine school-attendance laws in different cities (although we
believe that very little variation exists among the largest cities in our
sample), to examine the minimum-wage laws prevailing in each city
to test the minimum-wage impact more directly, or to compare the
educational achievement scores of school systems in slum areas
relative to other schools in a city to observe educational quality
differences.

THE FINDINGS

Industrial Structure

The structure of the urban economy determines the extent of age segregation in the labor market. Cities dominated by industries that tend to discriminate against young workers and have developed powerful institutional and legal barriers to their entry have higher rates of unemployment for youth and for slum youth in particular. The struggle for control over preferred jobs that are limited or secure for a specific segment of the labor force residing in the urban centers has resulted in the establishment of laws, rules, and institutions, such as trade unions and employees' associations. Control over jobs is fundamental to the economic survival of workers. Consequently, the urban labor market becomes structured in a series of fairly well-defined compartments or sectors. Unorganized and weaker members of the urban labor force cannot compete effectively with the dominant white labor force, which is organized and protected by laws, institutional arrangements, and political pressures. White males in the urban labor force may be government employees, union members, or professionally licensed or certified. White-collar office or managerial workers are adequately protected against job competition from blacks, Mexican-Americans, Puerto Ricans, and Indians, as well as from youthful and female members of the labor force. This division of workers has resulted in a widening gap in unemployment experience and economic status between the two groups.

Analysis of the factors accounting for unemployment among slum youth provides considerable support for the concept of segmented labor markets in the urban economy. The existence of powerful barriers to entry into the preferred, high-income, stable employment sectors dominates the conventional forces, such as the supply and demand for labor, the quality of the labor force, the location of employment opportunities, and so forth. The industrial structure of the urban economy measured by the shares of employment in each of the major industries accounted for more than 75 percent of the variation in unemployment rates for youths aged fourteen to nineteen, sixteen to nineteen, and twenty to twenty-four.* In labor markets dominated by the construction and manufacturing sectors, there are higher youth unemployment rates than in markets with a large retail sector.

---

*The industrial structure used in this analysis was that reported in Table 2.2 for the central city containing each slum area.

The impact of the industrial structure on youth unemployment varied with age. For the workers twenty to twenty-four years of age, manufacturing was the most significant sector in contributing to higher unemployment rates. Workers aged sixteen to nineteen years were most sensitive to the share of employment in the retail trade sector; the larger the retail sector, the lower the unemployment rate. The share of employment in the construction sector had the largest adverse impact on unemployment for the total youth labor force, fourteen to twenty-four years of age.

Finance, insurance, and real estate, wholesale, transportation, and services were all statistically insignificant in explaining youth unemployment rates. Government employment was also not significant. This may be explained by two counteracting trends. Civil service requirements, such as age, certification, and testing, operate to reduce the employment opportunities for youth in government. However, the growth of new governmental programs in the social welfare and anti-poverty area may have offset the standard institutional factors and expanded employment opportunities for youth in slum areas.

The evidence indicates that a complex, interrelated set of factors has developed and segregated job opportunities for adults and youth. Labor markets characterized by a large share of employment in manufacturing and construction demonstrate the greatest degree of employment segregation. The institutional barriers used to prevent or restrict the entry of young workers into these segregated sectors are, first and foremost, the trade unions, which control or greatly influence the number of people eligible to work in these preferred industries. The degree of unionization in the industrial sector is probably the most significant factor accounting for the impact of the employment shares on youth unemployment. Manufacturing and construction have the greatest degree of union strength relative to the other sectors in the urban economy, and it is not surprising to observe the adverse impact on youth unemployment. Moreover, the union's principal device for rationing jobs during adverse economic times is the seniority system, which discriminates against younger workers in favor of older workers. Consequently, even if young workers were permitted by unions to enter the occupation or industry, they would have a greater likelihood of becoming unemployed than older workers.

In addition, custom, mores, or laws have restricted the entry of youth into many occupations and industries. Legal factors have often set limits on the labor supply of young workers. Child-labor laws and compulsory school-attendance laws set the lower parameter on the eligibility and size of the youth labor force. Although many legislative acts have promoted health and welfare of children as their primary objectives, they have also resulted, whether by conscious design or not, in restricting the youth labor force. Adult attitudes and prejudices regarding young workers have often been influenced by the extension of these legal structures beyond their relevant context. The application of these laws and rules, although well specified, often spills over beyond the realistic time period and is used to justify employment discrimination and segregation based on age. Conventional views, such as "the longer children stay in school, the better off they will be," or "teenagers should not do strenuous physical work because it is unhealthy," are used to rationalize employment discrimination against young workers in the interest of these workers. "All children should attend college" is a popular middle-class American view that permeates all economic and social classes. The result is an unparalleled expansion of college enrollment in the past decade. The passion for college education, regardless of its economic or social value, has, as its by-product, a sharp reduction of the young labor force and a built-in bias against youngsters not in college and seeking full-time productive employment. If college is beneficial for all youth, then employers or unions that entice youngsters into the labor force are depriving them of the "opportunity of a lifetime." This tortured logic provides an excuse for exercising an initial prejudice against young workers.

The prejudice against employing young workers may be based on perfectly reasonable and justifiable grounds. The unions recognize that shortages of labor mean less job competition, higher wages, and more union power. Consequently, school-attendance laws and higher education are vigorously supported by the union movement, not only because education is valuable for all Americans but also because it is consistent with the union's basic economic and political objectives. Employers find their predilection for older workers justifiable, partly because they do not want to antagonize the union or destroy harmonious union-management relations, but primarily because young workers are less desirable economically than older workers. Young workers have lower productivity because of greater inexperience, absenteeism, lateness, turnover, and the need for more training time.

The blending of interests of the employers and unions, reinforced by the dominant value system, which places health and education of children above all else, has resulted in a segregated labor market. The degree of segregation varies among urban labor markets. To the extent that segregation is substantial, youth unemployment will be high.

The educational-certification syndrome so aptly described by Ivar Berg in Education and Jobs: The Great Training Robbery[2] is another practice restricting the participation of young workers in the labor market. Getting a college degree for its own sake, regardless of whether it is necessary to perform in the economy, is a permanent feature of the job-search process. The requirement of an educational degree operates to reduce competition, afford protection for those with

degrees, and prolong the period before entrance into the labor market
as a full-time worker. Professional certification and licensing,
controlled or influenced by professional associations, societies, and
state governments, also tend to segregate the labor market and isolate
youth from competing for jobs. The number of eligible workers and
the length of time required to qualify for degrees, licenses, and
certificates are often controlled by the workers and their institutions,
which determine policy for their own benefit and not in the interest
of the general public, and by publicly approved devices, such as laws
and licenses through state and municipal governments. A notable and
controversial example of entry control is the apprenticeship system
in the construction-trade unions. This device allows unions to select
potential journeymen from a large pool of applicants. Criteria for
selection are solely in the hands of the union officials, and charges of
discrimination, prejudice, and nepotism have recently plagued the
apprenticeship system.

The American Medical Association has virtually the same effect
in controlling entry into the medical profession, exerting its control
on several levels, from medical school admission procedures to the
certification procedures at specialty board examinations and hospitals'
decisions on applicants to meet intern and residence requirements.

Job control and job security, designed to protect the employment
and improve the earnings of workers, are obtained by segregating the
urban labor market. Consequently, employment opportunities for youth
are reduced substantially and unemployment rises. The methods
employed are defended in the name of consumer protection and in the
interests of youth themselves.

The unfavorable impact of the structure of the urban labor market
on youth unemployment indicates that a general increase in employment
in all sectors will not help to reduce unemployment. Only the expansion of the retail trade sector is likely to alleviate high youth unemployment among slum residents. Unfortunately, there is limited if any
growth in employment in the retail trade sector, particularly in the
central business districts of the major cities. In some cities employment in retail trade has declined. Most of the growth in retail trade
employment has occurred in suburban areas that are inaccessible to
youngsters in the city, particularly poor, minority group youngsters,
without cars or adequate public transportation to the suburbs. Between
1951 and 1966 retail employment increased by 30.0 percent in the
county containing the central city but by 130.8 percent in the suburban
rings. The relative change in employment in the retail sector should
be helpful for youngsters living near suburban shopping centers and
those who have access to automobiles; however, it does not look very
promising for black youth residing in slum areas of major cities.

The concept that a tightly segregated labor market reduces
employment opportunities for youth in the urban economy is supported
by the insignificant impact the growth of employment had on reducing
unemployment of youngsters fourteen to nineteen years of age. The
considerable differences among the urban labor markets in the growth
of employment did not contribute to explaining variations among the
unemployment rates of fourteen to nineteen year olds in these areas.
Under normal labor market conditions, without artificial barriers
isolating some segments of the labor force, the demand for labor should
be a primary factor in reducing unemployment, including youth unemployment. Assuming that the labor supply does not grow proportionally
faster than the increased demand for workers, rapid employment growth
in the city should create more job opportunities for young workers and,
thus, reduce their unemployment rate.

The findings indicate that employment growth was not significant
in reducing unemployment among fourteen to nineteen year olds but
was a major factor in reducing unemployment for twenty to twenty-four
year olds. Their similarity to adult workers allowed this older group
of young workers to find jobs in the segregated labor market when
employment expanded substantially in the city. However, the employment growth occurred in areas of the urban economy that were closed
to workers fourteen to nineteen years of age—e.g., finance, insurance,
real estate, government, transportation, construction, services, and
manufacturing. Retail trade expanded only slightly and in some cases
declined. The conclusion is clear: the growth of employment per se
will not reduce unemployment among fourteen to nineteen year olds
residing in slum areas; however, it will reduce unemployment of young
adult workers (twenty to twenty-four years old) in slums.

If industrial structure segregates the labor market, then employment growth can have a favorable impact if it occurs in areas
dominated by youth employment. Therefore, it is reasonable to expect
that differential growth in youth-sensitive or youth-dominated jobs
should account for differences among localities in youth unemployment.*

----

*To derive an index of youth-sensitive employment a national
nine-industry-by-nine-occupation matrix of employment by age was
used to obtain the number of persons aged fourteen to twenty-four that
were employed in each cell of the matrix. The absolute figures were
aggregated by industry and transformed into percentages to obtain the
share of youth employment by industry for the nation. These percentages were applied to absolute employment in the appropriate industrial
classifications for each of the labor markets of our cities containing
the slum areas in 1959 to obtain a measure of youth-sensitive

Surprisingly, no relationship was found between the growth of employment in youth jobs and youth unemployment in slum areas.* Perhaps the employment growth was insufficient to absorb the new nonwhite workers entering the labor force. Perhaps white youngsters absorbed the newly created youth jobs at the expense of nonwhite youngsters in ghettos. Ghetto nonwhites may be prevented from obtaining employment by the inaccessibility of jobs oriented to youth in the suburbs; by racial discrimination; by limited job information; by the excessive labor-supply response of nonwhite youngsters, given the number of new jobs; or by a combination of these factors. Thus, a dismal picture emerges: employment growth even in jobs employing young workers and accompanied by increases in the educational attainment of nonwhite youngsters did not reduce unemployment or explain variations among slum areas in youth unemployment.

Labor Supply

A growing supply of labor with a relatively fixed amount of employment opportunities for young workers in the ghettos is likely

---

employment. For 1966 national employment data by the same nine industrial categories was used from County Business Patterns. To this was applied a nine-industry-by-nine-occupation matrix that was extrapolated from a national industry occupation matrix for 1960 and 1975 developed by the U.S. Department of Labor. Since data for employment cross-classified by industry, occupation, and age was not available for 1966, it was assumed youth aged fourteen to twenty-four comprised the same share of employment in each cell of the matrix as they did in 1960. The data were then aggregated to obtain the share of youth employment by industry. These national percentages were applied to employment data by industry of each of the cities containing the slum areas in 1966 to obtain a measure of youth-sensitive employment. Source: U.S. Bureau of the Census, U.S. Census of Population: 1960, Occupation by Industry, Final Report PC (2)-7C (Washington, D.C., 1963); and County Business Patterns, CBP-66, 4, 5, 6, 7, 10, 12, 15, 16, 18, 19, 22, 23, 24, 25, 27, 32, 34, 37, 40, 44, 45, 49, and 51 (Washington, D.C., 1967). Tomorrow's Manpower Needs, U.S. Bureau of Labor Statistics, Vol. IV: The National Industry-Occupational Matrix and Other Manpower Data, Bulletin No. 1601, Appendix G (Washington, D.C., 1969). (Our study used advance data from this report.)

*In some equations a positive relationship exists contrary to our expectations and is statistically significant for the entire group fourteen to twenty-four years of age.

to result in higher rates of unemployment among these workers. Two measures of the size of the potential youth labor force were tested: labor-force participation rates and net migration rates into the cities. As Table 5-3 shows, there were sharp differences in labor force participation rates of youngsters in these slum areas. For all age groups the labor force participation rate was not significant in explaining the differences among the slum areas in youth unemployment rates. In general, the higher the labor force participation rate for fourteen to nineteen year olds, the lower their unemployment rate, but the statistical relationship was not significant. Apparently, two sets of forces are operating to offset the relationship. First, if employment is increasing and the unemployment rate of young workers is low, more youngsters may seek employment, thus raising the participation rate. On the other hand, if unemployment is high and jobs are scarce, youngsters may enter the labor force to help support their families, and the unemployment rate may continue to worsen. These two conditions may occur simultaneously. Thus, no significant relationship between the youth's participation rate and unemployment rate emerges from the findings.

The rate of net migration into the cities at times seems to be significantly related to the unemployment rate of older members of the youth labor force.* The more net migration in the preceding six years, the higher the unemployment rate of youngsters twenty to twenty-four years of age, perhaps because of competition from new migrants in this age cohort entering the city's labor force.**

The net-migration rate into the city had no relationship to the unemployment rate of youngsters aged fourteen to nineteen years. This seems to suggest that the migrants were not teenagers and did not have teenage children and that, therefore, very little increase in this segment of the youthful slum labor force occurred when net migration rates were high.

Female Labor Force Competition

Given the nature of the jobs available to or sought by youth—predominantly part-time, casual, low wage, with flexible hours and low skill requirements—we would expect youth to experience considerable

---

*In some cases the opposite relationship was found, but it was not statistically significant.

**The rate of net migration used in this analysis was that reported in note to Table 2-11 for the central city containing each slum area.

TABLE 5.3

Labor Force Participation Rates of Youth:
Slum Areas, 1966

Slum Area	14-19	16-19	20-24	14-24
Harlem	32.5	43.4	69.6	47.5
East Harlem	27.1	38.2	59.3	39.0
Brooklyn	27.7	39.7	64.0	42.3
Philadelphia	35.9	52.0	62.8	45.2
St. Louis	32.6	45.7	70.0	43.6
San Antonio	30.6	42.7	66.0	40.6
Phoenix	36.5	49.0	65.4	45.7
New Orleans	27.6	37.3	70.6	42.4
San Francisco	31.2	44.9	73.4	53.7
Boston	35.0	48.2	64.7	48.2
South Chicago	20.4	30.8	66.1	31.4
West Chicago	26.7	39.8	68.5	38.8

Source: "Urban Employment Survey of 1966," unpublished data prepared by the U.S. Department of Labor, Bureau of Labor Statistics.

competition from the female labor force. The more intense the competition, measured by the female labor force participation rate, the higher the unemployment rate among slum youngsters.* For youngsters aged twenty to twenty-four, we found that such a relationship was not significant. Apparently, competition between this group and females was limited. Considering that this age group resembles adult workers in seeking full-time work in more stable industries and occupations, the failure to observe a significant relationship is understandable.

An opposite and significant relationship was found between the female participation rate and the unemployment rate of sixteen to nineteen year olds. The more females there are in the labor force, the lower is the unemployment rate among sixteen to nineteen year olds living in slum areas. This suggests that the youngsters may drop out of the labor force because they were not successful in competing

---

*The female labor force participation rate used in this analysis was that for females aged 16 years and over living in the central city containing each slum area. Monthly Labor Review (U.S. Department of Labor, Bureau of Labor Statistics); unpublished data supplied by the Bureau of Labor Statistics, 1968; and special tabulations prepared by the U.S. Bureau of the Census, 1969, based on annual averages from the "Current Population Survey of 1967."

with women for part-time jobs. Employed women may provide sufficient secondary income to reduce the pressure on youngsters to
enter the labor force; thus, they may inflate the measured rate of
unemployment among youth.

In summary, higher female labor force participation rates were
not significantly related to higher unemployment rates among slum
youths aged fourteen to twenty-four and among those aged twenty to
twenty-four. Higher female participation rates were significantly
related to lower unemployment rates among sixteen to nineteen year
old slum youths. This suggests that young teenagers leave the labor
force when faced with female competition, but that for older youths
this trend may be counteracted by the necessity for many of them to
support themselves and remain in the labor force.

Wage Level and Minimum Wages

The relationship of the level of wages prevailing in an urban
labor market and the unemployment rate of youth, particularly youths
residing in slum areas of central cities, has several important policy
implications. First, as we have noted, much controversy has been
generated over the impact of the minimum wage on employment opportunities, particularly for marginal workers. (Marginal workers are
defined as the unskilled and uneducated and normally include teenage
and other young workers.) The argument is based on the theory that
establishing artificial wage floors above the marginal revenue productivity of workers will force some firms to reduce their staffs and
force others out of business. In either case employment would be
reduced, and young workers in low wage-competitive industries would
be the first to be affected. Thus, minimum wages would contribute
to the rising level of youth unemployment. Some economists argue
that the increase in the minimum wage has been a major contributor
to the high rates of youth unemployment during the recent period of
economic prosperity. In order to test the impact of minimum wages
in urban labor markets on youth unemployment in slum areas, the
average wage level was used.* The crude test of the hypothesis was
the following: the lower the wage level in a given labor market, the
greater the impact of the federal minimum wage on the community,
and the higher the rate of youth unemployment. (Data on prevailing

---

*The wage level used in this analysis was that reported in
Chapter 2, p. 54 (footnote), for the central city containing each slum
area.

minimum wages in the cities of our sample would have been desirable but were not available.)

An alternative hypothesis is based on the existence of wage rigidities in the local market. Wages do not adjust downward, even in periods of heavy unemployment. Unemployed workers cannot, and do not, offer their labor services at lower wages than employed workers; thus, they remain unemployed—perhaps because of insufficient or inaccurate information, commutation and transportation problems, housing barriers, and so forth,or perhaps because of the existence of noncompeting groups of workers in the labor market, representing different levels of skills and education, accounting for full employment in some occupations and heavy unemployment in other occupations. The lack of substitution among workers may account for an area characterized both by high wages and a high rate of unemployment. Moreover, the noncompeting groups hypothesis seems more likely to apply to young adult workers, for the reasons cited earlier. Young workers would experience even greater difficulties in finding employment in a labor market where high wages reflect skill, education, or productivity. Strong trade unions would create an additional employment problem for young workers seeking to enter the skilled urban labor market. High-wage labor markets may be an indicator of the extent of job segregation of adults and youth. High wages reduce the degree of substitution and raise youth unemployment.

For all subsets of the youth group aged fourteen to twenty-four, the wage level was positively related to the unemployment rate.* Moreover, the relationship was statistically significant. The minimum-wage hypothesis is not supported by the results. However, the noncompeting groups hypothesis and the segregated labor market concept are supported by the results, indicating that, in urban labor markets characterized by high wages, it is more difficult for young workers to find employment while competing for adult jobs. Low-wage areas have substantial employment opportunities for youth, and competition and substitution between youth and adults occur more frequently. Rising levels of wages, greater union strength, and rising educational requirements may operate to reduce employment opportunities for youth and, given the rapid growth in the supply of young workers, would account for rising unemployment. Furthermore, competition from white youngsters and female workers for the limited number of jobs

---

*In the equations that included the welfare case rates, the relationship between the wage level and unemployment rate was not significant. In all other cases it was significant.

available to youth would aggravate the unemployment problems of
nonwhite youth in ghetto areas.

Adult Unemployment Rate

The adult unemployment rate* in the slums was not related to
the unemployment rate of either the fourteen to nineteen year olds or
the sixteen to nineteen year olds in those areas. This provides further
evidence that the younger segment of the youth labor force is influenced
by a different set of factors than the adult labor force. The unemployment rate of youngsters twenty to twenty-four years of age was very
closely and significantly related to the adult unemployment rate,
supporting the view that the two groups of youngsters are influenced
by different forces in the urban labor market. The twenty to twenty-
four year olds are subject to the same forces as the adults residing
in slums, while the youngsters are not. The degree of segregation in
the labor market affects the youngsters below twenty years of age, and
the adverse impact increases according to the age of the youngster.

Structural Barriers

The analysis indicates that the industrial structure of the urban
economy, as reflected by the employment shares of the various industrial sectors and the wage rate, has a critical impact on the level of
youth unemployment in slum areas, particularly that of fourteen to
nineteen year olds. The traditional economic factors reflecting the
supply and demand of these workers were insignificant in explaining
slum youth unemployment, as compared with the structure of the labor
market and the institutional and legal factors segregating youth from
adult workers and reducing job opportunities for young workers.
However, there are a number of interrelated social and economic
factors, often institutionalized in the operation of the urban labor
market, which affect the employment prospects of nonwhite youth in
the ghetto areas of our largest cities. Here, we are concerned with
the impact of educational factors and the educational requirements of
jobs, the health of the young workers, alternative sources of income,

---

*The adult unemployment rate refers to persons aged twenty-
five years and over. Source: "Urban Employment Survey of 1966,"
unpublished data prepared by the U.S. Department of Labor, Bureau
of Labor Statistics.

housing segregation, employment discrimination, and the spatial location of employment.

The concept of a dual labor market for nonwhite workers, particularly slum dwellers, would be even more applicable in determining opportunities for slum youth. Thus, we would expect to find that these structural forces would be of greater intensity for young workers and account for higher rates of unemployment than for adult workers living in slum areas.

Educational Gap

Ignoring, for the moment, the large variations in the quality of education, it is important to see whether quantitative differences in education account for the differences in unemployment rates among youth living in different slums. Moreover, it is extremely important to test whether the difference between the amount of education required by employers in a given labor market and the amount of education supplied by the young nonwhite population account for these differences in youth unemployment.

The higher the demand for educated workers, the lower the unemployment rate for youth in slum areas.* This finding appears to be inconsistent with the expectation that in labor markets requiring high educational attainment, young workers would be at a severe disadvantage because of competition from adult workers, fewer employment opportunities for youth, more prevalent age discrimination, and their inadequate educational attainment. However, the result can be explained by a noncompetitive groups hypothesis and is consistent with the job-discouragement hypothesis. Where the job requirements are sufficiently high, we find a more segregated and formalized adult-youth labor market dichotomy. The prevalence of jobs with high educational requirements reduces the number of job opportunities available to youngsters. Aware of the limited nature of the job market, many of them consequently drop out of the labor force. In markets where the delineation is not clear--where wages and educational requirements are low--there is more competition, and more young workers enter the labor force, raising the unemployment rate of these workers in slum areas.

---

*The educational supply of labor used in this analysis was that reported for Table 3-1 (p. 59, single asterisked footnote) for the central city containing each slum area.

A higher level of education possessed by youths in slum areas was not significantly related to lower unemployment rates.* Two factors may account for this finding: (a) there may have been systematic differences in the quality of education among youth in different slums, and (b) educational-attainment levels are unimportant for youth in obtaining employment because of the age and racial discrimination operating in the urban labor market. In many jobs age and experience are more important than formal education for obtaining employment. Frequently, the young workers in slum areas possess considerably more education than many older workers but still have considerably higher unemployment rates.

The finding provides considerable support for the notion that factors other than education are critical in obtaining employment. In the choice between hiring a nonwhite youngster with a high school diploma and a white youngster with a tenth-grade education, a forty-year-old woman with nine years of education, or a thirty-five-year-old white man with eight years of education and some work experience, the employer may place the nonwhite youngster at the end of the queue in a restricted, segregated labor market for low-wage, dead-end, casual employment. This choice framework is consistent with the findings of our survey of Harlem youth. Their low expectation of future returns from education and the existence of high returns from illegal activities make it reasonable and easy for youngsters to choose the illegal market place over school and work.

The educational gap did not emerge as an important factor in explaining differences in youth unemployment rates among slum areas, except for sixteen to nineteen year olds.** For that group the larger the gap, the lower the unemployment rate. In a labor market characterized by high educational requirements, nonwhite youth with high levels of education have a higher labor force participation rate. However, since there is no relationship between the demand for education required by employers and the supply of education of nonwhite youth

---

*The educational supply of labor used in this analysis was that of the population in each slum area for the respective youth age cohort. Source: "Urban Employment Survey of 1966," unpublished data prepared by the U.S. Department of Labor, Bureau of Labor Statistics.

**The educational gap used in this analysis was derived by subtracting the educational supply of labor of the respective youth age cohorts from the educational demand of labor of the central city containing each slum area. Also, see the previous footnote in this chapter and Table 3-1.

and because of factors such as age, color, and experience, the nonwhite workers are not eligible to work in the skilled and educated sector of the urban labor market. These educated nonwhite workers can and do find employment in the low-wage, low-educated sector of the urban market or become discouraged workers. The result is to push out other nonwhites with lower levels of education and, thus, raise unemployment rates for nonwhite youth.

Raising educational-attainment levels, therefore, would not overcome the institutional factors segregating slum youngsters into a period of unemployment and limited opportunities in the labor market.

Educational Achievement

Two extremely crude measures were used to observe the impact of educational achievement or quality in accounting for differences in youth unemployment among slums. First, scores on a standard U.S. Army qualifications test were used to observe achievement levels.[3] These scores were obtained for states by color and, therefore, are only a crude approximation of the actual differences among youth in the various slum areas of each state. Higher army scores were associated with lower unemployment rates for sixteen to nineteen year olds and twenty to twenty-four year olds but the weakness of the data limited the statistical significance of the finding.

The other measure used was the local school system's educational expenditures per child.* It would be better to have the expenditures made in the past fifteen years to measure the benefits received by the youngsters fourteen to twenty-four years of age. Further, expenditures may reflect not higher quality of education but higher costs of operating a school system. Third, high current expenditures for education may be a response to high levels of youth unemployment because insufficient resources were allocated in previous years. Fourth, expenditures may not be uniform between the slum area schools and the rest of the city's schools. Given all these limitations, it was not surprising to observe no significant relationship between educational expenditures per child and youth unemployment rates in slum areas.

_____

*This measure is derived by dividing each local school system's total current expenditures for each school year by its respective average daily attendance of pupils for that year. "Selected Statistics of Local School Systems 1966-67," National Education Association—Research Division, Research Report 1968-R-11 (1968).

Welfare

The effect of welfare on youth unemployment can operate on two levels. First, it may affect the labor force decisions of young mothers and fathers aged fourteen to twenty-four, who may be eligible for or receiving welfare; thus, it may indirectly affect the measured rate of youth unemployment. Specifically, broad eligibility or a relatively generous welfare payment level may dampen the labor response of young workers and help contribute to a reduction in unemployment.

Second, the availability and level of welfare payments may affect young workers aged fourteen to nineteen, whose parents may be eligible for, or receiving, welfare. High welfare payments reduce the need for youngsters to enter the labor force to supplement family income. The result may be a smaller labor force and a lower youth-unemployment rate. The statistical evidence relating the welfare case rate of the cities and the youth unemployment rate of the slums does not support this hypothesis.* Although the higher the case rate in a city, the lower the youth unemployment rate in the slum, the relationship was not significant.

In sharp contrast the welfare payment rate had a critical influence on the unemployment rates of ghetto youth. The more generous the level of payments per recipient, the lower the youth unemployment rate. The relationship was strongest for the oldest age group, supporting the view that welfare benefits operate as a significant opportunity cost, reducing the incentive of the eligible welfare population to enter the labor force and work. The same relationship and interpretation holds for the sixteen to nineteen year olds. However, the relationship is considerably weaker for the fourteen to nineteen year old group. Since the majority of fourteen and fifteen year olds are not heads of households or parents and, therefore, are not directly eligible to be recipients of welfare benefits, the payment level has less impact on their labor force decisions than on those youngsters sixteen to twenty-four years of age.

In either case the existence of heavy welfare caseloads is not sufficient to affect youth unemployment rates. The critical factor appears to be the impact of the level of welfare payments on the decision to enter the labor force. When welfare benefits are high, the incentive to work is less, and the unemployment rate lower, especially for youngsters aged sixteen to twenty-four. Direct benefits

---

*The welfare measures used in this analysis were those reported in notes to Tables 3-8 and 3-9 for the central city containing each slum area.

appear to have greater impact than indirect benefits, that is, the level of welfare payments has a stronger effect on older youth receiving direct benefits as heads of households or parents than on fourteen to fifteen year olds indirectly receiving benefits through their parents. The implications are obvious: if we reduce welfare payments and case-loads without providing jobs at wage levels that compete with welfare benefits, the level of youth unemployment in ghettos and other poor areas will rise substantially.

One additional explanation of the differential effect of the welfare case rate and payment rate is worth noting. Welfare benefits, of any level of payment, are conditional on the recipient's having no other earned income. In short, a 100 percent tax rate existed for most welfare families; a dollar earned is "taxed" by a welfare dollar lost. Where welfare benefits are high, the cost of losing these payments is greater, and, therefore, the need to work is reduced.* In these conditions the young worker will tend not to work or seek work. Thus, the measured rate of youth unemployment is lower where welfare payments are higher. The welfare case rate is not related to the youth unemployment rate in a similar fashion, perhaps because of the lower cost of losing the welfare benefits. If jobs are available at salaries higher than welfare benefits, then more people will be willing to seek work and forgo welfare benefits or supplement low levels of welfare payments.

Health

Poor health is often cited as a major factor contributing to unemployment. However, although it is obvious that poor health contributes to reducing family income, it is by no means clear whether it raises the unemployment rate, even when it forces workers to leave their jobs. First, poor health may cause a worker to withdraw from the labor force altogether, so that he is not counted among the unemployed. Second, if poor health causes a reduction in family income because of unemployment (measured or otherwise), other members of the family may seek employment in order to restore the family income to its previous level. The effect on the unemployment rate of thus increasing the labor force will depend on the demand for labor, as well as the qualifications of these new workers. If jobs in the

---

*Some locations, such as New York City, have established experimental programs allowing welfare recipients to earn income without a 100 percent tax on benefits.

secondary labor market are scarce and the skills and experience of
the new workers are limited, their addition to the labor force will
probably cause unemployment to rise. If the opposite conditions
prevail—if the secondary workers are more skilled than the primary
worker and the labor market demand for them is higher than for the
primary worker—unemployment will be reduced.

One additional complexity may alter the relationship. If health
conditions affect all family members, as is likely to be the case among
poor families lacking proper diet, medical care, housing, and living
in close contact, then the poor health of the family would reduce the potential growth of the secondary labor force.

Since our measure of health in a given area is the incidence of
tuberculosis per 100,000 population, our expectation is that the higher
the incidence of tuberculosis, a communicable disease, the lower the
unemployment rate, as a result of withdrawals from the labor force.*
However, we expect that the higher the incidence of poor health, the
greater the need for young workers to support their families. In the
tight and segregated labor market for nonwhite youth, an increase in
the labor force will result in higher rates of youth unemployment.

The results indicate no significant relationship between health
and youth unemployment. Contrary to our expectation the unemployment rate of young workers is not lower in slum areas afflicted with
especially poor health. What can be inferred from this relationship
is that poor health does have a tendency to push additional young workers
into the labor market, but this is offset by the fact that some of these
youth are also victims of poor health and drop out of the labor force.
If we had a measure of the health of the young workers and the condition of health among family members, it would be possible to specify
the effect of these offsetting forces. Improving the health of a slum
area, although obviously desirable for other reasons, would probably
have only a slight effect on slum youth unemployment. The result
would probably be more youngsters dropping out of the labor force
because their healthy fathers and mothers continue to work, thus
offsetting the increase of any new healthy young entrants into the
labor force.

Finally, it is interesting to note the differential impact of health
on youth unemployment for younger and older age groups. The sixteen
to nineteen-year-olds had a stronger relationship than the group aged
twenty to twenty-four years. Since the older group is less likely to
be living with their parents, they may be less likely to support their

-----

*The health rate used in this analysis was that reported in
Table 3-4 for the central city containing each slum area.

parents during times of poor health. Thus, they tend not to have an impact on the youth labor supply and unemployment rate of their age group.

Crime

One of the most controversial hypotheses in the literature on the youth labor market is that youngsters confront a choice between work and leisure and, more recently, between legal and illegal work. Specifically, young nonwhites in slum areas may simply prefer leisure to work and may have sufficient income from relatives and friends to subsist at an acceptable standard. Furthermore, many young non-whites are forced to make decisions early in their lives: whether to pursue an income-producing activity that is illegal or a less remuner-ative but legal career. Differential costs in the form of direct work costs and risks exist for both income-generating activities, as well as differential benefits, not only in income but in status, conditions of work, opportunity for higher income in the future, scheduling, flexibility, authority, and so forth. Given the alternatives it is under-standable for young blacks and other minority groups in slum areas to select illegal activities as a means of earning an income. What is the effect of such choice on measured rates of youth unemployment? We can assume, first, that a nonwhite youth engaged in illegal activi-ties will probably respond in the affirmative if asked whether he is employed. Otherwise, it would be difficult to account for his con-sumption patterns and living standards, which are quite visible in his home. Second, he may actually perceive himself as employed, since he is working for his income. Third, he may fear that if he acknow-ledges his state of unemployment, the government may ask him to participate in programs that would interfere with his income-producing activities.

In an area of high crime, where large flows of income from illegal activities are generated, the need is reduced for many youngsters to enter the labor force in a regular job, both because of the avail-ability of illegal opportunities and because transfers of illegal income make it less imperative for them to seek legitimate employment. However, many sociological studies report that unemployment breeds crime—that is, that the lack of opportunities to earn an income forces people into a life of crime. This implies no choice framework but a form of compulsion in order to survive. However, it may provide a choice between the level one is working to subsist on and the alternative activities that generate different incomes. If unemployment stimulates crime, we should observe a strong positive relationship between the index of criminal activity used as a proxy for income earned from illegal activity and youth unemployment rates.

The results do not support either hypothesis.* No significant relationship was found between crime and unemployment among slum youth.** Apparently, offsetting forces are operating to reduce the significance of the findings. For the older group the appeal and benefits of working in illegal jobs are stronger than for youngsters. It may well be that illegal activities are not open to very young workers or that at the earlier age the choice framework is dominated by leisure considerations rather than by alternative incomes. However, the fourteen to nineteen year old who lives with his parents has no need to defend his standards of consumption by stating that he is working. Therefore, although criminal activities are occurring in his slum area and he is a participant, he may be registered as unemployed. The older youngster living alone is more likely to claim that he is employed.

Spatial Barriers

Geographic factors have been viewed as vital in affecting the unemployment of minority workers living in slum areas. The rapid growth of suburban areas surrounding the central cities has led to a general dispersion of employment opportunities. Of particular importance to the youth labor market is the movement of wholesale and retail employment out of the central business district and into suburban areas. Moreover, a wide number of service jobs, the kinds that are often filled by young workers, have followed the affluent middle and upper classes to the suburbs. In order to detect the importance of these spatial factors we selected two measures: (a) the extent of residential segregation, and (b) the spatial dispersion of jobs between the central city and the surrounding suburban area.*** Our hypotheses were the following: (a) the greater the spatial distribution of jobs, the higher

---

*The crime rate used in this analysis was that reported in Table 3-10 for the central city containing each slum area.

**The relationship approaches the range of statistical significance only for the sixteen to nineteen year olds. In some equations crime was inversely related to youth unemployment, but it was not statistically significant.

***The measures of residential segregation and spatial distribution used in this analysis were those reported in Chapter 2 (p. 38 footnote) and Table 2-7, respectively, for the central city containing each slum area.

the unemployment rate of slum youth; and (b) the greater the degree of residential segregation, the higher the unemployment rate of slum youth.

Neither factor was found to be related to slum youth unemployment in a statistically significant way. However, the relationships deserve some comment. Greater dispersion of jobs was associated with higher unemployment for the groups aged fourteen to nineteen and sixteen to nineteen years, but the opposite relationship was found for those aged twenty to twenty-four years.* The older age group is more likely to travel by private car, has greater knowledge of locations in suburbs, and has more responsibility than those sixteen to nineteen years of age. Moreover, the job market for these older youth may not be so dependent on part-time service and retail jobs, and the central city residential location may have sufficient employment opportunities so that wide dispersion of jobs does not present a serious employment barrier to older youth. Moreover, if whites have moved into suburban areas, the competition for jobs in the central city may be considerably less than before.

The higher the index of residential segregation, the higher the unemployment rate for the oldest age group of minority youth residing in the ghetto, while for the group sixteen to nineteen, the more segregated the residential community, the lower the unemployment rate. This is consistent with the interpretation of the impact of spatial distribution of jobs on youth unemployment.

For older ghetto youth, with more access to suburban areas than younger people, spatial distribution was not a serious problem; however, if the nonwhite workers were dependent on job information in the suburbs, being highly segregated in the ghetto would cause them to have higher unemployment rates. On the other hand, workers aged fourteen to nineteen, who under no circumstances can obtain jobs in the suburbs because of difficult travel conditions, may be better off living in a highly segregated residential area. First, a heavy concentration of nonwhites may mean more that middle-class and upper-class nonwhites are residing in the ghetto because of housing discrimination. This may result in more part-time and full-time employment opportunities for ghetto youngsters in service activities, babysitting, domestic work, barber and beauty shops, supermarkets, liquor stores, and department and clothing stores. Second, in areas that are segregated the information flow regarding jobs and working

---

*Moreover, in some cases a positive but insignificant relationship is observed between spatial distribution and unemployment rates of twenty to twenty-four year olds.

conditions is better. Information flows are more accurate, move
faster, and carry more data.

In summary, residential segregation and spatial distribution of
jobs do not have clear and significant relationships to youth unemployment. The nature of the relationships vary by age level within the
cohort fourteen to twenty-four years of age, but none are statistically
significant. Overall, the spatial factors reflected in these measures
seemed to offset each other, and no clear relationship is established.

Racial Discrimination

In our earlier analysis we discovered that racial discrimination
was an important factor in explaining nonwhite unemployment rates
among cities and the ratio of white to nonwhite unemployment within
a city, as well as the slum unemployment rates, but that it was a much
less important factor in explaining slum unemployment rates.* We
find no significant relationship between the unemployment rate of slum
youth and our two measures of discrimination—occupational distribution of nonwhites to whites and occupational distribution index adjusted for educational differences between whites and nonwhites.**

This indicates that the industrial structure, age discrimination,
alternative incomes, and other factors play a more significant role in
screening out ghetto youth from jobs in the urban economy.

For a nonwhite youth in a slum area, the urban labor market consists of a series of barriers, which become progressively more difficult to negotiate as the worker comes closer to obtaining a stable, rewarding, productive job. The obstacles are partly accidents of history,
antiquated rules, laws, and attitudes and partly devices designed to
protect valuable property in the form of preferred jobs from competition, economic fluctuation, and the vagaries of the marketplace. A
system of rules and institutions has emerged to control the undesirable
consequences of a competitive local economy. But protection is af-
forded only to those who are inside and organized, not to the new groups
who are feared and excluded. A natural alliance of business, workers,

---

*The two measures of discrimination used in this analysis were
those reported in Tables 3-5 and 3-6 for the central city containing
each slum area.

**For workers fourteen to nineteen and sixteen to nineteen years
of age a positive relationship is found but for workers twenty to
twenty-four years of age, the opposite relationship exists.

and government has formed to monopolize the job property for those members of the work force who already possess it.

Evidence presented earlier supports the contention that a segregated labor market exists, with a series of cumulative and ever more difficult employment barriers. Nowhere are these barriers higher than those facing nonwhite youth in urban slums. Because the labor market does not generate sufficient employment, an elaborate job-protection system emerges. As employment expands, young workers are screened out because they lack the education, experience, and skills required. As youngsters succeed in obtaining more education, a system of certification, licensing, and apprenticeship is established, which they must satisfy to enter the job, or occupation, or profession. If all these barriers are overcome, racial discrimination is employed as the last barrier to entry into the privileged arena. Legal restrictions, educational requirements, unions and professional associations, age, and finally racial discrimination place the slum youngster at the end of the hiring queue in an economy that never needs enough workers to reach the end of the line. The segregated structure of the urban economy and the multiple employment barriers account for the intolerable levels of youth unemployment in our slums.

SUMMARY OF THE MAJOR FINDINGS

Employment growth was a significant factor in reducing the unemployment rate of the older segment of the youth labor force residing in slum areas. The greater the growth of employment in the city, the lower the unemployment rate of twenty- to twenty-four-year old workers. However, the growth of employment did not have an impact on younger workers in slum areas.

The level of wages prevailing in the urban labor market was significantly related to the unemployment rates of both fourteen to nineteen year olds and twenty to twenty-four year olds. The higher the wages in the urban economy, the higher the unemployment rates for these two groups of young workers.

The welfare payment rate had a very strong and significant relationship to the level of unemployment of both groups of young workers. The higher the payment rate, the lower the unemployment rates of young workers in these slum areas. In cities where the payment rates for welfare recipients were low, the unemployment rates for young workers were high.

The only other economic factor having a significant relationship to the unemployment rate of young workers was the net-migration rate. The larger the rate of migration into the city during the preceding three years, the higher the unemployment rate of the older youngsters, twenty to twenty-four years old, in the city's slums.

The labor force participation rate of the twenty to twenty-four year olds in the ghettos was not a significant factor contributing to higher unemployment rates for this group.

Similarly, the unemployment rate for the younger age groups was not significantly affected by either the net-migration rate or the labor force participation rate of these youngsters.

For both age groups of youngsters, the size of the dependent population as measured by the welfare case rate had no relationship to unemployment rates.

The female labor force participation rate had a significant relationship to that of fourteen- to nineteen-year-old slum youth: the higher the female participation rate, the lower the youth unemployment rate. In contrast, the higher the female participation rate, the higher the unemployment rate of twenty to twenty-four year olds, but the relationship was not significant.

The adult unemployment rate had a significant impact on the unemployment rate of youngsters aged twenty to twenty-four but was not related to the unemployment rate of younger members of the youth labor force residing in the slums.

A measure of change in employment for youth-related jobs had no significant relationship with the unemployment rates for either age group of the youth labor force residing in slum areas.

The cyclical industries index was significantly related to the unemployment rates of both the fourteen to nineteen year olds and the twenty to twenty-four year olds. The higher the proportion of available jobs in construction and manufacturing and retail industries, the higher the unemployment rate of young workers.

The size of the manufacturing and construction sectors had a definite impact on the unemployment rates of both groups of youngsters. The larger either of these industrial sectors, the higher the unemployment rate of young workers in the ghetto areas.

In contrast, the larger the retail sector in the urban economy, the lower the unemployment rate for young workers of both age groups in the slums. This finding appears when we examine the retail sector by itself, rather than as a part of the cyclical industrial mix.

The wholesale sector bore no relationship to the unemployment rate of either group of young workers. However, the finance and service sectors had a negative but not significant relationship to the youth unemployment rates in the slums. The larger the finance and services sectors, the worse the employment prospects for ghetto youngsters of both age groups. A similar relationship was observed between the size of the transportation sector and the youth unemployment rate: the larger the transportation sector, the higher the unemployment rate for young workers, particularly fourteen to nineteen year olds. It was less significant but still adverse for the twenty to twenty-four year olds.

Although the government sector's employment did not have a significant impact on youth labor market, it did have a favorable relationship. The greater the share of government employment in a local labor market, the lower the youth unemployment rate. While the government sector does not provide much employment opportunity in the civil service for the youngest group of workers, it does offer opportunity for the older group. Moreover, entrance requirements are primarily of an educational nature rather than for licensing or apprenticeship, which may be controlled by unions and employers. It may therefore be easier for ghetto youngsters to enter government employment than it would be to enter the construction, manufacturing, or financial sectors of the urban economy.

The higher the educational demand by employers in a local labor market, the lower the unemployment rate for the young workers residing in slum areas. This relationship is significant for the older group of youngsters, as well as for the total group aged fourteen to twenty-four.

For all young workers fourteen to twenty-four years of age, the larger the gap between their educational attainment and the level required by employers in the labor market, the higher the unemployment rate. This relationship is significant for youngsters sixteen to nineteen but it is not significant for those twenty to twenty-four years of age.

The measure of educational achievement—the army test scores of youngsters in an urban labor market—was not related in a significant way to the unemployment rate for either age group. However, the relationships for the younger and older subsets differed. The higher the scores, the higher the unemployment rate for the fourteen to nineteen year olds; the lower the scores, the higher the unemployment rate for the twenty to twenty-four year olds.

Health and residential segregation were found to have no significant relationship to the unemployment rates of either group of youngsters. Both factors had positive relationships, that is, the worse the health and the greater the degree of residential segregation, the higher the youth unemployment rates; but the relationships were not significant.

In contrast to the relationship of significance between the crime rate and the unemployment rate of the slums, there was no significant relationship between the crime rate and the unemployment rate of youngsters in the slum areas. The relationship was positive but not significant.

The spatial distribution of jobs into the suburbs did not have a significant impact on the youth unemployment rate. Apparently, these youths do not compete for jobs in those sectors that are moving to the suburbs at the fastest rate.

Models

The basic economic model, containing the employment change, wage level, participation rate, net-migration, and welfare payment rate, accounted for 87 percent of the variation in the unemployment rates of twenty to twenty-four year-olds in slum areas and for 70 percent of the variation for the fourteen to nineteen year olds.

The industrial-structure model, containing the employment shares of the construction, manufacturing, retail, wholesale, finance, and service sectors of the local urban economy, accounted for 75 percent of the variation for twenty to twenty-four year olds and 78 percent for fourteen to nineteen year olds.

The basic structural and institutional model was the least effective in explaining the differences among slum youth in unemployment rates, accounting for 47 percent of the older group and only 30 percent of the younger group. When the model included the educational attainment of youth instead of racial discrimination, its explanatory power increased substantially. For the younger subset, fourteen to nineteen, the model now accounted for 51 percent of the variation in youth unemployment; for the older subset, twenty to twenty-four, the model accounted for nearly 61 percent of the variation.

The model explaining the most (80 percent) variation of the total youth group fourteen to twenty-four consisted of the employment change, wage level, participation rate, adult unemployment rate, and welfare payment rate. The model had two significant factors: (a) the higher the employment change, the lower the youth unemployment rate; and (b) the higher the welfare payment rate, the lower the youth unemployment rate. The wage level, adult employment rate, and participation rate, while all positively related to the youth unemployment rate, did not approach a significant relationship.

The best model for the explanation of the unemployment rate of sixteen to nineteen year olds was a combined economic and structural model, consisting of the educational gap, spatial distribution, youth employment change, net migration, female labor force participation rates, and cyclical industrial mix. The model had three significant factors: (a) the larger the share of cyclical industries (construction, manufacturing, and retail), the higher the youth unemployment rate; (b) the higher the female labor force participation rate, the lower the unemployment rate; and (c) the greater the educational gap, the lower the unemployment rate of youngsters sixteen to nineteen years of age. The combined model accounted for 88 percent of the variation of youth unemployment rates.

An economic model consisting of the employment change, wage level, participation rate, welfare payment rate, and adult unemployment rate accounted for 98 percent of the variation in unemployment rates of workers twenty to twenty-four years of age. All but the wage level were statistically significant. The higher the payment rates and the greater the employment change, the lower the youth unemployment rate, while the higher the labor force participation rate and the higher the adult unemployment rate, the higher the youth unemployment rate.

"MAKING IT
AND GETTING BY":
EMPLOYMENT PATTERNS
AND UNEMPLOYPMENT PROBLEMS
OF BLACK YOUTH IN HARLEM

The available information and statistical data on the employment patterns and unemployment problems of black youth, particularly those residing in slum areas of our cities, are not sufficient in quantity or quality to enable us to understand the complex forces influencing the behavior of these youth, much less to design government policies and programs to alleviate their extraordinarily high rates of unemployment.

These data must be supplemented by qualitative data on the behavior, habits, attitudes, life-styles, expectations, means of acquiring incomes other than work, and employment and educational experiences of youth in urban ghettos. For example, without some crude notion of the magnitude and the distribution of incomes generated and transferred throughout the ghetto and the city from illegal market activities, such as gambling, narcotics, robbery, theft, prostitution, and protection, it will be difficult to design training and employment programs that will attract large numbers of hard-core unemployed youth at modest training allowances and marginal wages. The design of programs and incentives requires additional qualitative data as well as experimentation to test the target population's incentives and responsiveness to new programs.

METHODOLOGY

Budget and time constraints prohibited a full-scale representative sample of unemployed black youth. More important than these constraints was the belief that a formal interview and questionnaire would not succeed in eliciting frank, honest answers about many activities that are currently deemed immoral or illegal. Therefore, a critical research decision was made to sacrifice appropriate sampling procedures and reduce the number of persons in our sample and the amount of comparable demographic and historical data in order to obtain a more reliable in-depth probe of the education and employment problems of black youth and their attitudes, perceptions, and experiences.

The field work was carried out by three seniors at the City College of New York, two of them male and one female, all black. They were extremely bright, sociable, and well informed about the literature and current events on unemployment, black power, ghetto life, and so forth.

The interviewers were instructed to walk the streets of Harlem during the summer of 1968 and to make contact with any individuals or groups of individuals that appeared to be unemployed, idle during the daytime hours, and between the ages of eighteen and twenty-four years. The interviewers found most of their subjects in school yards, parks, pool halls, bars, employment agencies, and community action agencies.

The interviewers were told to be casual and informal, but were not given any specific instructions regarding the initial introduction to the subject. Stress was placed upon establishing good rapport and opening up the subject to a thorough and frank discussion of each youth's sources of income and his activities, attitudes, expectations, and experiences regarding jobs, wages, school, and training.

The interviewers reported great difficulty in contacting people who were articulate and willing to spend a long period of time discussing these areas. When such people were found the interviews often consumed parts of several days, and sometimes the interviewer spent an entire day with the subject as he went about his daily activities. In the cases in which there was continuous contact over a period of time, the background material and the contents of the interview were greatly enhanced. The personality, perception, and adaptability of the interviewer in this situation are critical. This is reflected in the survey: sixteen of the twenty-five interviews were done by one of the interviewers.

Despite all the inherent difficulties and obvious methodological weaknesses of the approach, twenty-five black youths between the ages of eighteen and twenty-five were interviewed. All but three were males. The inability to find female subjects remains a major puzzle of the study. It is a well-documented fact that female blacks in ghettos have the highest unemployment of any demographic group. (Specifically, the female youth unemployment rate in Harlem in December, 1966, was 19.9 percent.) However, the interviewers were not only unable to interview many young women but were not even able to locate many. As a result of the preponderance of men in the sample, most of the statements and insights are biased and cannot be interpreted to include problems and policies for female youth.

An extremely important input of the fieldwork was the comprehensive report written by the interviewers after completing each interview. The reports provide both factual and impressionistic material on the problem of youth employment and life in the ghettos of Harlem and point out where the biases of the reporters may have influenced their findings.

There are serious limitations in both the approach and the potential bias and error of the material reported from the subjects. There was no attempt to verify the factual material given to the interviewers. The interviewing and recording process has inherent potential for the biases of the interviewer to dominate or at least influence the written reports. The groups of subjects interviewed were in no way selected to provide sound statistical results or analysis, nor can any generalizations be drawn from such limited numbers and so unrepresentative a sample. In addition, the number of interviews is extremely small, and the number of females is insufficient to gain much insight, much less any understanding, of the unique problems confronting them. Finally, limiting interviews to one area precluded our learning about intercity differences of the problems of slum youth.

Despite these serious limitations, the qualitative impressions and supplementary data gained by establishing contact with the target population are extremely important. A view of life in the ghetto from the perspective of the ghetto dwellers provides important clues and insights that are useful in designing programs and policies. Furthermore, conventional sampling has not been able to produce information on the illegal activities and income of the population in the slums and cities. Finally, the interviews can serve as a test of the usefulness of an exploratory probe to determine whether these types of field studies are worthwhile in understanding the problems of urban ghetto dwellers.

GENERAL BACKGROUND

Our sample of twenty-two male and three female youngsters between the ages of eighteen and twenty-five, all resided in Harlem at the time of the interview, during the summer of 1968. Eight of the males were then employed, primarily in part-time work. Thirteen of the sixteen who gave information about their place of birth came from New York City, not all from Harlem. Three others were born in the South.

Ten of the respondents lived with their parents, three lived alone, and four lived with their girlfriends. One respondent lived with his wife, and one female lived with her baby. The other six did not provide this information. In general, the males living with women were older than those who resided with parents.

Most of the households had at least one employed member, usually in a semiskilled occupation with a governmental or quasi-nonprofit institution—e.g., the Post Office, Veterans Administration, nurse's aid, Welfare Receipients League. Information on the educational level of the subjects' parents was sketchy. Out of eleven responses, only one reported a parent with fewer than six years of education; five had parents (or a parent) who were high-school graduates, and two had parents with some college education.

For the most part, families suffered neither extreme economic hardship nor heavy unemployment and seemed to be relatively stable and cohesive. Ten of sixteen respondents reported having a good relationship with their families. Eight stated that their parents did not overburden them with criticism of their attitudes and modes of behavior. One respondent said: "My folks do right by me. They kick into my kitty regularly." One of the interviewers described his relationship with his father as "more of a close-friend relationship than a father-son one." On the other hand, one respondent who was unemployed was a disappointment to the other members of his family, who had good jobs and educations: "My brother and sister think I'm a dark sheep, a waste." Very few of the respondents expressed animosity toward their parents; in fact, one can say that the family system seemed quite protective and supportive rather than hostile and antagonistic to the children.

Housing conditions of the respondents were at best adequate. All the respondents lived in the same area, and nearly all the buildings were in similar condition—"smelly and dirty," according to one interviewer, and so stifling in the summer heat that the doors of the apartments were "opened wide and you could see bodies readjusting their positions to catch any shift in the wind's direction." A respondent reported that her family had no heavy blankets; in winter their apartment was so cold that they slept in their clothes and wrapped themselves in bedspreads. When it rained, there was such severe flooding that "it got so deep we had to wear boots in the house." At the opposite extreme, another home was described as "cozy, with two gold cloth sofas in good condition, a table, lamps and numerous books and photographs of the family."

The material from these in-depth interviews revolves around four interrelated areas—employment, education, service in the armed forces, and illegal activities (hustling and narcotics).

EMPLOYMENT

Long-term unemployment was quite extensive among the youth. Seven of the seventeen who were unemployed had been out of work for more than one year. One respondent, a high school graduate (general diploma), had been unemployed for over three years; he was last employed as a stock clerk after graduation and was currently a narcotics addict. Another long-term unemployed respondent was last employed for six months as a janitor, at $33.00 a week. After completing only nine years of schooling (the least amount of schooling in our sample), he had been unemployed for a year and a half.

Eight of the respondents had been unemployed for less than six months. The disparity in the periods of unemployment and the remarks of the respondents suggest two distinct categories of respondents: (a) those who had been unemployed for more than a year and who were no longer in the labor force, and (b) those who were unemployed for less than a year and were still seeking employment.

Of the eight youths in the sample who were then employed, none had held his current job for more than a year. Three were working with community action agencies; the others were employed as mechanic, truck loader, carrier, musician, and clerk. In contrast, almost half (eight) of the respondents who were unemployed at the time had previously had a stable employment experience, holding down their previous jobs for one year or longer.

As one would expect, the types of jobs these respondents had held and the level of wages were among the worst offered in the urban economy. The occupations, predominantly low-skilled, low-wage jobs in the least stable sectors of the urban economy, included assembly line worker, janitor, kitchen helper, hospital attendant, guard, and feeder, in addition to the ones mentioned above. However, three respondents had held higher-wage, higher-skilled jobs—as clerk-typists and computer operators.

Wages on these jobs ranged from a low of $33.00 per week as a janitor to a high of $135.00 per week as a computer operator. Of the fifteen respondents who reported income data, four earned less than $60.00 per week, three earned between $60.00 and $80.00, five between $80.00 and $100.00, and three more than $100.00 per week. The three highest earners, two former computer operators and a hospital attendant, were unemployed at the time of the interview. One computer operator was laid off after a substantial cutback in the work force of the company and had been unemployed for almost a year. He refused to take employment below his skills and qualifications and would not work for less than $100.00 per week. He was living at home with his parents, whose combined annual family

income was approximately $13,000. He received support from his
parents and from unemployment compensation.

The other skilled computer operator was fired after an argument
with his supervisor about Muhammed Ali. He had received nine
months of training in an IBM school while in the military service. At
the time of the survey, he had been unemployed for one month.

The hospital attendant had been employed for over two years
and had received substantial increases over his starting salary of
$85.00 per week. He was earning approximately $110.00 per week
when he voluntarily quit the job. The reasons given were boredom,
some fears of the nature of the job, and the people he had to work
with.

The high reservation wage required by these two respondents
indicates the difficulty of inducing many youngsters into the labor
market and into jobs paying below $100.00 per week. Moreover, the
other working conditions of a job in terms of psychic satisfaction
seem to be important to most of the respondents.

Many of the respondents indicated dissatisfaction with their
present jobs or their employment experience. Discontent focused on
two major areas: wages and opportunities for promotion. Dead-end,
low-wage, repetitious, and boring jobs were cited as the prime
sources of dissatisfaction and high turnover. One illuminating quote
conveys the message: "After two years of blind regimentation in the
Army, I just couldn't take any more of that governmental orders
crap. Most black people feel that that kind of money makes you
middle class and respectable, but it didn't impress me at all, not
at all." The same person commented on another job, at a large
department store: "Anybody could have done the job. . . . I have
never been on a job that allowed promotion or advancement due to
one's own initiative and creativity."

Another respondent described his unhappiness with his job and
the reason he left:

> They were making me do all the loading and dirty work.
> I mean, there were eight or nine of us on the floor, most
> of them Puerto Rican. My supervisor was black—of
> course the boss was white. Every time the boss pres-
> sured the supervisor, the supervisor would get on my
> back. Out of all of them, I had to lift the heavy stuff,
> even had to sweep—that was too much to take. . . .
> Besides, my thoughts were on auto mechanics and that
> was on my mind—not warehouse.
>
> I get a few jobs fixing people's cars. It is not
> steady, but it's good enough. . . . I don't have to turn
> anywhere else for money even though I don't know how

long this will last. Plus I figure I am helping my mother
since at least I don't have to go and ask her for money.

He then gave up looking for jobs "because they said I did not have an
auto repair license or a high school diploma. So I just gave up trying
to get a job. I knew that auto mechanics was what I wanted all the
time. You know, I was always interested in cars."

The desire for higher wages was repeatedly expressed in the
interviews. Even the unemployed respondents indicated a very high
reservation wage before they would seriously consider working. For
example: "All the black troops returning from Nam and they offers
them a $60.00 a week job for which they are supposed to be grateful.
I go on welfare before I work for $60.00 a week." Another comment
about a reasonable wage was: "I'll work for $2.25 per hour, nothing
less. Anything that brings in $80.00-$96.00 per week. That's good
for a start. But this $1.50 an hour-$60.00 per week shit, that's
out."

On the other hand, the low wages were often accepted by youth,
provided that there were some compensating features of the job. A
case in point, which also reveals the migratory power of the big city,
was offered by a respondent from the Carolinas:

> I came to New York because all my friends—and I had a
> lot of close good friends—were leaving. . . . There are
> just naturally more opportunities here than down
> there. . . . A lot of kids come up to make money in the
> summer, buy school clothes and so on, and then go back
> to school in the Carolinas.

It took a while to get a job:

> I didn't have experience so I had to take what I could get.
> I got a job pulling racks in the garment district. A com-
> pany by the name of Ideal Trucking Co. They gave me
> the minimum pay—what was it, $1.50 an hour. I got
> interested in packing, so I applied for a packer job at
> $70.00 a week with the Jeffrey Store. All my home boys
> worked there, so it was really nice, a grand job working
> there. You might even say it was hard hours, working
> from 8 in the morning until 11 or 12 P.M., but then the
> overtime was real nice, and some weeks I could take home
> $138.00, $140.00. Nobody wanted to stay in North
> Carolina. You know, by the time you get out of school your
> friends want to do things for themselves, and either you
> come up North or get drafted.

Four of the respondents indicated positive attitudes toward their jobs. These jobs were in the computer field and in community service. One respondent, who received his computer training in the military, had considerable praise for the high-salaried field. "As many blacks as possible should pursue the field; you're judged on qualification and knowledge." A respondent who worked in the community felt that she was performing a necessary service in gathering and distributing information on jobs and housing.

Another type of job sentiment was apathy or indifference. One respondent, who had been a guard for a protection agency, said, "It was just a job." The low wages and the low-skilled nature of the work involved in most of the jobs available to these youth did not encourage much commitment to the job. While lateral occupational changes could result in moderate increases in income, it was difficult to move vertically in the occupational structure. One twenty-year-old respondent had held six jobs since graduation from high school. His most recent job was as a truck loader, earning him $90.00 a week.

The job-search pattern was quite varied. Of the twenty-one respondents seven used the state employment agency; only one of them used any other placement service. Six others went to local community agencies, such as Haryou, and were placed in jobs. Another six respondents relied on personal friends; five used personal friends as their only source of job information. Four used commercial agencies; one also used the state employment agencies. None of the respondents indicated using newspapers or other printed media regarding jobs. Nor did they indicate that they knew of and/or used the local television show providing job information.

A difference in the use of job information was discovered between high school and nonhigh school graduates. The high school graduates relied more heavily on community agencies (five respondents) and private agencies, while the nonhigh school graduates used the state employment service and their friends exclusively.

There was no discernible pattern of placement among those recently employed: three found their jobs through their friends, two through the state agency, and one through the community action agency. The three jobs paying the lowest wages were referred by the state employment agency. The jobs with the highest salaries, those in the computer field, were secured through community agencies.

Several of the respondents revealed strong negative feelings about employment agencies, particularly the state agencies, which they charged with lack of interest and concern and the low quality of jobs referred. The general attitude is typified by the following comments:

The first time I went in they told me to come back twice.

Then they sent me downtown for a dishwasher job. I
wouldn't take it. Second time it was another waste of
time. That's all they do: waste your time. You sit and
sit and they look through some cards and all the jobs are
for dishwasher.
      The third time I got a job that paid every two weeks.
I didn't even have enough money to pay for the subway
trips and they were paying $125.00 every two weeks. So
you see it was just another pay-day and you know I was
seeing everybody getting paid. I ain't had no money.
I asked them to lend me some to start with but they say
they didn't have no petty cash. So I couldn't even afford
to hold on to the job for two weeks and I left. The fourth
time I waited three days to get an interview. All they
had was bull shit jobs. I just asked for an excuse to go
to the bathroom and ducked out of there.
      What they got to give you? Nothing. What they got
don't pay well, and what pay well they don't want to give
you. . . . It's always this thing that I don't have
experience.

      The four respondents who had enrolled in vocational-rehabilita-
tion programs did not receive the needed training, and they questioned
the value of these programs. A respondent who wanted coast guard
training was sent to a Job Corps center in Cleveland, Ohio. After
his arrival he discovered he could not receive the training he desired.
The other respondent in the Job Corps had been in a center in Morgan-
field, Kentucky. He described the center as an "army base" and
Job Corps itself as "a whole lot of talk." He waited two months for
training in auto mechanics and then left when "they let some white
boys in before us . . . we was on the list two months before they just
come."
      Attitudes toward public programs were apparent in responses
relating to Haryou-Act and a narcotics program known as "People's
Program." Haryou-Act offered one respondent a free ride. He was
very satisfied with the job "cause all I do is pick up a weekly check."
He was hired to organize youngsters and encourage them to go for
job training and continue their education. Instead, he spent his days
on a park bench.
      The concept underlying the People's Program was that an ex-
addict was the best qualified person to help someone presently
addicted. But the outcome of this program did not resemble its
original plan. The respondent reported that the head man was getting
paid by a number of other programs, including his own. Many of

the respondent's fellow workers were falsifying time cards and collecting other workers' salaries. Although these programs were meant to aid disadvantaged youth, they only succeeded in further alienating them.

Those who responded to a question concerning their goals and aspirations revealed very realistic and specific employment or occupational goals. However, not all the youths did respond. The types of jobs desired included clothing salesman, plumber, carpenter, policeman, steel worker, and computer systems analyst. (The last was realistic, for the person was already employed as a computer programmer.) The income aspirations of the respondents varied considerably, from $7,000 to $15,000, most of the respondents falling between $7,000 and $10,000 per year.

The dominant theme running through the statements of all respondents was the high value placed on doing some activity that was highly enjoyable to them. If it wasn't a source of pleasure, it wasn't worth doing for the monetary rewards. When one subject was asked what would he do if his desire to become a policeman was not fulfilled, he replied, "I don't know, nothing. . . . A man can only be happy doing what he wants to do."

Many respondents showed a sense of realism in their occupational choice; for example, one responded: "I dreamt about a lot of things. I thought and dreamt, man. But you know, I know I can't be like no doctor or so. . . . I guess I thought about being a salesman—selling clothes. Maybe that's what I like."

Despite the specific and realistic occupational goals that many of the respondents expressed, there was a pervasive absence of any attempt in the past or strategy for the future to obtain these jobs. In several cases the high school diploma was either necessary or perceived to be necessary for entering these occupations. After being informed of the need for a high school diploma, these respondents gave up the pursuit of these jobs. It is not clear whether they felt they were unable to obtain a high school diploma or that, even with the diploma, they would not be able to obtain the job. One respondent who wanted to be a steel worker related this anecdote referring to his attempt to become an apprentice:

> They would pay me but I know it wouldn't at first mean doing too much exciting. Basically, you have to stay around the men and see how they work, get them coffee, take orders, and that sort of thing. A friend of mine was once told by the Apprentice Center that he was too young, you had to be eighteen to apply. I went to them when I was eighteen and they say you need a high school diploma. I gave up.

Job discrimination, personally experienced or perceived by the youngsters, was a consistent response of the subjects. The effect of discrimination was to harden their hostile attitude toward whites and sharply reduce their incentive to obtain better jobs, training, and education. Often, the respondent rationalized his behavior or attitudes by citing discrimination as a powerful outside force eradicating all his personal efforts and accomplishments. One person, discussing his friends, commented: "Not too many of them finished high school. Sometimes I think I'm better off than them since I graduated. Don't have to hear no shit about we only hire high school grads. They mean white high school grads anyway." This response indicates a sense of hopelessness and despair; whether or not the perceived discrimination exists, the perception of discrimination has had and will have an adverse effect on the individual.

A comment of a different person reinforces the limited role education can play in solving the employment and income problems of blacks in urban areas. "Knowledge is insurance for the future. And you got to be trained. But you see they say somebody got to do the dirty work. And that somebody they say got to be black people." Again allegiance is paid to education; however, the but clause, indicating that it is not the same for blacks, runs through the thoughts and statements of many of the subjects interviewed. For youngsters enrolled in school, who are convinced on one level of the need for education but are also cognizant of the inadequacy of education to solve their problems and the absence of any of the promised rewards of education for blacks, high dropout rates should result. The players in the system do not believe the system can or does work for their benefit.

The theme of constant rejection also runs through the interviews. Hostility and apathy are the two most common consequences among youth. One youth indicated that the rejection took many forms. Often, logical reasons were offered, but in the end he always felt it was because he was black. "The employers would say, 'The job has been filled, we think you're overqualified, you wouldn't like the job, it is too far away from your home,' all sorts of shit. Lots of places they don't want black people to work there, like Home Life Insurance."

An unemployed black youth commented: "Times are hard. I don't think a young man like me should have so many problems, it's no good. Times are hard, times are very hard."

In the eyes of the black youngster discrimination is everywhere. One young worker revealed his perceptions on this subject, as follows:

I was out on my own since I was 17 so I have had to make it for myself . . . . It wasn't a matter of choice—like saying I left home because I wanted to. I had to do it, and push

hard for myself. I was making $2.00 an hour and then
this guy came in and made more money than me . . . .
And he didn't have no diploma either. Yes, I found out
how much he was making—$2.75 an hour . . . . He was
white.

EDUCATION

The greatest point of similarity in the sample of Harlem youth
was the experience of dropping out of school. Eighteen of the twenty-
five cases had left high school at least temporarily. Ten had graduated
from high school, six after having dropped out earlier. All three
southern-born and educated males in the sample had graduated from
high school and did not drop out of school before graduation. Only four
New York City-educated students had completed high school without
dropping out at any time.
Ten of nineteen respondents had been enrolled in an academic
curriculum, five in vocational, and two each in commercial and
general curriculum areas. It is tragic to discover that many students
enroll in a program in which they are not interested and which cannot
provide useful and valuable skills in a labor market making increasing
educational demands of new entrants.
The experience of the respondents with school was, for all but
a few individuals, extremely unsatisfactory. Negative attitudes were
expressed toward teachers, administrators, and the entire educational
system. Most respondents recognized the value of education for
obtaining better jobs; however, the process itself was sufficiently
distasteful to reduce their incentive to continue school or training.
Boredom, frustration, and discouragement with the school
system dominated the responses of the youngsters. Dropping out was
seen as a rational course of action because the schools were very
hostile to these youngsters. Some youngsters dropped out because
of the curriculum. "I was enthusiastic I guess until the 12th grade.
In the 12th grade they started giving us the same thing over and over
again. Like what we was doing was nothing new. I cut loose."
Others dropped out because of conflicts over curriculum with parents
or guidance counselors: "I wanted to do auto mechanics but she
[mother] wanted me to take up more like an academic type thing.
I left school at sixteen and went to Alabama. I just wanted to get
away for a break. I wasn't going to work or nothing. I spent time
with my family." Others dropped out for financial reasons.

I was doing very well in my skills but not so well in the
other stuff [academic program]. I thought if I could go

out and work I could help out [the family] a little [mother
was ill]. They [guidance counselors] tried to persuade
me to stay in school, but I kept telling them that my
mother was sick and I had to get money, so they finally
let me go.

Some students were misdirected by teachers and counselors
and placed in the wrong programs; the result was often a dropout:
"I was in a "1" class [bright students] and was given an academic
program when I got to high school. I could not switch over to the cut
program so I got fed up and dropped out."

The remarks of the respondents on conditions in their schools
and the methods of operation are illuminating:

Classes are so big the teacher has a hard time. She can't
take no more than a minute to solve individual problems.
You can ask questions but you can't get long explanations.
She has a lesson she has to get across in a small time.
She has to keep up. . . . In school you can't expect too
much personal attention just as on a job you couldn't
expect a boss to spend too much time with you alone.

Another respondent described his elementary and high school
experience:

It was all right [elementary school]. The teachers tried
with you. I think they tried and gave you attention. But
high school, I went in September and never went back
except to sign out. You could see that was no school.
Dope fiends and winos all over the place. I sized that up
in one day. Why waste my time there. The teachers
don't care a fuck. When you drop out, one less nigger.
They make their money, they're white, that's all they
care. Come in and go out is their speed.

Another respondent reported a similar experience:

I thought they gave us a raw deal. Teachers were working
by the clock. If you had a problem teachers often suggested that you quit school. By being concerned about us
and not the bell, the clock, and the bucks, those whiteys
and negroes [teachers] could have helped us a hell of a
lot more.

On the problem of communications, one respondent said:

Teachers were poor then and now. Teachers were unable
to communicate with blacks. If they could have related to
us better some of us would have been better off. I
recently went back to school [JHS 120] and the kids run
wild; teachers either can't deal with them or won't deal
with them. No one I respected tried to talk me out of
leaving school.

The respondents' views give the general impression that the
school is an institution set up to benefit the teachers and administrators
at the expense of the students. Overcrowded conditions, disinterested
or incompetent teachers, poor communications, misguided direction
and counseling, rigid curriculum, inflexible rules and lack of concern
and responsibility are the messages received from these interviews.
Forces both within the school system and outside, from peers, parents,
and the illegal market of the urban economy, operate to encourage
the exodus from the schools. The motivation to graduate is severely
reduced by the attitude that

You don't learn nothin' in school. It's a waste of time.
At the hospital I was making more than guys I know
finished high school. So it ain't nothin'. . . . Besides
I can't understand getting a high school diploma only to
go in the Army. You going to get killed so it ain't worth
it.
        You know they say the kids are lazy. You stay away
from school and when you return they look at you like you
dumb. They say, what happened? You stupid or something? But they are stupid. Kids are not sick, they are
smart. A place you don't like you just stay away from.
It's as simple as that.

And finally, personal circumstances and events complicate the
students' attempts to remain in school.

I was on the stuff [heroin] for ten months to a year. I
first took it in school and then I started it in the neighborhood and everywhere, man. I kept telling myself that I
wanted to stop and get treatment but since I was under age
I knew I would have to go to the hospital with my parents
and I didn't want my mother to know. One Friday night
last February I got high and she saw me and found out.
So I said there is no more need to hide. So the next
Monday we both went together to (a hospital) for treatment. . . . They give you medication to cut the need,

counselling, discussions every week, what you can do to
avoid repetition. . . . While getting treatment I piled up
excessive absence [from school] . . . .

      Eighteen is the bad age in high school. They try to
get you out of school and they don't really encourage you
to go to night school. They tell you you should enroll but
no help. You got to be straight if you are in at eighteen,
one slip and you're out. . . . A card came to my home
telling me to return the books. I knew that was it. They
were threatening all the while to evict me because of my
age and the school was overcrowded. I was lacking in
only two subjects: Chemistry and English 8. I was going
to take them the next year and then graduate. I could go
to night school and finish. I took the Regents in American
History and passed. I was to take it in Chemistry but I
was absent in it so much I knew I could not pass so I
figured I would do it next term.

He never graduated.
      A web of rules strangles all but the strongest and most capable
students, forcing the others out of a competitive and often ruthless
school system. "Catholic school was fine—I dug!," said one respondent, "but public school in this place is a shame." The young
man was expelled from school after a two and one-half month absence
because of a broken collar bone,

> even though I had a doctor's notice, but I guess it was
> 'cause I was on trial basis and plus. . . . the attendance
> officer is a very nasty old woman—the cause of many
> people being thrown out . . . . You know they have a
> student-faculty court set up for dismissals due to disci-
> plinary problems. Well, at court she lays it on thick—
> this cracker—and the accused student can't say very much
> to defend himself from being dismissed. I became bitter
> after that.

At the school he had attended previously,

> there are, I think six guidance counsellors for something
> like 5,000 kids. At Brandeis I think there are ten. And
> that's a big goddamn school. You know that school operates
> in 3 shifts. Ten counsellors for what?—10,000 kids?
>   What I did learn was because of interest—personal
> interest. . . . Most kids naturally come into public school
> without that interest to begin with and little is done to make

them interested. In Catholic school, the Brothers and
Sisters are people who care. Just them caring makes
you care. You get interested and you work. Public school
nobody cares. You just take notes, and then they tell you
you got a test tomorrow. . . . I tell you if you enter class
late at the start of the term you go through that term without
even knowing the teacher's name. At least it is so up to
the mid-term and then you try to find out her name for the
exam booklet. . . . The place is a machine with those
shifts. Ding! Bell! One group comes in. Ding! Bell!
A next group comes in. The public school system is a
farce.

There are many students who for a variety of reasons remain in
school and succeed in graduating with a diploma. However, the value
of their education is greatly diminished by the lack of any real
achievement and accomplishments. One respondent who had finished
high school said: "School was kind of a fun thing. Cats goofed off
and no one paid much attention. Teachers didn't give a damn, they
just put in their time and got the hell out of there. Teachers didn't
give a damn and they demanded and got no discipline. Guys went wild.
I put in my time and made everyone happy."

Those who had received their education in parochial schools or
in southern schools tended to have more favorable attitudes toward
the school system. All three respondents who went to school in the
South had graduated from high school. One of them stated that "all
teachers were helpful and on the ball." The students' favorable
perception of the attitudes of their teachers in these school systems
may be due to the existence of a common bond between students and
teachers: the shared religious orientation in the parochial schools
and in the southern schools the fact that both students and teachers
were black.

Although many of the interviewees cited unfavorable experiences
they had had in school, many responded favorably regarding further
schooling and training. All respondents seemed to indicate a positive
value for skills and training in order to obtain better employment.
Twelve of seventeen respondents indicated a desire to return to school
or training. Two had gone back to school and received high school
equivalency diplomas. However, no one in the sample had received
any training or enrolled in any government training program. Some
interviewees were totally ignorant of the opportunities for training
that were available. Others were aware of some of the programs
but had negative opinions or misinformation about them.

In summary, we can conclude that at least some of the students
in the slum areas, perhaps most, are not benefiting from their

educational experience. What is obviously missing is a mutually
desired, tangible, and concrete goal and a system of incentives drawing
together student and teacher in a cooperative effort. These interviews point to many areas in which improvement is needed before
learning can proceed in the schools: (a) in better communication among
parents, students, teachers, and administrators; (b) guidance
counseling; (c) class size; better and more flexible curriculum; (d)
courses related to future occupations; (e) closer contact with employers
and the labor market; and (f) more understanding, concern, and, most
important, respect toward black students on the part of the school
system. Finally, regardless of the improvement in the schools and
in the skill achievements of the students, little will be gained unless
real or perceived employment discrimination is eliminated. "A
black man can have more degrees than a thermometer, but it won't
help him get a decent job. That territory is whitey's turf."

MILITARY SERVICE AND TRAINING

The four respondents with experience in the armed forces
presented a mixed and often confused picture of military life. The
military offers opportunities but it also has many elements of overt
discrimination. Equality does not exist "if you're black, and in the
military you got to be three times better than those whitey's. I would
never go back into the service. Charity begins at home, the fight is
here."

Most of the hostility and bitterness about the service is a result
not of experiences in the military but of the severe emotional letdown
after discharge. The emotional aftereffect is greater because of the
expectations built up in the service. One respondent spoke about his
brother, a Vietnam veteran:

> And he can't even get a job. Now isn't that a bitch! In
> 1961 they had the war but it was different. Now they
> glad to get anybody—lowering IQ's and all of that. But
> I won't go—never. . . . I am not in agreement. I won't
> fight for them crackers. Tell me to fight for somebody's
> freedom then I get back here and it's the same shit.

Another respondent on the service: "I left school in April, and December 10, 1965, I went into the service. . . . That's right, I can't
forget that date, can't forget it. One of the happiest times in my life."
After getting out of the service and looking for a job:

Too many no's. Everywhere I went they said I had a lack
of experience. I tell them about my experience overseas
and they say that don't count. . . . The Veterans say they
will offer help, but I don't know. I started to go to them
but I say I would try on my own for a start. . . . I went
to companies and agencies—everything. I went, for
instance, to the Ajax Construction Company in Jersey.
It is run by Italians or Jews, I don't even know. They
wanted 2 years' experience. One year overseas on heavy
equipment, driving a fork lift and working at ammunition
storage—they said, "We don't take that." I see that as
experience. I just got tired, went away. . . . it made me
a hell of a lot bitter. You're catching hell overseas and
you come home for a job and there's nothing here. . . .
They don't want to be bothered with this when they get out.
They want to work.

He went "to four or five agencies. At all of them I said that I would
operate lift vehicles and, you see, I would train to work other vehicles
on my off-time. They let you do that . . . . But no. They give me
the run-around."

After coming home from Vietnam, another respondent stated:

I fell in with the wrong set and I don't know how to pull
myself out of it. I got to pull myself away because I
ain't doing nothing now. Like I lost all my momentum
and I don't want to do nothing. I don't know what's
wrong with me. You know . . . a lot of people tell me
that I have college ability; they say I conversate [sic]
well. You know they even went so far to even have a
professor come from some college to talk to me. . . .
They say I had good potential. . . . I went a couple times
to class . . . .
      They talk about important things, not that shit that
don't mean nothing. They talk about more constructive
things like ghetto problems. . . . They weren't phonies—
they were men!
      I am in a confused state. My mind is not stable. I
can't cope with myself. . . .
      It has a serene . . . it is hard to have a different
outlook. This country's outlook is too hard and brutal.
This is a developed and great country, true, but it has no
serenity, if you see what I mean. Like dig this. The
other day a kid on 8th Avenue asked a man for 10

cents—one dime. I tell you—and the man stabbed him in
his jugular vein. But—shit! I tell you I walk with my
M-16. I hate violence but I love life.

I should have re-enlisted. I shouldn't have got out
so quick. If I re-enlisted I would've got a better education
and more out of life. This I regret. A better education
and I would have a better job ultimately. . . . Another
six months to another three years. . . . I reinlist and I
would go back into school—which is what I didn't know at
the start—and learn engineering. I like outdoor work and
working with my hands.

Asked how he felt about himself overseas, he said:

We were men. I had my obligation and my job to do and I
did it. I didn't really have men under me but in my fork-
lifting job I knew what I was doing and the men working
with me listened to my instructions and we worked
together in companionship. When I was overseas I saved
my money that I earned and won. . . . When I came
back I told my mother, "Mom, I saved $1800—let's take
this money and move out of here." She didn't want to
move. You know, she say, it is the same everywhere,
and she been living there a very long time. I couldn't
understand that. . . . If I could help them move it would
have helped me keep feeling responsible. It won't be fair
to say that she not moving was the cause for me getting
this way, but after that I didn't have much to care about.

"I didn't want to come back," he said.

I was real scared coming back on that plane. You know
everyone else was happy. Some had wives or girls they
were dying to see and they couldn't wait to land. I wished
we didn't land. I was quiet and alone. When the plane
landed and we came to the discharge desk I nearly felt like
running way on back to the plane. I didn't know what to do,
I was so confused. Something tell me stay another six
months—re-enlist. But like I just went along with the
crowd. . . . I took a cab all the way from the airport to
right here and, just like I thought, nothing changed. It
was early morning, five o'clock, and quiet. The door, the
house, the street was all the same. I felt kind of sick.
I pulled out my things and just stood there. Everything
was the same.

ILLEGAL ACTIVITIES

Background data on the subjects in the sample indicate a very high arrest record for the fourteen who responded to the question. Eight were arrested, four of them for assault, grand larceny, or narcotics. A large number of respondents were connected with either the use or sale of drugs, particularly marijuana and heroin. Out of nine specific responses, six were using heroin and three were smoking marijuana.

Several of the respondents reported that their police records did not hinder them in their search for employment. One respondent commented that "nobody ever turned me down 'cause of them [arrests]; usually they just ignore them because they are minor offenses." This was probably due more to the type of position the respondent was seeking rather than to his personal history.

Only one of the respondents had a record of repeated arrests. Most had been arrested once, were not convicted, or else pleaded guilty to a lesser crime and were put on probation. What is startling is the respondents' casual attitude toward their arrests and toward the judicial system. One respondent stated, "You always get sentenced and then they suspend it. . . . "

The attitude toward selling narcotics was summed up by one respondent: "Like, who hasn't?" And the attitude toward taking drugs is expressed by the following comment: "I use everything from heroin to marijuana. Been using it off and on for four years. As long as you don't abuse them, nothing's wrong with narcotics. It helps you avoid reality every now and then and you need that or else you go crazy. I don't abuse drugs, they simply make me see into myself better." Belief in the pervasiveness of the use of drugs came through in practically all the interviews. For example, one respondent, commenting on the use of marijuana, stated: "Everybody does, I do that until I die. I would never consider myself on the level of the out-and-out junkie. I see nothing wrong with smoking if you don't overdo it."

The drug scene starts early in the life of a ghetto youngster. References to narcotics use and selling in the schools were numerous. Said one respondent:

You know, it is all over school. They sell it and smoke it in the bathroom. I didn't know too much about it then. Like one day this guy came up to me and asked me if I was straight and I didn't know what he mean. It is only later I found out it mean you have dope or take dope. But they are messed up. I know it is bad, man, messed up a

lot of real nice girls. I see those girls turn on the hot
water pipe and stand in front of it so that steam could go
up their noses and clear up all that comes from the dope.

According to the interviews and personal observation, hustling
was pervasive in Harlem. Nearly every respondent had some contact
with an activity that could be considered hustling, from panhandling
to selling heroin. Many of the respondents were aware of the risks
and penalties for these assorted illegal activities, and most preferred
the safer activities, such as gambling and running numbers, despite
the higher incomes associated with narcotics. One comment was:
"I hustle to make a fast buck, better than work, it is true you get 30
days for numbers and 30 years for dope, but I never worry with
numbers. People hustle at numbers cause it's safer." Another
comment was:

> I just hanging around. If things get too boring during the
> summer I'll find something to do. . . . This is America,
> man—you can always make money pushing numbers or
> something. . . . It's 3 o'clock now. You can see them
> coming out of the sidewalk. Tonight they go back in with
> $800 and put it on the dressing table.

The option to hustle is always available and, thus, acts as an
effective safety valve for economic as well as social and personal
pressures. People can approach their lives in a more relaxed manner
and with greater flexibility. It is unnecessary to plan about the future.
The option of hustling or using drugs is ever-present and available.
The attitude is best expressed by one respondent:

> I figure what is going to happen. What you going to be
> you'll be. I might be wrong. But working,shit. . . .
> You got all those people who work and suppose to do
> right and they ain't nowhere. Then you get guys who do
> evil and they make the money. Those guys who sell the
> dope got all the money wrapped up: cars'n everything.
> They don't do nothin' for it. They don't take the stuff
> either. That's why I say what is going to be is going to
> be . . . .
>   I'll do something this summer. I won't work for
> nobody . . . . Sell something . . . . Push something . . . .
> Reefers?
>   I might run numbers; don't know. . . . If I sell
> anything it will be cocaine. That don't harm you. Every-
> body takes cocaine, them movie stars; all of them . . .

to keep them calm. Sure, even the President in the White
House takes it to keep cool. . . . But they killing us:
killing us in Viet Nam and with dope. They don't take it
but sell it to niggers who sell it to niggers. That's how
they gonna get rid of us all.

One extremely articulate respondent provided a series of comments incorporating many of the attitudes, values, perceptions, and
even general behavior toward hustling as a way of life. Moreover,
it provides some interesting facts about the earnings from hustling
compared to regular work.

On hustling:

I have scarcely gone legit in my life. I have never really
worked in my life. Look now: I'm not working, but I pick
up a check every week. . . . Look, I got into numbers,
understand. I used to dress plain and simple—used to
wear a lot of khaki stuff—you know, khaki shirts. Nothing
flashy . . . .I started out as a watch-out in the corridor.
This banker told me he would start me off at $65 a week.
Then another one came along and say: "Listen, I'll top
that for you. I'll give you $75 a week." And so I take it.
It is tax-free, you know. So? So, I started to move on
up. Another banker gave me $90 a week and from time to
time he would up that. Soon I was making $160 a week . . .
I had this girlfriend—nice chick—and I really fell for her.
We was in love, or at least I thought I loved her . . . .
        You ever see what happens to those young people who
get married—straight people who get married and come and
live around here? They break up and go to pieces.
Numbers bankers move down the street with fancy clothes
and Cadillacs. Marriage don't last. And the straight guy
goes to pieces. The other guys, they know how to survive
and play the game. Life is a game . . . .It is survival of
the fittest. You have to know how to play the game . . . .
So you got to be strong . . . What is to be is to be, yes,
but I believe you got to get up and get it. I can't sit down
on this park bench here and expect things to come right to
me. I got to see what I want and go out and get it.
        So, like I was saying, I found out that my girlfriend
was seeing a numbers banker . . . so I said if that's what
she likes, I am going to go out and get like that. . . . So
I started stealing. By now I was taking the customers'
slips with their requests in the corridor and take it to the
back room. I was in a big numbers joint now—I won't

tell you where it is—with three people—three!—in the
corridor collecting. So I started dipping into the money.
First time I took $60. . . . I never took any of the policy
slips because that way they could find out through the
customers. Then I took $100 . . . I started buying ex-
pensive suedes and dressing real good.

You see, they thought I was stupid. They thought I
was too stupid to steal. But you see, I only used to play
stupid. I could hear them counting money in the back room,
and they had two people with the banker in the back—a
woman and somebody else—and they thought one of them
was stealing. . . .

Plus I started playing and I hit—hit for $1,000. But
I still was stealing. . . . You know, I would see a gold
watch and want it. By the end of one week I stole $600
and took home over $700. Then I hit—hit for $13,000.

I went back to my family and was going to help
them. . . . They knew what I was doing. . . . They didn't
want to come with me. I wanted to get my own place and
run my own business. . . . Then I found out who was my
friends—my so-called friends. That's the trouble with
black people: they too petty; they go for hamburgers. . . .
We got our own lawyer and went over to the police to get
a "business license"—actually, that is just the side money,
you know, you give them so that they don't interfere with
you. But then my friends wanted to make me a co-worker
with them. Co-worker! That means working for them.
And I was putting in the most money. If I had to work for
anybody, then it was best that I stayed with the bankers I
was with before. At least if we got busted I wouldn't get
rapped the most . . . . I never been busted. It's just
luck, that's all.

You see we got to do like the Jew fellow. He and his
friends are in for business and they serious about it. They
get the money by false ways at the start but then they invest
it in legitimate business. . . . I don't think hustling
should be singled out as bad. They have other higher ups
who rob and cheat and nobody says nothing about it.

On seeing a robbery:

Just robbed the lady's pocketbook!
Sure, I'm annoyed. Why? Cause, like I said, too
petty! Now if a cop were around he would get a bullet in
his back that would kill him dead just for something petty.

They grab at hamburgers. There is probably no more
than $2.00 in that goddamn purse. I mean to say if you
gonna get busted or killed it might as well be for something big. Just like when they riot, they go for the stupid
stuff. You ever see what they take? A shoe, a jacket,
a ring. What they should do is go midtown where all those
diamond centers are and burst a few of them for the real
stuff. . . . If I ever was to pull something, I would take
about $100,000. . . .

It's hard for one guy to rob a bank, I guess. I don't
know if it's ever been done do you? But you say you come
off with $100,000 and they catch you . . . . You get a good
lawyer and offer to pay him $10,000. . . . If you get a
sentence and the money isn't found, after you serve you
have the money to keep, right? I think so, ain't it? The
lawyer knows this, so the longer sentence you get the
longer he has to wait. So he go talk to the judge. He
might even promise to cut the judge in. So you get 8 or 10
years at the end of which you have at least $80,000.

On seeing the pocketbook thief reappear: "There goes the guy.
I knew he was going to eventually come around that way. They'll
catch him. He's too stupid. You see him? He's got a patch by his
eye which can't come right off and I think people here know him."

And finally, the rapid deterioration of a human being, from a
respected and productive member of the armed services in Vietnam
to a hard-core narcotics addict, desperately seeking help but completely unable to help himself and living in constant fear of being
without narcotics and harming someone in order to obtain narcotics,
is sadly depicted in the following anecdote:

You know, when I got back from overseas, like I wanted to
make up for all I was missing—to get to do much as I could
out of life. [A friend wrote to him.] I knew from his
letters that he used to take drugs and you know he would
go through this thing about how great it was and so on. But
I couldn't pay it no mind [But he went to his friend when
he came home] and he and his friends were all high with
the stuff and they asked me why I don't have some and join
them. I say no at first but then I join them . . . . I went
back a few times . . . They look at me and say that I got
the habit . . . . I say "never—I'm as good as I ever
was . . . ." But what they said was true. One day after I
had this urge and my body starting hurting . . . it's a
bitch, boy.

He needed money for drugs: precisely $4.00.

That would last me till Saturday night, Sunday morning.
I have an uncle who lends me money so I can get the stuff.
He don't approve of it but he sees and knows what I went
through once—the pain and everything—and he don't like
to see me suffer. So he gives me some money. He is also
trying to get me to hospital and back to school . . . If I
can borrow $4.00 I will pay back after I see my uncle
tomorrow.

He pointed to some children.

You see them: snortin'! The one in the blue shirt now . . .
These young kids, they not doing it for the reason other
people used to do it which was to survive by forgetting.
They do it for kicks but they don't know what they playing
with. If they only knew what it will turn them into.
    When I was overseas I felt like a man, but now that
I come back here I don't feel like a man no more. Overseas everybody has a responsibility . . . to do what you
have to do . . . and we are men. So a buddy comes up to
you to borrow money and you lend him because you won't
have to go asking him back for your money—he's going to
bring it to you. Not like out here. I came back with a
load of money and you know I don't really know how to
value money—or I didn't know then. I needed clothes so
I bought about $180.00 worth of clothes.

He tried to get help for his addiction:

I went to this hospital here on 123rd Street and asked them
to take me, and they look at me and say "we don't have
facilities for dealing with dope fiends." Oh! They got me
so mad. They don't even know what a dope fiend is. I
am trying to help myself and this is the way they react. . . .
This morning I went to another hospital. . . . I waited and
waited and they was a lot of dudes hoping to get accepted
but they only took six. Of all those cats, they said they
only had room for six. Some of those addicts used to go
stealing pills and that kind of stuff as a narcotic substitute
but an aide tell me that most of the time it is vitamin pills.
He say: "I hope they all get as strong as a horse, the
bitches."

He is afraid that he might hurt someone trying to get money for drugs. "I think the remorse after that would be too much for me. I would have to kill myself."

The respondents indicated a very heavy involvement in the illegal economy of New York City. The youngsters engaged in a full range of income-generating activities, from armed robbery to running numbers. A large segment of the income generated in the Harlem area seems to be derived from the distribution and sale of heroin. The size of the addict pool and the number of people required as workers in the heroin distribution system in New York City indicate the importance of the illegal drug industry as a source of both employment and income for many youngsters and adults living in the slum areas of Harlem, Bedford-Stuyvesant, and East Harlem. A recent study by the Hudson Institute[1] estimated the number of addicts in New York at 70,000, with 50 percent estimated to be residing in the three slum areas. The number of employees in the distribution system at the lowest level of street dealers and jugglers to service the addict pool is estimated at 8,000, with average earnings probably exceeding $10,000 per year.

Of the total population of the three slums, one out of eleven people, or more than 9 percent, are heroin addicts, according to the Hudson study. Among the Puerto Rican population in these slums, the percentage is 11.4 percent, or 8,750 Puerto Rican addicts. And among the young males fourteen to twenty-four years of age in the three slums, there are an estimated 11,700 addicts, or 26.5 percent of this age living in the slum areas.[2] These figures greatly exceed the number of youngsters out of work and indicate the extent and severity of the heroin problem. However, they also indicate the real amount of unemployment in the slum areas among youngsters. The illegal economy, which, in addition to the heroin industry, includes gambling, robbery, theft, shoplifting, prostitution, numbers, and protection, runs into hundreds of millions of dollars, and the youngsters and adults engaged in these activities are generating incomes for themselves and their families and friends in the ghetto communities and the rest of the city and are not counted as unemployed members of the ghetto or city labor force.

By way of illustration, the retail value of heroin sold or consumed in New York City is estimated to be $463 million (925 kilograms of pure heroin at a price of $5.00 per 10 milligrams). The amount of theft by addicts to purchase the retail heroin has been estimated to be $577 million.[3]

From an independent source of data, the Urban Employment Survey of 1966, initiated by the U.S. Department of Labor, it was possible to estimate the dollar amount of income reported by slum dwellers without identifying the source. The total income earned from legal sources in Harlem was $399,068,544 in 1966 (74,676 families with a mean income of $5,344 per year; see appendix to this chapter for the derivation of the estimate of illegal income in Harlem). A conservative estimate places 10 percent of the population of Harlem engaged in illegal activities, at the average income earned of $6,000 per year. The total illegal income thus amounts to $90 million, or 22.5 percent of the earned income during the year. The estimate is considered conservative, because 38 percent of the population in the survey had unaccountable sources of income. The amount of income generated from all illegal activities in the city may be as high as half a billion dollars. In light of these figures, the $90 million estimate for Harlem seems reasonable. By way of comparison, if Harlem has one-fourth of the heroin addicts in the city, it also has the same percentage of revenue generated from the distribution of the drug, which amounts to over $115 million per year. This does not include the highly profitable large-scale businesses of gambling, including numbers, prostitution, and bootlegging.

Anyone living in and studying the slums of our major cities is aware of the pervasive impact of illegal activities and income generated by them. Recently, two more studies have attempted to demonstrate the magnitude of two forms of illegal economic activity in New York City slums, particularly Harlem. "The Black Mafia Moves into the Numbers Racket"[4] stated, "There are an estimated 100,000 numbers workers in the five boroughs, with the bulk of them active in the black ghettos of Harlem, the South Bronx and Bedford Stuyvesant." Aside from the sizable employment effect, the amount of income generated by the numbers business is estimated to range "from an ultraconservative $300 million to well over $1 billion, with most sources crediting the higher figure." The importance of the illegal economy to the residents of slum areas is suggested by a remark of Livingston L. Wingate, executive director of the Urban League, in response to the legalization of off-track betting in New York City.

> Wingate contended in essence, that crime was one of the nation's six largest industries, that numbers was Harlem's "thing," that authorities had done nothing about police corruption, which, he argued, made the police partners in crime, and that what people wanted was not whitey coming in from downtown but a piece of the action for themselves.[5]

Wingate's remarks were reinforced by Basil Patterson, a state senator from Harlem and the 1970 unsuccessful Democratic candidate for lieutenant governor of New York.

When you are four years old in Harlem, you are aware of
the numbers racket . . . You see the numbers runners
taking their bets; you see the cops taking their payoffs;
you know that the man who knows the cop by his first name
is always the numbers guy. Those of us who have always
lived in the community, where policy has always operated
openly, with the open cooperation of the police force, have
a suspicion when we see the system changed and a new ball
game coming in. None of us wants to be put in the position
of defending a racket. It's an awfully difficult position
we're put in. But Wingate touched a resonant chord in the
community; he expressed a gut reaction I think what the
people are saying is: "Prove to us that you are not trying
to keep us out of something we are reaching into. Is this
another device to wean away money that would have
remained in black pockets or will you try to spread it
around more equitably?"[6]

On another front, a study by the Small Business Chamber of
Commerce in Harlem[7] estimated the cost of crime in Harlem at a
staggering 2 billion dollars a year. Nearly $1.8 billion was estimated
to be related to the narcotics problem, crimes committed by addicts.
Even if the addicts receive one-third of the value of the stolen property,
$600 million will be distributed into the narcotics distribution system.
If the workers in the lower echelons of the system receive only one-
fourth of the total funds, an additional $150 million of illegal income
is distributed in the slum areas. Moreover, if one-third of the value
of other stolen goods, not associated with narcotics, is available,
an additional $67 million is distributed.

It is not important to obtain a precise estimate of the income
received by the residents of slum areas from illegal business activities. What is essential is to recognize that illegal activities supply
substantial income to residents of poverty areas, as well as other
members of the urban population. The impact and consequences of
the illegal money on unemployment and employment, on labor force
behavior, and on wage rates, taxation, and manpower and poverty
programs are not known and must be examined carefully.

Government programs and policies and the regular legitimate
labor market cannot compete effectively with the opportunities offered
in the illegal marketplace. It cannot be profitable to pursue economic,
educational, and manpower policies that do not recognize the problems
and barriers presented by the opportunities in the illegal economy.

Hustling often is an economically and socially rewarding way
of life for many people. Moreover, it contributes to a quasi-stable
social existence in slum areas capable of exploding from the

tremendous economic and social tensions generated by poverty,
uncertainty, hunger, disease, and insecurity. There are many in the
outside society who derive benefits from the system: large profits,
a source of cheap labor, a casual labor reserve unattached and seeking
part-time work, graft and corruption of officials, preservation of the
status quo (no waves, no costs). But there are people who suffer
cruel and permanent damage from the system. The girls forced into
prostitution to support their children, the narcotics addicts unable
to satisfy their craving for drugs, and finally the public at large,
paying exhorbitant costs in terms of crime and the enforcement of
justice by police and courts. An attempt to alter the illegal activities,
like all economic and social processes, will cause a disturbance to
the general equilibrium of the larger system. The implications must
be known and steps must be taken to avoid all undesirable consequences.
Methods must be developed to guide youngsters into more productive
legal activities, while reducing the high rewards from the unproductive
and illegal activities. Opening up new opportunities, while simultaneously closing down others, will be required to avoid severe economic
pressures. The larger system must change before we can expect a
smooth and orderly change from an explosive subsystem of the slums.

CONCLUSIONS

In contrast to the broken home and unsatisfactory family life
depicted by Patrick Moynihan and supported by an array of statistics
on family desertion, welfare families, and so forth, the respondents
in the sample were not from broken homes. They had siblings who
had achieved some degree of success in school and in the labor market
and had educated and employed parents who were not confined to low-
wage occupations. The stable family structure and the psychological
and economic support of their parents reduced the hardships of a
life of low income and high unemployment for many of the black
youngsters. The support provided by the parents or other relatives
and friends operated to reduce the need to work on a permanent basis
and allows the youngsters to exist on a subsistence wage. Nevertheless, serious unemployment and social problems afflict these subjects.
Job turnover was prevalent alongside long-term unemployment.

Long-term employees usually receive higher wages, with a high
correlation between the duration of employment and wage level.
Consequently, it is in the interests of the employer to replace long-
term workers with new workers, as long as skill and productivity do
not differ. Since most such jobs are low-paying and unskilled, a
ready labor supply exists to replace the worker. Productivity is often
not increased by lengthy service in these marginal jobs, and, hence,

replacement at no cost to the employer is assured. To the employee
the opportunity cost of changing jobs is very low; wages and job content
are undesirable, and the opportunity to acquire income from other
sources is always available. The system thus forces both the employee
and the employer into a high-turnover, casual employment sector of
the urban economy. The lack of future opportunities that might lead
to a radical change in life-style (outside the ghetto) is the real factor
in the low opportunity costs of even higher-wage jobs. This would
account for blacks giving up some well-paying jobs that are dead-end
and do not allow the opportunity to break out of ghetto life. The
incentive to work hard in order to be able to effect a change in one's
way of life is absent in such jobs. In addition, underlying racial
prejudice acts to reinforce the "getting by" theme.

The theme of "getting by" dominates the lives of these black
youth. The frustration encountered in the world of work and "whitey"
is too much to endure for the meager rewards it offers to relatively
unskilled and uneducated blacks. The availability of alternative sources
of incomes and an attitude of being on one's own are powerful com-
petitors to the regulated middle-class world.

The urban labor market for black men without specialized skills
and education offers no opportunity for an individual to break through
the barriers of life in the ghetto. At best, the segmented urban labor
market offers marginal employment and wages to allow people to
"get by"; at worst, it offers the conditions of subsistence in a sea of
affluence and wealth. There is no hope of a structural change in the
earnings and, hence, the life-styles of blacks in the ghettos. There
is no incentive to hold a marginal job with subsistence wages because
of the lack of opportunity to rise in the occupational and income
classes.

On the other hand, opportunities for personal freedom, status,
dignity, and, most important, economic success do exist in the slums
of our cities. When confronted with the choice of working long hours
at a monotonous, often dirty job, at low wages and with no economic
security, subject to exploitation by a white employer or working
relatively few hours at one's own choosing, at high wages, with
social acceptance by peers and the community at large, a rational
man will choose the latter. Hustling by satisfying the tastes of
consumers for goods and services deemed illegal or immoral by the
white-dominated society is a logical and rational option chosen by
many young blacks in the urban economy. The value system of the
ghettos and slums differs substantially from that of small town,
middle-class America.

Blacks living under conditions of poverty, prejudice, and
discrimination, facing a hostile environment that offers more barriers
than pathways of upward mobility, must adopt a rational system of

improving their economic status in the urban environment. The market
for gambling, numbers, prostitution, and narcotics is large and highly
profitable. The transfer of income from these activities into the
ghetto is substantial, although specific data and estimates are difficult
to obtain.

The development of illegal activities operates in the subculture
as a nondestructive release from social and economic tensions.
Instead of sporadic or permanent explosions, crime, narcotics
selling, and gambling operate as social depressants built into the life
of the ghetto. Moreover, the authorities are reluctant, and with good
reason, to interfere drastically with many of these activities, despite
their illegal and immoral nature. Narcotics may be to the black
man in our cities what alcohol was to the American Indian in the old
West. Both reduce the ethnic group image, status, and culture until
they are destroyed from both within and without. Both substitute a
material depressant, limiting the mental and physical strength of the
addicted individual. Both force the individual to act in a manner
destined to antagonize the dominant group and ultimately compel it to
destroy or contain the individual and his group. And both offer a
source of income to a few members of the minority group who served
as the salesman for the white supplier.

A record of criminal activities and arrest did not seem to present
a problem for black youth in securing employment. It was never
mentioned in any of the interviews. This finding, although quite
surprising, supports the notion of the low cost attached to entering
and engaging in illegal activities. There is no great social stigma
attached to being arrested; in fact, it is often viewed as a mark of
courage and honor among the young. Second, the job opportunities
are already limited by a variety of other barriers, so that the additive
effect of an arrest record is relatively unimportant. Third, the law-
enforcement and court system does not inflict substantial deterrents,
thus reducing the costs of apprehension. Once apprehended, one can
calculate the penalty expected with great accuracy. Given both the
low probability of arrest and the limited penalties imposed by the
judicial system, the rewards of hustling often justify the activities
on rational, benefit-cost grounds.

Too often, the black youngster assimilates white middle-class
values, which unfortunately contributes to more difficulties and
barriers in the labor market. A case in point is the high status
attributed to "white-collar office work" and the correspondingly low
status attributed to blue-collar craftsman occupations. Objectively,
white-collar office employment does not confer many economic
rewards—the wages are often considerably lower than many blue-
collar factory or craftsman jobs; fringe benefits are lower, unionization is negligible, job insecurity is greater (no seniority, no union),

and so forth. Ironically, it is precisely the appeal of the status of white-collar jobs that has contributed to the relatively low economic benefits of such employment. The fact that the supply of workers for these jobs is greater because of the high status attached to such employment prevents unionization and keeps wages low. Blacks accepting this value system are expressing an unusual trade-off, substituting a white-collar job as a clerk at less than $100.00 per week for a job as a truck driver or butcher at $200.00 to $300.00 per week. This misdirection of the labor supply causes still greater wage disparities between the two sets of occupations, benefiting one at the expense of the other.

Many black youth in ghetto areas subscribe to the accepted values of the society-at-large, such as the importance of education and training, employment in meaningful and responsible work, and dependence upon one's own resources, and such goals as a successful career, the accumulation of wealth, and the achievement of status and prestige through possessions and a respected occupation. Unfortunately, all too often, black youth are denied opportunities to realize these goals. Often, the accepted means are found to be too difficult or too frustration-ridden. On the other hand, the alternative of illegitimate activities more readily facilitates the achievement of some measure of success for black ghetto residents.

Distrust and hostility toward whites were primarily generated in the school system. The black students felt that their teachers did not care about them and were not held responsible for their work. Their activities and attitudes toward black students reinforced the concept that teachers were being paid to teach but did not care and did not perform their jobs. The theme that nobody cared about black students was prevalent among the black youths interviewed. In and out of school others receive the rewards, while the black youths suffer irreparable damages educationally and psychologically. An ironic postscript to the black man's educational experience in the military was offered by one respondent. "My best skill in the Army was shoot to kill . . . they taught me that and may yet regret it."

The city school systems have failed to train and educate a substantial portion of black youngsters. A serious mismatch exists between the needs of these black students and the services provided by the educational institutions. A severe communications gap, preventing a productive exchange of information, ideas, and services, is a root cause of many of the deficiencies in the school systems in serving the minority groups of the cities. The extent of the misinformation and the communications gap is revealed by the large number of subjects who were involved in academic programs in the high schools. Their lack of interest in school and in academic subjects in particular was obvious to the most casual observer; yet, the school system

offered them no option to switch to another program or school. More
over, an academic diploma may not be, and often is not, so desirable
as a certificate of graduation from a fine vocational high school. Unfortunately, there are too few "fine" vocational schools in the New
York City area where many minority students can enroll.

The experience of the subjects with the armed forces is illuminating. Military experience provides semi-integration into a disciplin
and controlled environment. The system both upgrades and alienates
black men. The alienation grows out of a sense of exploitation and a
perception of inequities. Post-Vietnam experiences provide an
abrupt and traumatic change in the treatment and expectations of the
black veteran. After paying his dues by fighting and defending his
country, the black veteran is rejected and exploited. Great expectations lead to great frustrations and disillusionment. The expectations
are not unrealistic. Life in the army provided a responsible job and
some skill training for the black soldier. He was accepted by the
dominant group, particularly when engaged in work assignments and
especially in combat. He was allowed to experience and taste life in
a different and often better environment. He feels he is owed a debt
by the society when he returns from the war, but often, cruelly
rejected, searches in vain for employment, respect, dignity, or even
concern on the part of his fellow Americans. Two choices exist:
hostility and aggressive external destruction or apathy and self-
destruction.

The interviewees expressed very strong hostility toward whites,
in part for exploitation and discrimination on the job with regard to
hiring, wages, promotional opportunities, dirty work, and lay offs.
For some, hatred and hopelessness were replaced by despair and
apathy.

APPENDIX: AN ATTEMPT TO ESTIMATE ILLEGAL INCOME IN HARLEM

In Harlem 172 out of 2,306 members of the labor force were
unemployed, according to the Urban Employment Survey of 1966. All
reported not having any earned income from wages, and 65 reported
income from public sources. Another 30 (it may be double counting)
received income from other sources, including the possibility of
illegal income. The maximum number of people receiving income
from identified sources other than work would be 95, and the minimum
(complete duplication) would be 65. However, 172 people received
income and did not work. Thus, 77 people, or approximately 3.8
percent of the measured labor force in Harlem, could not account
for their gross annual income. Moreover, 47 out of the 172 reported

annual family income of over $5,000, 61 reported over $4,000, and 100 over $3,000 without working, or 58.1 percent of the unemployed.

Examining the data of those not in the labor force, 1,453, or approximately 42 percent of the population, we find 832 having an explicit source of income other than wages, 411 from public assistance, of which 344, or 83.7 percent, is Aid for Families with Dependent Children, and 421 receiving income from other sources. Thus, 621 people have incomes that are not accounted for, or 42 percent of the total not in the labor force. Thus, only 28 percent of those not in the labor force received income from direct accountable sources such as public assistance, and 72 percent received income in transfer payments as gifts or in illegal sources of income.

Thus far, we can add the unemployed with income without source (107) and those people not in the labor force (1,042) and have a total of 1,149 (out of a population reporting of 3,489, or almost 33 percent) who can possibly derive their income through transfer payments (gifts) and illegal sources of income. Eliminating the reported other sources of income, we still find a total of 698 people, or 20 percent of the total reporting, who had not reported any source of income but who reported annual income. One-fifth of the Harlem adult population received income that was not from work, welfare, gifts, unemployment insurance, home relief, charity, and so forth. We are assuming the only other source of income is illegal activities.

Of those not in the labor force, 46.9 percent, or 681 people, reported gross annual income in excess of $3,000, while 33.1 percent, or 480, reported income in excess of $4,000, and 335, or 23.1 percent, reported income in excess of $5,000. Only 344 were on Aid for Families with Dependent Children, and the bulk in this group fall in the range between $1,500 to $3,000. We can assume that the lower range must be receiving their income from public assistance, unemployment insurance, and gifts and charity. The conclusion is that those earning above $4,000 without working—480 people, or 33.1 percent of those not in the labor force—derive their income predominantly from illegal sources. An estimate of their income would be over $5,000—on the average probably closer to $6,000.

Turning to part-time workers, a portion of their annual income also appears to be derived from illegal sources. Only 27 people, or 8.7 percent, earned more than $80 a week and at a full work year would have made $4,000, but 140, or 47.1 percent, reported income in excess of $4,000. Clearly, 113 out of 297 part-time workers have undisclosed incomes, assuming part-time workers receiving benefits and transfers cannot receive them at income levels in excess of $5,000.

Full-time workers reporting income of over $5,000 were 850 out of 1,567, or 54.2 percent, while only 11, or 0.7 percent, earned

more than $99 per week.* Again, a large discrepancy exists, even
when adding 105 full-time workers receiving all forms of public
assistance and 208 receiving other income. The tentative conclusion
indicates a large number receiving income from identifiable legal
sources. There would be very few, if any, individuals with incomes
of $5,000 or more who would be receiving large transfer payments.
Nevertheless, if we deduct the 313 full-time workers receiving all
other sources of income, including public assistance, and we still
have 537 full-time workers (while only 11 earned enough hourly wages
to reach that standard of income), then this yields a descrepancy of
526.

Adding up the number of people who reported gross annual income
but had no way of accounting for the source will provide a crude
estimate of those receiving income from illegal activities.

Category	People with Unaccountable Sources of Income	
	Number	Percent
Unemployed	77	
Not in the Labor Force	621	20
Part-Time Workers	98	
Full-Time Workers	526	18
Total	1,322	38

*The assumption is that those people with gross annual income
of over $5,000 who do not earn $99 per week or more do not receive
funds from public assistance and gifts, since they have fairly high
earnings but are dependent on other sources of income (illegal) to
account for the discrepancy of what they earn from wages and what
they report for gross annual income. If we included the group with
gross annual income of $4,000-$4,999, who would normally have to
earn $80-$98 per week to reach such a level without other sources of
income, then we would have 1,077 full-time workers and 140 part-
time workers earning gross annual income of $4,000 or more, and the
corresponding category in wages in excess of $80 would be 769 full-
time workers and 27 part-time workers. The result would be 113
part-time workers with wages not likely to be from regular channels
of public assistance and gifts, as well as 308 full-time workers falling
into that category.

The income received by these individuals is difficult to estimate accurately. However, there is enough data to make a calculated guess that would be reasonably accurate. Most respondents who have earned illegal income cannot hide their consumption of goods from a census enumerator. Thus, in response to questions regarding gross annual income, they are more likely to give an estimate (in their perception) of what would be consistent with their visible consumer purchases. Thus, we find a large number of people with reported incomes in the $4,000 and above range without any source of income reported. Presumably, a substantial number may be earning $10,000 or more. If we assume a lower limit of $5,000 for an individual without any detectable source of income and we take 20 percent of the total population left of 150,402 in Harlem receiving income assumed from illegal sources, or approximately

30,000 people x $5,000 = $150 million of illegal income.

At $10,000 it would be $300 million. A very low estimate of income derived from illegal sources would be 10 percent of the population, or 15,000 people, at $6,000, it would amount to $90 million per year of illegal income. This would be 22.5 percent of the total income of Harlem, according to the Urban Employment Survey of 1966. The $300 million figure would be approximately 75 percent of the total income of Harlem.

**A REVIEW
OF THE FINDINGS:
IN SEARCH
OF A FOUNDATION
FOR POLICY**

Rapid economic growth and substantial expansion of employment dominated the national economy during the decade of the 1960's. Prosperity and affluence reached many communities throughout the country. Yet, the major cities were in a state of crisis.

Although unemployment in the nation dropped substantially between 1960 and 1966, many of our largest cities did not experience a proportionate decrease in unemployment. There was considerable variation in the distribution of economic benefits among the cities and slums. Some cities and most slums within these cities even experienced a deterioration in the employment conditions, with unemployment rising. Rising expenditures and declining tax revenues, the exodus of middle-class whites, the dramatic rise in the welfare case load, the great influx of blacks and Spanish-speaking minorities into the major population centers, the overloaded and ineffectual urban educational systems, and the civil disorders and urban riots provided ample proof that the cities of the nation were in serious trouble.

The situation in many of our major urban centers has worsened since 1966. Rising national unemployment between 1969 and 1971 has aggravated the already severe employment problems of nonwhites, slum dwellers, and youth. The demographic pattern set in the early 1960's has continued, as more whites leave for the suburbs and more blacks arrive in the cities from rural areas, particularly in the South. Unemployment, crime, welfare case rates, and poverty have all registered substantial increases during the last two years, in part because of the general recession.

This study has attempted to explain this selective prosperity among cities and slums and to identify the factors that account for it. Additional objectives were to explain the variations among the cities in nonwhite unemployment rates and to identify the factors accounting for youth unemployment in slum areas. The findings, it is hoped, will lead to improvements in public manpower and economic policy, particularly in the operation of the urban labor market.

Although the data presented are drawn almost exclusively from the early 1960's, the persistence of these social and economic trends and the fact that the conditions identified prevailed in periods of both recession and prosperity make the findings useful for understanding the future problems of urban labor markets and designing policies and programs to improve the economic status of all urban dwellers.

DEMOGRAPHIC AND ECONOMIC CONDITIONS

Urban labor markets displayed great diversity in population traits, function, activity, size, institutional factors, industrial structure, labor supply, spatial configuration, transportation systems, government structure and organization, housing conditions, poverty, and unemployment. The composition of the population and the labor force in the thirty largest cities changed substantially between 1960 and 1966, as a result of the large outflow of the white population into the suburbs and the smaller inflow of black and Spanish-speaking people from rural and southern areas. Moreover, the population of the cities became increasingly dependent, with a larger proportion of children and old people, owing to natural growth and migration patterns.

Population movements have resulted in larger percentages of nonwhites in most—not all—of the largest cities. Some urban centers have a proportion of nonwhites aged sixteen years and over far below the national figure of 10.6 percent in 1966. But in fifteen major cities in the country, over 20 percent of their population aged sixteen years and over were nonwhite in 1966.

As the composition of the population of the major cities has changed, the composition of the labor force has changed concomitantly. The percent of nonwhites aged sixteen years and over in the labor force was 11.2 percent in 1966. Six of our thirty cities had a nonwhite labor force in the same age group in excess of 40 percent in 1966. Moreover, even in cities where the proportion of nonwhites in the population and labor force was low compared to the national average, both grew substantially between 1960 and 1966.[1]

There were sizable variations in unemployment rates among slums, cities, and nonwhites in cities in both 1960 and 1966. In most cities the unemployment rates of both nonwhites and whites decreased between 1960 and 1966. However, whites experienced greater declines, resulting in a widening of the gap between the races. Although the available data are not directly comparable, they do show that the highest ratios of male nonwhite/white unemployment rates in 1960 were 2.8 in Milwaukee and Chicago, while in 1966 the ratio of total (male plus female) nonwhite/white unemployment rates were as high as 4.4 and 4.3 in Pittsburgh and San Antonio, respectively. In five cities out of thirty, the unemployment rate of nonwhites increased.[2]

Welfare case loads varied greatly among our largest cities, but were significantly higher in the eastern cities. Twenty-seven of the thirty largest cities experienced increases in welfare case loads during the period of rapid economic growth, and in seven cities the increases were in excess of 100 percent.

Welfare payment rates also varied greatly, with extremely low payments in southern and southwestern cities and highest payment in western and eastern cities. The percentage increase in the level of welfare payments from 1960 to 1966 was not substantial, despite rising wages and costs of living. Increases in welfare payments in most of the thirty cities were less than 5 percent per annum.

The labor force participation rates in the cities also varied greatly, especially in the 1966 period of prosperity. The changes in participation rates were not uniform or in the same direction. Seven cities actually had decreases.

The largest cities also had vastly different experiences with respect to migratory flows. Southwestern and western cities experienced substantial in-migration, while northeastern cities such as Boston and New York experienced substantial out-migration. Part of this out-migration reflects a shift of old residents of the city into suburban areas greater than the inflow of new migrants. Nearly two-thirds of the cities lost people. By 1966 the size of migratory flows into most of the cities seems to have been reduced significantly.

Employment growth was negligible in urban labor markets in 1956-59, but substantial between 1962 and 1966. However, the growth was not uniform; in fact, one city experienced a slight decline in the latter period, some cities experienced a growth of employment in excess of 20 percent, while others grew at a rate of 5 percent, particularly the older northeastern cities.

Changes in employment by industry were noticeably different among the cities. In most of the largest cities, manufacturing employment increased significantly during the past two decades, but the suburban areas experienced a larger absolute and relative increase. Older cities in the northeast thus experienced an over-all decrease in manufacturing employment. In contrast, southwestern cities experienced substantial growth in manufacturing employment, in some cases exceeding their own suburban growth in this sector.

The service sector experienced the largest employment increase for both central cities and suburban rings, followed by finance, real estate, and insurance. (Contract construction experienced a modest increase in all but four cities.) (The transportation sector grew in all labor markets but two.) The smallest employment gains for central cities were registered in the wholesale and retail sectors. In contrast, the retail sector experienced substantial growth in the suburban rings.

The industrial mix of employment in the thirty cities is extremely varied. With respect to changes in the industrial mix, the manufacturing share of employment decreased substantially; only three cities experienced an increase in the share of employment in manufacturing. In contract construction two-thirds of the cities experienced an increase in the share of employment. Transportation's share of employment increased in twenty-two cities during this period, while most cities experienced a decline in the share of wholesale employment. The share of employment in the retail sector remained fairly stable. Finance, insurance, and real estate experienced a growth in twenty-five of the thirty cities. The largest increase in the share of employment occurred in the service sector, with every city experiencing an increased share, ranging from 10 percent to 20 percent.

The cities exhibit great variations in the index of spatial distribution—that is, the percentage of jobs outside the county containing the central city, ranging from 60.6 percent for Boston to 2.7 percent for Memphis in 1960. There were no discernible patterns of spatial distribution based on age, location, or structure of the economy.

In twenty-five of the thirty largest cities, substantial employment growth occurred, but the growth in surburban rings was much greater than in central city countries, raising the index of job dispersal, in some cases at a rate of 25 percent. The result was a 16.2 percent increase in the over-all spatial-distribution index in 1966.

Changes in the spatial distribution of jobs vary greatly by industry. The contract construction sector remains heavily (85 percent concentrated in central city countries. The transportation and public utility sector is also heavily concentrated in the central cities, with most cities having approximately 80 percent of the share of employment inside the city. The location of manufacturing sector did not show a consistent pattern. Some cities had as much as 95 percent of manufacturing located inside the city's labor market, while others had over 50 percent located outside the city. Those cities with the heaviest concentration of manufacturing had the greatest job decentralization in this sector.

For the most part the retail sector exhibits a fairly stable share of employment located inside the city. The finance and insurance sector also exhibits a heavy concentration of employment in the central city, with most cities having 85 percent of the total employment in this sector in the central city. A great deal more variation exists in the service sector, with suburban rings having as little as 2 percent and as much as 54 percent of the service sector's employment share.

In summary, manufacturing, retail, and services experienced the greatest job dispersal and have the heaviest concentration in suburban rings. The manufacturing sector demonstrates the greatest propensity to locate outside the central city. Lower land costs and better transportation facilities seem to be the propelling forces behind the relocation of manufacturing employment.

The spatial distribution of jobs has increased over the period 1960-66. However, not all industries experienced an increase in job dispersal, the increases were not uniform by cities, and not all industries in all the cities experienced a movement out of the city. Moreover, the employment problems of city residents may be more affected by suburbanites commuting to the city for employment than by the movement of jobs to the suburbs.

SOCIAL AND LABOR MARKET
CONDITIONS

From 1960 to 1966 the educational attainment of the employed labor force, used as a measure of employers' educational requirements, rose at a uniform but modest rate, approximately 5 percent, for all thirty cities. By 1966 employed workers in every labor market in the thirty cities possessed an average of at least twelve years of schooling. The striking feature was the uniformity among the cities with respect to the education possessed by workers and required by employers in both time periods.*

In contrast, the quality of the labor supply, measured by the educational attainment of the population aged twenty-five years and over, varied substantially among the thirty cities. In 1960 only two cities had a population with an average of eleven years of school or more. By 1966, when the employers in all the cities required workers to have an average of twelve years of school, there was not a population in any of the cities that had an average attainment of twelve years. The range of educational attainment among the cities was 11.1 grades to 8.7 grades in 1960 and 11.9 to 8.8 in 1966. The result was a growing gap between the educational requirements and educational

---

*As stated in the first single asterisked footnote on p. 59, this is due in large part to the national data used to calculate the educational demand of labor for each city.

attainments. Imbalances in excess of two years were found in nine
cities in 1966. The gap widened in the seven-year period despite
increases in the educational attainment of the population. In fact, the
gap for the unemployed and those not in the labor force population is
even wider than our data indicate, since the educational-attainment
figures include the employed labor force, which contributes 90 percent
more of the labor supply and has a higher level of educational attainment than the total labor force and population.

Two measures of discrimination (or, more accurately, racial
imbalance in the occupational structure of the urban economy) were
calculated in the study. The first is a crude measure based on the
proportions of employed nonwhites in the better jobs in the occupational
structure of the urban labor market compared to the corresponding
proportions for white workers. A sharp variation exists among the
thirty cities, from a low of 1.31 to a high of 3.72. Although southern
cities tended to have the highest measures of discrimination, there
were several nonsouthern cities with indexes over 2.00 in 1960. With
only two exceptions the measure of discrimination increased between
1960 and 1966, despite economic growth and efforts to promote civil
rights.* In some cases the growth was alarming; for example, the
index for Memphis rose from 2.94 to 6.19, or over 110 percent. By
the end of 1966 twenty-one cities had indexes of racial discrimination
in excess of 2.0, most of them in the northern industrial states. The
southern cities continued to demonstrate the highest degree of racial
discrimination, with four of the six southern cities registering indexes
in excess of 4.0.

Employment opportunities for nonwhites in terms of desirable
and preferred occupations have decreased relative to whites in the
major cities, and their relative occupational position has worsened
significantly. This does not mean that nonwhites have not moved into
better occupations. In fact during the 1960's there was a sharp
increase in the number and proportions of nonwhites in better-paying
and higher-status jobs. But our measure does reflect a more rapid
growth of whites compared to nonwhites in these better jobs.

The second measure of discrimination adjusts the nonwhite/
white occupational distribution by nonwhite/white educational differences among the cities. According to this index the range of employment discrimination in 1960 was 0.25 to 2.31. By 1966, the range
had widened from .37 to 4.64. Despite the six-year period of economic
progress, the employment discrimination index in 1966 was higher
than 1960 in every large city except San Diego. Nearly two-thirds

----

*See p. 73, first single asterisked footnote.

of the cities had indexes in excess of 1.0, indicating considerable
discrimination. The differences in discrimination were as much as
374 percent between 1960 and 1966 and were not confined to southern
or western cities. The measure of employment discrimination was
higher by 350 percent in Detroit, 374 percent in Cleveland, and by
338 percent in Chicago.

A similar result is found by using the ratio of occupational distribution by color to educational attainment by color. All the measures
indicate a substantially higher index of discrimination in employment
in every urban labor market except one, regardless of geographical
location. Southern cities had the highest measures of employment
discrimination, but northern cities also were significantly higher in
1966 than 1960.

In contrast to the unsatisfactory trend in the area of education
and discrimination, the health of the population (measured by the
incidence of tuberculosis per 100,000 persons) improved substantially.
The variations among cities are still enormous. In 1960 the rate ran
from a low of 17.8 per 100,000 to 84.3. By 1966 all but five cities had
experienced a decrease, but the variation was still large, from 15.2
to 79.6.

The cities experienced substantial increases in personal and
property crime and in heroin addiction between 1960 and 1966. However, there was considerable variation in these measures among the
cities.

Finally, the cities also differed considerably in population
density, ranging from 25,940 persons per square mile in New York
City to 2,349 in Phoenix in 1960. In 1966 New York was still the most
concentrated center, with 26,752 persons per square mile, and
Phoenix again was the low, with 2,741. Eleven cities reduced their
population densities, while the remaining cities experienced increases,
led by gains of 23.5 percent and 22.3 percent in Memphis and Houston,
respectively.

STRATEGIC FACTORS IN
URBAN UNEMPLOYMENT

The Growth of Employment

In periods of recession or of prosperity, the growth of the
national economy, resulting in a rapid increase in the absolute
number of jobs, is a critical precondition to the reduction of unemployment in individual cities. However, the findings of our study of
the thirty largest cities in both 1960 and 1966 indicate that although

national employment growth can have a favorable impact in reducing urban unemployment, it was not a significant factor in accounting for the differences in unemployment rates among urban labor markets. The implication of this result is clear: policies designed to stimulate the growth of the national economy are necessary, but gains will not be sufficient to achieve full employment in our major urban labor markets.

Moreover, our present restrictive monetary and fiscal policies, resulting in a national unemployment rate in excess of 6.0 percent, are contributing to substantial increases in unemployment in our largest cities and especially in the slum areas of these urban centers. To contend that piecemeal social policies of manpower training, welfare reform, unemployment compensation, and the like are either sufficient or useful in coping with unemployment, given economic conditions in the nation, is deceitful. The evidence is clear that, even if we succeeded in reaching the Council of Economic Advisers' target of 4.5 percent or even 3.5 percent unemployment, this growth would not be of sufficient strength that unemployment in our largest labor markets would be significantly reduced. This is not to suggest that these full employment policies are not urgently needed to improve the material welfare of the citizens, but a great deal more is required in other areas of social and economic policy.

Employment growth in the city had a favorable and significant impact on the measures of the ratio of nonwhite to white unemployment rates in both 1960 and 1966 and on the unemployment rate of workers aged twenty to twenty-four years old living in slums in 1966. Nonwhites experienced a proportionately greater decrease in unemployment relative to white workers when employment growth was increasing significantly; and conversely, in labor markets that were sluggish, nonwhites did not do so well as whites in reducing their unemployment rate. Although employment growth seems to have contributed to the reduction of unemployment among twenty- to twenty-four-year-old slum youth, there was not a significant relationship between employment growth and unemployment rates of teenage workers living in the slum areas.

In 1966 the nonwhite unemployment rate and the unemployment rate in slum areas were not significantly lower in labor markets that experienced more rapid employment growth. This evidence thus indicates that employment growth does not necessarily result in less unemployment, particularly for minority groups and slum dwellers. The social and economic forces operating in slum areas and among minority groups are so powerful that they offset the beneficial impact of rapid employment growth. Moreover, the growth of employment itself may trigger the social and economic forces that result in higher rates of measured unemployment in slums and among minority

residents of the cities. For example, prosperity and new opportunities
may stimulate a large increase in the labor force by reducing the
number of discouraged workers and the number of workers engaged
in illegal activities by stimulating more people to leave school or the
welfare rolls to enter the labor force or by encouraging more people
to move into urban areas where employment opportunities are perceived to be abundant or income transfers and welfare support higher.

Labor Supply Responses

The idea that employment growth may cause an oversupply of
labor and, thus, higher unemployment is not clearly supported by
some of the empirical relationships. For the larger urban labor
markets, the higher the labor force participation rates in both 1960
and 1966, the lower the unemployment rates in the cities. For the
slum residents in both 1960 and 1966, no significant relationship
exists between labor force participation rates and the unemployment
rate; similarly for the labor force participation of youth aged twenty
to twenty-four residing in the slums during 1966.

In contrast to the mixed findings for the slums and for youth
residing in slums, the labor force participation rates of nonwhites in
the cities were significantly related to their unemployment rates in
1960 and 1966 and also to the ratio of nonwhite to white unemployment
rates in both periods. The higher the nonwhite participation rate, the
lower both of these unemployment figures. Where unemployment is
low, labor force participation rates are considerably higher. This
suggests that labor force participation rates rise when conditions in
the labor market are tight and jobs are available but they do not
overreact to cause an excess supply of workers. Moreover, the
participation rates for nonwhites are so responsive to the level of
unemployment that when unemployment is high, these groups withdraw
from the labor force, and when unemployment is low, they re-enter.

The relationship that emerges suggests that it is not an excessive
labor supply response to employment opportunities that prevents the
growth of employment from being reflected in lower rates of unemployment in these labor markets but the fact that the labor force
responds to high unemployment by withdrawal from the labor market
and to low unemployment by re-entry. This is especially true in
the case of nonwhites.

Another finding tends to confirm this view. All the relationships
of the different unemployment rates for cities, nonwhites, slums,
and slum youth indicate that the labor supply response, measured
by net migration, was not a significant factor in accounting for these
different levels of unemployment in either the recession of 1960 or

the prosperity of 1966. The only exception was a high rate of nonwhite migration associated with a high rate of unemployment in the city and slum area in 1960.

Wage Level

Higher levels of wages in the urban labor markets were associated with higher levels of unemployment in the cities in 1960, but the relationship was not significant in 1966. In only one case was the high wage rate/high unemployment rate relationship established during the prosperity of 1966, and this was among slum youth. For slum youth aged sixteen to nineteen and twenty to twenty-four, there was a significant relationship between the level of wages and the unemployment rate.

These findings are subject to several conflicting interpretations. However, the findings relating high youth unemployment and high wages suggest that low-wage areas, more likely to be affected by state and national minimum-wage laws, were not significantly related to higher youth unemployment in slum areas of the cities. It does suggest that high-wage areas tend to have labor market characteristics that make it exceedingly difficult for minority youth residing in slums to obtain gainful employment. The age segregation of the labor market, accentuated by the characteristics of the minority residents of slums, results in fewer job opportunities for young slum workers in high-wage areas and, thus, higher levels of unemployment. Discrimination by age and race intensified the segregation of the job market and penalized young black workers in ghetto areas. Thus, if job growth occurs in areas precluding the employment of youth, particularly black youth, it will not result in lower unemployment.

Welfare Case Rates and
Payment Levels

The impact of the current welfare system on the operation of the urban labor markets is the subject of much controversy. The policy recommendations in the Nixon Administration's Family Assistance Plan and in the New Jersey Negative Income Tax Experiment suggest the importance of welfare in the decision to participate in the labor force.

The relationship between the welfare case rate in a city and the level of unemployment is unclear. In the recession of 1960 there was no significant relationship between the welfare case rate and the rate of unemployment in the city, the slum, and among nonwhites.

ever, in 1966 the higher the welfare case rate, the higher the
l of unemployment in the city, slum, and among nonwhites. This
ult seems to suggest that, when the labor market is extremely
loose, as in 1960, people who are on the welfare rolls do not seek
work and are not in the labor force. However, some cities with high
case rates had low unemployment rates, while in 1966, when the
economy was growing rapidly and unemployment was low, some cities
with high welfare case rates had high rates of unemployment. This
suggests that people on welfare continue to seek employment, do not
drop out of the labor force, and thus contribute to higher levels of
unemployment. The increase in job opportunities compels them to
say that they are seeking work in order to appear willing to accept
work instead of welfare. It also suggests that, while employment
growth does not necessarily reduce unemployment, it also does not
reduce welfare case rates. Because of the structural impediments
and the characteristics of the welfare recipients, predominantly
children and mothers, welfare case rates are not very responsive to
changing economic conditions. It is also possible that the cities with
high welfare case rates may be more restrictive with regard to the
number of people receiving welfare, thus forcing many potential
welfare recipients into the ranks of the unemployed.

The fiscal conditions of the cities make this possibility a reality
in many cases. Cities may be faced with the need to accept more
people on welfare, while cutting the welfare payments. Moreover,
if a city has a reputation for high payments and relaxed eligibility
requirements, as New York City has, this may stimulate in-migration
of poor people who cannot obtain welfare in their home states and,
thus, may swell the number of unemployed in the slum areas and in
the city as a whole.

The level of welfare payments had a greater impact than the
case load on the operation of the urban labor market and on the unemployment rate of the city, slum, and slum youth. In 1960 the higher
the welfare payment rates, the higher the unemployment rate in the
city. While the same relationship held in 1966, it was not significant
in this period of prosperity. Thus, raising payment rates for welfare recipients was not useful in reducing labor force participation
rates and, thus, measured unemployment rates in the cities.

However, for residents of the slum areas, raising the welfare
payment rate had a very significant effect on the reduction of unemployment rates in 1966, but not in 1960. The higher the payment
rates offered in the cities in 1966, the lower the rate of slum unemployment. Thus, for poor people in the urban labor market, the payment rate seems to have been an alternative to work and, therefore,
reduced the labor force participation rates and the level of slum
unemployment. This effect could operate not only on the welfare

mother and her children, particularly teenage children, but might also have an indirect effect on the male head of household's decision to work.

This interpretation of the impact of welfare payment rates on slum unemployment rates is further supported by the findings on the relationship between welfare payment rates and slum youth unemployment rates in 1966. The higher the payment rates, the lower the unemployment rates of young workers aged fourteen to nineteen, sixteen to nineteen, and twenty to twenty-four years. A high level of welfare payments operates as an economic incentive to drop out of the labor force and, thus, reduces the competition among the remaining labor force members for the scarce employment opportunities for slum residents and slum youth. The result is lower rates of unemployment for young workers. Moreover, the transfer of income among other members of the ghetto also may reduce the necessity to work or to seek work on a full-time basis, thus lowering measured rates of unemployment. In addition, it allows the potential workers of the ghetto more time and flexibility by providing them with limited working capital to enter or experiment with illegal income-producing activities. The income and work in this sector seem to be a very important aspect of the operation of the labor market of the ghetto and thus, indirectly, of the city.

The policy implications are disturbing but clear: if we raise welfare payment rates to compete with market wages for the jobs for which welfare clients are eligible and suitable, labor force participation rates will fall. The result will be lower rates of unemployment in the city and slum. The new Family Assistance Plan program, designed to encourage workers to enter the labor force and seek work—"workfare instead of welfare"—assumes a high level of demand for female labor and the creation of new job opportunities. The fact of the matter is that there are not enough jobs today, and not enough jobs are being created for the future. Moreover, as the labor force participation rates of women rise, the female labor supply will continue to expand, without inducing welfare mothers to work. The solution is to create a sufficient number of jobs for female workers. Our current preoccupation with controlling inflation results in fewer jobs and more unemployment. The level of unemployment will rise even faster if we encourage welfare mothers to enter the labor force by reducing welfare payments or further restricting eligibility. To increase the supply of female workers without increasing the demand for them in a less than full-employment national economy and in an urban labor market constantly experiencing an excess supply of labor will obviously result in more urban unemployment and reduced incomes for dependent children and their mothers.

Industrial Structure

The industrial structure of the cities, measured by the shares of employment in the major sectors of the local economy, did not contribute significantly to the explanation of different unemployment rates among the thirty largest cities in the United States in either 1960 or 1966. The only sectors that had a significant relationship with the unemployment rate of the city in both periods were manufacturing, transportation, and retail. The larger the manufacturing and transportation sectors, the higher the rate of unemployment. The larger the share of employment in the retail sector in 1966, the lower the unemployment rate in the city. The remaining sectors—wholesale, construction, government, service, and construction—were not significantly related to the city's unemployment rates.

Moreover, the relationship between the industrial structure and the slum unemployment rate in 1960 was quite similar. The only difference was in the service sector; during the recession of 1960 the larger this sector, the lower the slum unemployment rate. However, the relationship between the industrial structure and the slum unemployment rates in 1966 was extremely significant, with each sector significantly related to the slum unemployment rates. The industrial-structure models explained 90 percent of the variations in slum unemployment during the prosperity of 1966. The larger the share of employment in the city's labor market in construction, manufacturing, finance, and wholesale, the higher the rate of unemployment in the slum areas of the city.

In contrast, the higher the share of employment in retail and wholesale, the lower the unemployment rate in the slums. Apparently, the industrial structure in a tight labor market represents a measure of the degree of job segregation in the labor market faced by slum dwellers, particularly blacks and Spanish-speaking minorities. These slum dwellers are barred from employment opportunities in finance, manufacturing, and construction because of racial discrimination and/or educational deficiencies. Employment growth in these sectors of the urban economy will therefore not contribute proportionately to reductions in unemployment among the labor force residing in slum areas.

An unexpected finding was the change in the relationship between slum unemployment and employment in the service sector. In 1960 a large service sector was associated with low unemployment rates in the slums; in 1966 it was associated with high rates of unemployment. Several factors could account for the change in this relationship. First, the skills composition of the service sector may have changed, with 1966 having a larger proportion of the total employment in this sector in more skilled occupations, such as medical and teaching personnel compared to janitors and domestics. Second, nonwhites, particularly the younger workers in slum areas, may have rejected the opportunities in the service sector because of their low wages, undignified work, and low status, and because of alternative sources of income insources available in 1966. Thus, a change in the skill composition of the jobs and in taste, as well as with respect to the workers' willingness and need to work in the low-wage, unskilled portion of the service sector may account for the fact that the size of employment in the service sector did not have a favorable impact on reducing slum unemployment in 1966.

For workers fourteen to nineteen years of age residing in the slum areas during 1966, only the retail sector was related in a significant and beneficial way to unemployment rates. The larger the retail sector, the lower the unemployment rate of this group. In contrast, the construction sector had an adverse impact on the employment opportunities of ghetto youngsters. The larger the share of the construction sector in a labor market, the higher the rate of unemployment among those fourteen to nineteen years of age. The manufacturing sector also had an undesirable employment effect on youngsters aged fourteen to nineteen and twenty to twenty-four residing in slum areas in 1966. Again, this confirms the view that economic growth in the nation or in a local labor market will not necessarily reach slum dwellers, particularly young workers in slum areas. Specifically, the growth of finance, manufacturing, construction, and even the service sector will not provide employment opportunities for sufficient numbers of slum dwellers and for nonwhites in general to lower unemployment among these members of the urban labor force. The structure of the urban economy, with the institutional rules and requirements imposed by government, employers, and trade unions, effectively segregates many slum dwellers from employment opportunities in the urban economy. The growth sectors, protected by certification, educational requirements, union shops, apprenticeship, tests, and licensing, are the first lines of effective defense against entry. If all else fails, racial discrimination in employment further limits the small number of desirable high-wage jobs in the urban economy. These findings are consistent with the strong relationship found between high-wage urban labor markets and high unemployment in the city and among nonwhites, slum dwellers, and youngsters residing in slum areas.

The employment situation and future prospects for the nonwhite labor force in the urban labor markets are extremely gloomy, even more so for slum dwellers and young workers. Even in times of rapid employment growth and only 4.0 percent or 3.5 percent unemployment of the labor force, in urban labor markets characterized by high wages and dominated by construction, manufacturing, finance, insurance, commerce, and high-skilled services, unemployment will remain high for nonwhites, ghetto dwellers, and youth in the slums.

Changes in economic and manpower policies and programs will not substantially improve this picture. The structure of a local economy is extraordinarily difficult to change, and it may not be worthwhile to try. It would probably be more efficient and effective to change the people to fit the jobs and institutions than to change the structure of local employment. Government programs and leverage should concentrate on opening up more job opportunities in the primary high-wage sector of the urban labor market by fighting job discrimination and exclusionary practices of employers and unions and on restructuring the secondary labor market by encouraging union organization, wage subsidies, decasualization, and less seasonality of employment.

Education

The quality of labor in terms of education demanded by employers in the urban labor markets was usually associated in a significant way with unemployment. Although higher quality was related to lower levels of unemployment for the city's labor force, it emerged as a significant factor only in 1966. In direct contrast to this finding, higher educational demand for labor was significantly related to the slum unemployment rate only in the recession of 1960. Young workers residing in slum areas in cities where employers demanded high-quality labor also experienced significantly lower unemployment rates during 1966.

One of the most interesting results was the absence of a significant relationship between the differences in level of educational attainment between the total urban population and a specific minority group and the amount of unemployment experienced by these workers. The level of education of slum residents, both adults and youth, did not have any significant relationship with their unemployment rates in either 1960 or 1966. Moreover, for slum residents, the association of education and unemployment was quite different from other empirical findings. The higher the level of education possessed by the slum dwellers, the higher the rate of slum unemployment. Apparently, slum dwellers have relatively less education than nonslum dwellers, even where they have high educational levels compared to other slums. Or perhaps, despite the higher educational attainments of slum dwellers, the gap between attainments and employers' requirements is greater in areas where slum dwellers have higher educational levels.

The higher the level of education possessed by the population in a city, the higher the level of unemployment in that labor market in the recession of 1960. Again, this result runs counter to other empirical findings, suggesting that a skilled, educated population may be bound by allegiance to occupational lines, income levels, and status and does not adjust so readily to changing economic conditions in the labor markets as a population with less educational attainment. Or it may be that these labor markets are not susceptible to the impact of a recession because they are characterized by more stable and less responsive employment sectors. However, the results of the industrial-structure model indicate that the cyclically sensitive sectors of manufacturing, construction, and retail are not significant in explaining differences in unemployment in either recession or prosperity. Thus, it appears that educational rigidities reinforced the preference and financial ability of the better-educated workers to wait for the appropriate job. This operates to raise unemployment rates in the short run in skilled urban labor markets during recessions.

This conclusion is supported by our analysis of the educational gap between the supply of labor and the employers' requirements and the effect of this gap on the unemployment rate. With the exception of youngsters sixteen to nineteen in slums during 1966, there were no significant relationships between the measures of educational gap and unemployment in either period for city or slum. For the youngsters the larger the educational gap between the level of educational attainment and that required by employers, the lower their rate of unemployment.

The tentative conclusion is that the level of educational attainment is not a significant factor in reducing unemployment or in accounting for differences in unemployment among cities, among slums, and among nonwhites. Again, this does not mean that education is unimportant or insignificant or that future investments are not urgently needed, but it does suggest that education is not a panacea for the unemployment problems of the urban population, particularly the more disadvantaged members. Moreover, it suggests that increased investments in education will not be fully effective unless accompanied by other major policies and programs designed to expand the employment opportunities available to urban dwellers, particularly nonwhite slum dwellers and youngsters.

Reallocating funds to other areas will have a better payoff than continuing to expand current levels of expenditure on education in urban areas. Changes in the quality of education and in the level of achievement rather than measured attainment are no doubt crucial to the relationship between education and unemployment of city residents. No significant relationship was found between either army scores on the achievement test or expenditures per pupil and the

unemployment of young workers in slum areas in 1966. If better
data and measures of quality of education and achievement were
available, a more significant beneficial relationship between unemployment and education might be found.

Spatial Barriers

Job dispersal out of the central city did not significantly affect
the level of unemployment in the cities or the slums in either the
recession of 1960 or the prosperity of 1966. Moreover, it did not
have any significant relationship with the unemployment rates of
youngsters living in the slums in 1966, nor for all nonwhites in the
city in 1960. Only in the case of nonwhite unemployment in prosperous
1966 was job dispersal a significant factor.

Ironically, although spatial distribution may weaken the foundations of the central city by eroding the tax base, it may not prevent
slum dwellers from finding jobs in the central city. The findings
seem to suggest that if job dispersal is great and nonslum residents
or white slum dwellers can move into suburban areas following the
jobs, there may be less competition for the remaining jobs in the
central city. Thus, the spatial distribution of jobs does not necessarily
adversely affect slum dwellers.

The finding of a significant and important relationship between
a high degree of residential segregation and lower unemployment
rates in city and slum reinforces the view that segregation may in
some respects be useful for nonwhites. A similar relationship was
found between residential segregation and nonwhite unemployment
rates, although it was not significant. Residential segregation may
serve as a measure of job-information systems or reduced competition between whites and nonwhites. Residents of segregated communities tend to have better information systems and more personal
contacts to facilitate the information process. Moreover, residential
segregation tends to segregate labor force members, restricting competition between nonwhites and whites.

Discrimination

In general, the measures of discrimination used in the study
indicate that during a recession the more racial discrimination, the
lower the unemployment rate of nonwhite slum residents, while in
times of prosperity discrimination is not significantly related to
unemployment rates in slums and among nonwhites. These findings
suggest that in a loose labor market, nonwhites are more likely to

accept jobs requiring low levels of skill and education than are white workers, who tend not to compete for these jobs even during a recession. Thus, while these nonwhites cannot obtain jobs commensurate with their skill and educational levels, they can more readily adjust to the lower levels of jobs available in a loose labor market. The other nonwhites bumped out of these jobs by more skilled or educated nonwhites become discouraged and drop out of the labor force. The result is the paradox that discrimination in the urban labor market lowers the unemployment rate of nonwhites and slum dwellers in a recession.

During prosperity we would expect discrimination to have a substantial effect upon slum and nonwhite unemployment rates, because the rapid growth encourages nonwhites to seek better jobs and stay in the labor force. But this was not the case. This surprising finding is perhaps explained by the fact that job growth only served to neutralize the factors at work during the recession, but were not sufficient to establish a significant positive relationship.

Health

Although the relationship between health and unemployment is subject to many interpretations, the research indicates that it is significant. The poorer the health of the city's population, the higher the unemployment rate in the city, slum, and among nonwhites in time of recession. In the slums during 1966 the relationship changed but remained significant: the worse the health of the city, the lower the unemployment rate in the slum area. Apparently, there were more forces in operation in 1966 that enabled sick workers to stay out of the labor force and, thus, reduced the measured rate of unemployment in the slums. Secondary workers entering the labor force and securing jobs, health insurance, sick leave, workmen's compensation payments, unemployment insurance, and more savings may have reduced the need for workers with poor health to continue to seek employment.

Illegal Income and Activity

The impact of alternative sources of work and income in the illegal sector of the urban economy was found to be extremely important for nonwhites and slum residents. The more opportunities there were to engage in these illicit activities, the lower the unemployment rates of these groups. In 1966 substantially lower rates of nonwhite and slum unemployment were found in cities with higher crime rates, measured by the extent of property crime per capita.

Moreover, we found that the greater the extent of heroin addiction, the lower the unemployment rates among slum residents and
nonwhites during 1966. Heroin addicts are not likely to be in the
labor force, while the suppliers of the heroin must state that they are
employed in order to account for their high visible standard of living.
People engaged in such activities as gambling, numbers, hustling,
narcotics, prostitution, stealing, smuggling, protection, and so forth
are actively working and receiving compensation. The result is lower
rates of unemployment and, perhaps, lower rates of labor force
participation among those whose income is generated by illegal
activities.

CONCLUSION

The research indicates that such economic factors as the supply
of, and demand for, labor and the prevailing wage rates influence the
unemployment rate of the city's labor force, while structural factors
are more important for nonwhites, slum dwellers, and youth.

Racial discrimination in employment is a major contributor to
the high rates of unemployment among nonwhites and slum dwellers.
More limited job opportunities have forced many of these urban
dwellers to seek opportunities to earn an income in the illegal sector
of urban economy. General employment growth, educational attainment, and job dispersal—considered to be strategic factors contributing
to high unemployment rates, especially for minority groups residing
in cities—were found to be relatively insignificant. Although improved
education and skills and increased job opportunities in areas accessible
to urban dwellers are prerequisites for employment, they will not be
sufficient to solve the employment problems of the disadvantaged,
unless they are accompanied by an effective program to restructure
the urban labor market and open up new pathways into the primary
high-wage urban economy.

Furthermore, the diversity of conditions that prevail among
urban labor markets supports the need for a multitude of programs
specifically tailored to the problems faced by the various cities and
the various groups comprising the urban labor force.

8

By the end of 1971 the U.S. economy was in a serious recession, with nearly 5 million workers unemployed. The unemployment rate had climbed from a low of 3.5 percent in 1969 to 5.9 percent in 1971.[1] The rapid swelling in the ranks of the unemployed resulted in serious unemployment problems for the cities and particularly for the minority group labor force in these urban centers. Although specific data by city are not available, preliminary evidence indicates that by the end of 1971 national nonwhite unemployment was 9.4 percent.[2] For slum residents it probably approached 15 percent, and for youth living in slum areas it was likely to have been in the neighborhood of 35 percent.

The fight against inflation has been waged with the urban disadvantaged as the front-line troops. The casualty lists of the unemployed mount daily. The numbers that desert the conventional way of the labor force because of frustration, alienation, and discouragement must be recognized as part of the costs of the battle to hold down prices. The modest gains in the employment of urban minority groups between 1963 and 1969 have been eroded by the current recession. It is futile to propose public policies to reduce urban unemployment in the face of national economic policy designed to curb inflationary pressures.

A basic issue confronting us today is the inflation-unemployment dilemma. Everyone can agree on the objectives of achieving full employment and stable prices, but the real issue is to establish a priority for these conflicting goals. Should we sacrifice some price stability for less unemployment, and if so, how much? Two years ago it was decided that inflation was the major problem, and policies were designed to give top priority to controlling price increases. Today, there is evidence of a substantial shift in policy, with more

emphasis on unemployment and less on controlling inflation. A rapid
expansion of the economy in order to achieve an unemployment rate
in the range of 4.0 percent would probably cause significant inflationary pressures; however, without such an expansion, the severity
of unemployment among the residents of our urban centers will in-
tensify. Depression-like conditions already exist in many of our urban
slums. In order to avoid the undesirable consequences of inflation
and to achieve a reduction of national and urban unemployment, an
expansion of fiscal and monetary policy is necessary, but, at present,
tight wage, price, and profit controls are a prerequisite to such expansion. The other alternative is to wage a more aggressive and
determined battle against inflation. Such a policy would cause higher
unemployment in the short run, until price increases could be brought
to a "tolerable" level, below 2.5 percent per year. At that point a
gradual expansion of the economy would reduce unemployment, without causing labor shortages, excessive demand, and inflation. Under
such a policy it would be several years before we reached a level
approaching full employment at 3.0 percent.

Unfortunately, we do not have the luxury of time. Millions of
workers remain unemployed, and their families are denied the income
to live a decent life in the richest nation in the world. An effective
full-employment policy is essential. A 3.0 percent unemployment
rate should be the target, and we must accept a higher rate of inflation, perhaps 3.5 percent to 4.0 percent per annum. However, as
noted, research indicates that rapid economic and employment growth
will not be sufficient to reduce the unemployment rate of residents
of cities, nonwhites, slum residents, and young workers, especially
blacks, in ghetto areas.

The 1972 report of President Nixon's Council of Economic
Advisers sets an unemployment rate of 4.5 percent as the target for
1972. To achieve this goal, it will be necessary to complement
government fiscal and monetary policies with greatly expanded manpower programs to reach the hard-core unemployed in the slums
of our cities and in the backwaters of rural America.

The evidence is clear: if our society chooses to put its major
emphasis on less inflation and more unemployment by setting a target
that is reasonable and tolerable by policy-maker's values, such as
4 percent unemployment and less than 3 percent inflation, then it will
be necessary to develop a comprehensive public-employment program
to absorb nearly 1 million unemployed workers and reduce unemployment rates to below 3 percent at current levels of the labor force.

But a public employment program should not be viewed as
desirable solely for lowering unemployment. It can also help to deal
with the problems of labor market segmentation and employment
discrimination. First, it opens up opportunities in a respectable,

well-paying sector of employment. Government offers growth and promotion, reasonably competitive wages, status and stability, all prerequisites for living and raising a family in urban America. Second, it lessens employment discrimination, emphasizes merit and productivity, provides experience and dignity, and offers the chance to move from public employment into the private sector. If minority groups are resigned to the secondary low-wage sector and the tertiary high-wage illegal sector, then there is little opportunity or experience to move into the primary high-wage urban economy.

Third, in properly designed public employment systems, training and educational opportunities are available to improve workers' skills and productivity, as are direct economic incentives, in the form of higher wages, better jobs, and the opportunity to move into the private sector. Fourth, a public employment program can also be used to provide more and better municipal services.

Expansion of the New Careers program under a large-scale public employment program would be extremely desirable. New Careers combines all the characteristics of a sound manpower program, such as entry-level low-skilled jobs, upgrading, training, occupational ladders, status, professional identification, interesting and useful work, and decent wages.

To illustrate the absorptive employment capacity of the public sector, let us examine a new sector—child care. From the Nixon Administration Family Assistance Plan to the bills proposed by Representatives Brademas, Chisholm, and Abzug, the employment generation conceivably could reach 1 million workers by 1976—not including the work force used in the construction and rehabilitation of physical space for early childhood centers. Thus, the single act of signing a law and a $1-billion expenditure will create an entire industry with direct employment opportunities for 140,000 people as teachers, teaching assistants, teacher aides, nurses, nurses' aides, and maintenance men. The magnitude is similar to the recently enacted Emergency Employment Act of 1971. A $10 billion public child-care program would create direct employment for 1.4 million workers. Many women currently receiving welfare will be able to train for employment in the child-care sector of the economy. The spread of child care to the private market has already commenced under pressure from the women's liberation movement and from unions and companies attempting to recruit a female labor force in suburban areas. The secondary employment effects in construction, training, furnishings, and supplies will also create thousands of additional jobs in this one sector of the future economy. Public employment and new careers, as well as private employment and training in this sector, will create ample opportunities for many urban workers currently unemployed or on welfare. Moreover, millions of children

will be receiving additional education, which may be vital in developing
their abilities to the fullest potential.

Public employment need not and should not consist of unproductive make-work programs. The child-care sector illustrates
the magnitude of productive employment potential in the public and
private sector, not only providing valuable services to children, but
offering mothers opportunities to be productive citizens in the home
or in the marketplace.

Research indicates that, despite our efforts to expand the
economy, we will not be able to achieve full employment without too
much inflation unless productive employment is developed in the
public sector. The Family Assistance Plan and the recently enacted
Emergency Employment Act of 1971, calling for a temporary two-
year public employment program, are at least beginnings. If we are
to substantially reduce unemployment among disadvantaged urban
dwellers and provide improved public services to the urban population,
a productive and expanded public employment program must be developed.

Even with public employment a great deal of effort and resources
must be devoted to improving the skills of the urban labor force.
Although the evidence showed that educational attainment was not a
significant factor in explaining differences in unemployment rates,
it will be virtually impossible to break down employment discrimination, as well as develop a work force capable of providing needed
public services, without raising the skills and productivity of the
disadvantaged urban labor force. Emphasis must be placed on achievement, not attainment. Furthermore, differences in skills and education
among subgroups of the labor force must be narrowed and eliminated.
Merely to raise the educational attainment of blacks, Puerto Ricans,
Mexican-Americans, and Indians will not be sufficient to break down
employment discrimination in the primary sector of the urban economy.
As long as there is an observable gap between nonwhite workers and
the rest of the labor force, it will be difficult for them to obtain desirable employment.

For all but that fraction of the high school student population
who clearly have the motivation and ability to perform in college,
the urban school system is failing. Many claim the curriculum is
repetitious, irrelevant, and boring. Peer approval and social acceptance
surpass achievement in the motivation of many students. Income
and leisure time are more important goals than a job after graduation
or admission to college. The school system has been used as a huge
factoring system, separating those qualified for higher education
from the majority who are to enter the labor force directly. Very
little attention has been given to how well prepared the bulk of the
high school population is to meet the demands of the world of work.

Most urban schools have been oriented to the minority at the expense of the majority. While job opportunities for high school graduates, particularly whites, remained plentiful or where parents could afford to support youngsters enjoying leisure or searching for employment, pressure on the school systems did not develop. However, demographic and economic conditions have altered the current situation. Now, the high schools of many cities are dominated by a majority of black students who cannot find decent jobs upon graduation—or any jobs at all for that matter—and whose parents cannot afford to keep them out of the labor force. The schools, in fact, tend to encourage dropouts so as to reduce overcrowding and disciplinary and drug problems. Pressure has developed to change the structure, curriculum, performance, and accountability of the local school systems.

Educational reforms are urgently needed in the urban school systems to narrow educational-achievement differences and otherwise improve the employability of minority youngsters. But conditions in the schools seem to be worsening, and achievement levels may actually be falling. The result is more severe employment problems for these youngsters.

There are four major areas of decision making in the field of education related to labor markets and the employability of the disadvantaged labor force. First, we must decide whether to concentrate on raising the absolute levels of education of all youngsters or on narrowing the gap in educational levels between black and white youngsters. Another critical decision is whether to focus on raising attainment levels or on raising achievement levels. A third decision is whether to concentrate on general education or specific skills achievement. And, finally, we need to decide on general goals with respect to educational levels for American youth; for example, should we encourage college degrees for all or college opportunities for all?

The research findings provide some policy directions on these major educational issues. First and foremost, raising educational attainment levels is not the most effective way of improving employability; we should, rather, concentrate on narrowing the attainment levels of blacks relative to whites. This will not be sufficient, however; we must also stress performance and achievement, particularly in skills designed to improve the youngster's productivity in the urban labor market and enhance his employment prospects in the primary high-wage sector of the urban economy. We must narrow the differences in productivity between blacks and whites by concentrating our resources on programs designed to develop specific marketable skills, not general academic attainment or achievement levels. Minority groups will not succeed in competing for the better jobs unless their productivity equals or surpasses that of their white counterparts. If blacks go to college and whites go to postgraduate

school, the educational gap will persist and will be used to keep
minorities out of the preferred occupations, regardless of whether
the additional education is needed to perform satisfactorily.

Finally, with respect to college education, it appears that a
great injustice is being perpetrated on many youngsters in our society.
The heavy stress on attending college, regardless of aptitude, talent,
and motivation, is a serious waste of resources and manpower. Job
requirements are inflated by employers in reaction to the higher
levels of education possessed by job applicants; job seekers are told
to attend college in order to get positions, occupations, and jobs that,
in fact, require only a high school education but are currently filled
by frustrated college graduates. The value of the college degree may
be declining and the devaluation may accelerate as thousands of
college graduates enter a loose labor market. Blacks, in pursuit of
the false idol, will negotiate their way through the college system
only to find themselves in a similar position in the employment queue
as before. It will probably be desirable to de-emphasize general
college education for all youngsters and concentrate on providing
training in the many industrial and technical skills required by the
complex economy of the future. We need a fundamental change in
values, emphasizing useful work that requires specific technical
competencies rather than empty, meaningless status symbols, inflated
educational requirements, and artificial certifications and licensing
arrangements.

What types of educational reform would support these changes
in values? The economic forces of the labor market will exert some
pressure for change. As college graduates flood the labor market,
equipped with no specific skills, the relative wages of this group
of workers should fall compared to those of skilled technicians and
productive factory workers and craftsmen. The economic benefits
of a college education should decline and contribute to a reevaluation
in light of rising costs of higher education. Under these conditions,
it will be easier to induce changes in the educational and training
establishments.

Pressure to change curriculum and improve the quality in
the vocational schools should be exerted by trade unions, employer
associations, and parents. These schools provide the largest institutional setting for the skill development of our youngsters. Fundamental changes in curricula, accountability, teaching staffs, and
resources are required to make them responsive institutions, capable
of supplying skilled manpower. These schools should develop a first-
rate, cooperative education program with employers and unions to
ensure relevancy, increase motivation, provide income support, expand
experiences, develop sound work and study habits, and improve
accountability and performance of the school system. Neighborhood

Youth Corps funds could be expanded and shifted into wage subsidies and training allowances under a cooperative school program in vocational technical schools.

An extension of these efforts to enhance the status and expand the supply of technical skilled workers would be the creation and development of technical institutes and community and junior colleges. These programs should in no way imitate or duplicate college programs but should stress a high degree of proficiency in the complex skills required by the labor market. These institutions of higher technical education should also develop a strong cooperative-education program to encourage greater enrollment and develop better linkages with the labor market. Too often, such institutions try to imitate four-year colleges and are used as second-chance institutions for youngsters, who then try to transfer into regular four-year colleges. This preoccupation with transferability has weakened the structure of these institutions and has prevented them from succeeding in the critical mission of providing technical education for the labor market of the future.

In order to bridge the gap between school and work, it would be desirable to have employment counselors in every high school to provide individual advice and general information on careers and job opportunities. This service should not be restricted to high school seniors but should begin at the sophomore year. Employment counselors should encourage the participation and cooperation of unions and employers in establishing cooperative education programs and field trips to workplaces. More emphasis in counseling should be given to the labor market and the world of work and less to admission to the college of the parents' choice. Local communities should organize school work councils comprised of employers, union leaders, government officials, parents, and students to reduce the fallout of youngsters leaving school and seeking work.

No matter how tightly the net is woven, there will be casualites in the search for jobs. Rather than encourage second-chance institutions, such as the Job Corps, Neighborhood Youth Corps, and Skills Centers, it would be desirable to use the public employment program to provide on-the-job education and training and to have the private sector absorb these youngsters in a contract system, with or without wage subsidies. If second-chance institutions are to develop, it may be worthwhile to experiment with a voucher system similar to the G.I. bill. This would stimulate a variety of new programs designed to provide marketable skills. The possibility of deception, fraud, and corruption is the obvious disadvantage. But with some governmental supervision the market forces should provide sufficient competition to weed out the inefficient firms.

Despite the real possibilities of an excess supply of college graduates, it is essential for more blacks, Puerto Ricans, Indians, and Mexican-Americans to have the opportunity to attend institutions of higher learning. The attainment, certification, and productivity gaps will not lessen unless greater proportions of youngsters from these ethnic groups enter and complete college. In light of this need the open-enrollment policy instituted recently by the City University of New York, and supported by large-scale remedial efforts, merits special attention and study. The results should have great relevance for policies on campuses throughout the country.

However, merely opening our college campuses to youngsters who may be unprepared to engage in college work is a meaningless gesture. Degrees are worthless unless they are backed up by productive skills; the youngsters will remain disadvantaged and at the end of the hiring queue. The urban school system has not been able to prepare many of these youngsters for college or for employment. Shifting them into colleges will not solve the problem. The failure of the elementary and secondary schools cannot be overcome in the colleges without large resources of manpower, time, and commitment. Two-year college-preparatory work, with heavy emphasis on skills remediation, may be required for many of these disadvantaged youngsters. Counseling to change attitudes and residence halls to change environments will also be useful, and perhaps critical, in overcoming their educational and psychological problems.

An important aspect of encouraging poor youngsters to enroll in colleges will be supplementary income to help support their families and replace their foregone earnings while attending school. The costs of these programs will be high, but without the necessary resources the programs will fail and the students will experience even greater frustration and disillusionment. One possible solution is a national educational bank, which would provide the full costs of attending college to students who would be required to repay the loans at low interest after entering the labor market. The payback can be based on a proportion of total lifetime income or at a fixed interest rate. Moreover, schools would have resources with which to provide stipends to the neediest students, thus expanding college opportunities. The educational bank system would also encourage the development of new schools with more specialization in programs, more competition among schools, and more accountability of faculty performance in the lecture hall and classroom.

But these programs and experiments will be no substitute for a high-quality, performance-oriented system of elementary and secondary schools and early childhood education centers. Incentive systems must be created to encourage greater efforts, diversity, and experimentation and to attract a pool of talented manpower.

Performance contracting, the voucher system, parent and not community control of school boards, budget allocations and personnel,
merit salaries, and economic incentives for students are new ways
of approaching the problem of improving the performance of the urban
school system. More experimentation and more research into the
learning process are required and should receive federal government
support. More emphasis on the employability and earning capacity
of the product might be a useful starting point in reassessing the
performance of students, teachers, and the school system. It is ironic
that we know so little about the learning process and the performance
of the educational system when it has had a 200-year history of public
support. It is time to challenge the myths, the established decision
makers, the bureaucracy, and seek to discover how to make the school
serve the students of our country and help them to reach their full
potential.

Government programs in the manpower field have concentrated
almost exclusively on training programs as the most effective device
to increase the employability of unemployed workers. In fairness
to the U.S. Department of Labor, there has been a great deal of sensitivity to changes in the clientele receiving manpower-training services over the past nine years. Originally developed to help workers
displaced by the alleged technological revolution of the post-World
War II era, the programs have shifted their orientation to disadvantaged minority groups in urban areas and, more specifically, to youth.
In the latest Manpower Report of the President, 60 percent of the
funds were allocated to manpower training of urban youth.

The new emphasis accurately reflects the need, for unemployment among ghetto youth usually averages more than six times the
unemployment of the adult labor force. Recent experience and research indicate the need to continue the expansion of on-the-job
training, particularly in the private sector. This approach tends to
develop into a creaming process; the most productive of the unemployed youth in urban areas are selected to participate in the programs. Two new formats seem to have several interesting advantages over the current Job Opportunities in the Business Sector (JOBS)
program. It seems useful to try a private contracting system to
place hard-core unemployed individuals in jobs. Companies would
estimate the costs of training and developing such a person to a
point of stable employability and would receive a cost-plus fixed-fee
incentive contract. The obvious advantage of this system would be
the incentive of the contractor to either hire the newly trained worker
or ensure his placement in stable employment. Merely training the
worker would yield only a modest reward, but providing stable employment at higher earnings offers a continuous return to the contractor. The pressure to place workers in better-paying, stable jobs

will help to open up the primary sector of the urban economy to the better-educated and trained members of minority groups.

An alternative to the private contracting system would be the development of a wage-subsidy training-employment program, oriented toward the most disadvantaged group of the urban labor force, urban black youth. A wage-subsidy program would provide training to up-grade workers' productivity, while also providing wages sufficient to motivate job stability. The size of the subsidy should diminish as the worker's productivity increases, until he no longer needs subsidization. The advantage of this program is that it allows a longer time period for raising the productivity of the workers compared to the fixed cost of the current JOBS programs. Flexibility, time, and higher wages may all be required to upgrade the skills and work habits of disadvantaged youth in the urban slums. More experimentation is clearly needed in on-the-job training and subsidized employment. The costs will no doubt be great, but so may the benefits, particularly in the long run. Great resources are needed to turn many people into productive workers in our complex urban economy; limited expenditures may result in more failures and a greater sense of hopelessness and waste. The failure of practical solutions is not a reason for retrenchment and elimination of programs, but it may justify the enlargement of programs and funds to the levels required for success.

A national commitment to the achievement of full employment is a necessary precondition to a successful fight against unemployment and poverty in the U.S. It is essential to achieve a full-employment target of 3.0 percent before any of the remedial programs affecting the labor force can have a significant effect on reducing urban unem-ployment. (A portion of the residual 3 percent would consist of fric-tional unemployment, occurring as workers changed jobs or re-entered the labor force.) Unless the full-employment target is achieved, it is deceptive to contend that we can effectively solve the problems of minority groups, particularly the wide differences in economic status that exist in the country.

In order to achieve full employment without contributing to excessive inflation, it will be necessary to simultaneously attack the deficiencies in the supply of labor and, perhaps more important, the major obstacles presented by the structure of the national economy, which are especially intractable and harmful in the operation of the urban economy and local labor market. Our efforts in education and training will not succeed in reducing unemployment and poverty among blacks, Puerto Ricans, and other minorities, unless we commit the nation's will and its resources to eliminating discrimination in employment, housing, and education. Employment discrimination and the segregation of jobs in the urban labor market will counteract

the benefits of more jobs and more education. Job opportunities in
the primary high-wage, high-status occupations and industries must
be opened up so that all workers can compete equally for the opportunity
to earn a livelihood.

The growth of employment in cities per se, even in the central
city itself, and in certain sectors of the urban economy, such as
construction, manufacturing, finance, insurance, real estate, and
transportation, will not be effective in combatting the unemployment
of the ghetto unless concerted efforts are made to break the strangle-
hold of the oligologistic employers, trade unions, and government
agencies that control access to the preferred employment in the local
economy. The segmentation of the urban economy and the substantial
barriers to entry into the primary sector faced by nonwhites mean
that the fruits of a national economic growth policy and a full-employment target cannot be achieved without a restructuring of the
institutional rules and the economic control over jobs by the existing
power groups in the local labor markets.

Local, state, and federal governments must exercise their
power to open up employment opportunities in the growth and high-
wage sectors of the urban economy. First and foremost, an all-out
effort is required against employment discrimination. The current
efforts of the EEOC and the U.S. Department of Labors' Federal Contract Compliance Office have been limited because they lack the
power of the injunction and manpower and resources to investigate
the subtle discriminatory practices. The limited appropriations
provided these agencies and the absence of effective power to challenge local groups in control of job opportunities to accommodate
change in the distribution of jobs have resulted in limited gains in
this fight against job discrimination. The result has been the con-
tinuation of higher rates of unemployment for nonwhite and slum
residents in the cities, despite economic and employment growth.

The EEOC and the Federal Contract Compliance Office of the
U.S. Department of Labor must be given substantially increased
appropriations and manpower to wage a successful fight against employment discrimination. The commitment of the White House to
support the EEOC effort and the power to use cease and desist orders
and injunctions against violators of the Civil Rights Act of 1964
would provide some of the leverage needed to eradicate discrimination.
In January 1972 the latest attempt to legislate increased powers to
EEOC achieved modest results. The resistance of the trade unions,
employers, and employed workers to the redistribution of desirable
and scarce jobs would be reduced considerably if the economy was
growing rapidly and employment opportunities were expanding. Job
control is conceived as a property right by many workers. It is
unnecessary from the point of view of race and social relations to

take jobs away from currently employed white workers and give them
to currently unemployed black workers. Only in a period of rapid
employment expansion will the opening up of new employment opportunities for minority workers be accomplished without racial
strife, hostility, and even bloodshed. The Administration's plan for
the employment of black and other minority workers in the construction trades, as in the Philadelphia Plan, by using a specified
quantity of black workers on a given construction job, is not very
comforting to white construction workers who have been unemployed
because of the sluggishness of the construction industry. Tight monetary policies, along with cutbacks in government construction programs in an attempt to curb inflation, have reduced the growth of
construction employment. The hoarding of limited, scarce jobs is a
major function of unions. When the members of the union are unemployed, a plan to give fixed numbers of jobs to new workers, particularly inexperienced black workers, will increase racial tension
and will surely reduce the likelihood of efforts to break down the
resistance of white workers and white-controlled trade unions to
opportunities for black workers.

Full employment will never be achieved unless a coordinated
set of policies is enacted simultaneously to guarantee every American
who wants to work and earn a living a job in the U.S. economy, be
it in the public or the private sector. This requires an expansionary
fiscal and monetary policy to stimulate the private sector; a growth
in government employment and public-service employment to absorb
the residual work force not employed in the private sector; basic
reform in the institutions responsible for developing our human resources, particularly for providing labor market skills to young
workers; and an all-out attack on racial discrimination in housing,
schools, and especially in employment. Improving the skills of the
disadvantaged labor force without full employment will create greater
frustration and disillusionment. No better example can be found than
the recent experiences of the many engineers, scientists, and technicians who were directly and indirectly employed through government
expenditures and now are unemployed. And full unemployment cannot be achieved in the short run without excessive price increases.
A public employment program is, therefore, an absolute necessity,
which will become even more compelling if federal policy to reduce
the welfare rolls is implemented.

In summary, lowering the unemployment rate to 4.5 percent
without excessive inflation by the end of 1972 can be accomplished
by expansionary fiscal and monetary policy and an incomes policy.
Over the next few years an increase in the public employment program, with heavy emphasis on new careers, could employ an additional

1.6 million workers, bringing down the unemployment rate to 4.0 percent.* The public service employment program should have the capacity to double in size, in order to absorb women on welfare and residual workers who are unemployed because of inadequate aggregate demand due to excessive concern about inflation. Complementing these policies should be more resources and manpower to open up new job opportunities in the primary sector of the urban economy and educational and training programs focusing on labor market skills and productivity, using on-the-job training and cooperative education wherever possible.

MUNICIPAL POLICIES

Cities and states can do little in the area of manpower policies and programs, industrial development, or housing and transportation to reduce urban unemployment. The power to solve the problems of the cities and their residents is largely in the hands of the federal government. Without the policies specified in the previous section, it will be impossible for cities to cope with unemployment and related social problems. But there are marginal contributions to be made at the municipal level, in local government employment, government contracts, pressure on unions and employer associations for cooperation in the fight against discrimination, housing and transportation policy, and, finally, growth and direction of industrial development and job creation.

Local Government Employment and Expenditures

The Manpower Report of the President for 1970 claimed that "total employment attributed to state and local government purchases represented over 15 percent of all jobs in the nation."[3] Government agencies directly employed more than 12 million, including 9.5 million in state and local governments.[4] In the next decade state and local

------

*This assumes that the size of the labor force will be the same as that of 1971 and that 1.6 million persons who were then classified as unemployed will be employed. Source: Employment and Earnings, U.S. Department of Labor, Bureau of Labor Statistics, Vol. XVIII, No. 7 (Washington, D.C., 1972), Table H-1.

governments may generate one-third of the 15-million new jobs to
be created. [5] As these figures indicate, local governments can be an
important vehicle in employing and training disadvantaged workers.
Changes in civil service requirements, upgrading of programs, training for the disadvantaged, experimental probationary periods, wage
subsidies, and new careers, all must be explored and implemented to
provide greater opportunities to the disadvantaged urban labor force.
The use of contract cancellations is a potent tool to force compliance
with local and federal antidiscrimination laws. Efforts must be made
to create bridges between the public and private sector to encourage
government workers to enter the high-wage primary sector of the
urban economy. Cooperative employment programs can be a useful
experiment to develop techniques of facilitating transfers.

A strong commitment by city officials and the creation of a
powerful enforcement agency against racial, sex, and religious discrimination are necessary to implement the laws and open up opportunities in our cities. It is also essential to develop the cooperation
of major employers, employers' associations, and trade unions in
the local urban labor markets. Workers organized in powerful trade
unions will not permit others easy entrance into the primary urban
labor sector. An understanding of the attitudes and fears of employed
workers in protected jobs would contribute to an accommodation
between the haves and the have-nots. All too often, the needs of the
other parties involved in the working of the local economy are ignored,
with the consequence that fear and failure prevail.

Housing and Transportation

The results of research on the merits of developing programs
to relocate slum dwellers to the suburban areas or to redevelop the
ghetto for the slum dwellers do not indicate a promising payoff in
the reduction of urban slum unemployment. Neither the distribution
of jobs into the suburbs nor the locking in of the ghetto dwellers was
found to be significant in raising unemployment rates or accounting
for the differences in unemployment among slums and nonwhites in
different cities. This does not mean that blacks should not have the
opportunity to move and work in suburban areas, or that open housing
in the suburbs and currently segregated communities in the city should
not be encouraged with more funds and greater enforcement powers,
or that transportation systems should not be improved. It does mean
that these measures should not have top priority in the effort to reduce
urban slum unemployment, particularly for nonwhites and youth.
Other factors—for example, job segregation and racial discrimination—
are much more significant.

Moreover, while it would be desirable to have employment growth in the city, such growth need not be in the ghetto. It would be irresponsible for the local government to impose additional economic costs and more disadvantages by requiring employers to locate in the slum area. Most cities have adequate public transportation systems connecting the central business district with residential areas of the city. If such is not the case, it would probably be a better investment to improve the public intracity transportation network than to give costly incentives to employers to locate in the slum areas.

The economic, social, and political costs and benefits for individuals and communities involved in moving industry into slum areas and moving slum dwellers into suburban rings must be carefully examined. It would be extremely useful to have research documenting the costs of operating in slum areas and suburban areas, purely from the viewpoint of the firm's locational decision, in order to obtain information on the true costs of subsidizing a relocation program. Rather than individual relocation of families, which some blacks may not want, an alternative would be to build new communities in exurban areas with access to suburban jobs.

Finally, if the integration of social and economic life is an objective of the American society and government, and if we want to stimulate the integrated development of suburban America, it will be necessary to develop and to implement simultaneously a comprehensive package of programs designed to provide housing, employment, training, wage subsidies, and job placement in the industries and firms leaving the central cities for the suburbs. Substantial resources and a strong commitment will be required to combine effective subsidies in housing, training, employment, and education with the relocation of many thousands of city and slum residents and the redirection of future migrants into new towns and communities in the suburban and exurban ring of the major metropolitan centers of the country. This vast undertaking would be directed at achieving a social and population balance of the ethnic groups in the country in the face of the location decisions of firms and industries. Without an all-out effort with largescale allocation of resources, such an objective can never be accomplished. A by-product of such a program may be the return migration into the cities of people who work in the central city. Ironically, the renaissance of urban America may come about through the development and subsidization of suburban and exurban America.

Industrial Development

The growth of the urban economy is a necessary prerequisite for full employment of the population of urban metropolitan areas.

Recent experience with the Area Redevelopment Act, the Economic Development Act, and the Appalachian Regional Development Program indicates the difficulty of attracting industry into depressed areas. Although this difficulty is probably substantially less for urban centers than for rural depressed areas, the competition among cities is greater. The standard devices of tax credits, subsidized rentals, property tax abatements, and training the labor force are available to all municipalities and states and do not provide a competitive advantage to any region or city. Such factors as transportation and distribution systems, proximity to markets and suppliers of raw materials, the quality of the labor force, the social and cultural amenities of life, climate, the municipal services, the costs of operation, and the residence of the top management are more likely to determine the location of plants and corporate headquarters than any policies subject to local governmental control.

Under these conditions it is extremely unlikely that major changes will occur in the location of firms inside and outside the city and among cities. Moreover, it will be equally difficult to change the structure of employment and the mix of industries in local labor markets. Aside from government employment the share of employment in the various major industrial sectors cannot be influenced to any significant extent by local policies. What changes occur will be determined by new technology, new resource discoveries, population growth, and changes in consumer tastes.

An educated and skilled work force will provide a reasonable inducement for most firms to locate in a metropolitan center. Since the problems in the urban labor market are so diverse, it is important for local officials and agencies to tailor policies and programs to meet the needs of their indigenous work force. Nevertheless, all cities must face the problem of improving the skill and productivity of the work force. Emphasis should be given to on-the-job training programs that will, of necessity, select the best of the unemployed and not the hard-core, long-term unemployed. In order to open up jobs in the primary sector to recent trainees, a large-scale cooperative effort to upgrade jobs and restructure the internal labor markets of large city employers, including municipal government, is required.

Industrial development schemes in urban centers have had some favorable but marginal impact by using site assembly and planning of industrial parks. Space limitations, particularly for manufacturing operations, have stimulated many plants to locate in suburban and exurban areas. In order to offset this movement, some cities, such as New York, have commenced industrial development programs in the central city with reasonable success, although the number of jobs created is minimal compared to the needs.

Improving the Local Labor Market

In most urban centers there will be jobs for the urban labor force. However, suburban dwellers commuting to the central city will continue to be a major source of job competition. City governments must develop programs in manpower training and development that raise the productivity and skills of the urban work force.

Experimental programs in the area of wage subsidies, cooperative jobs between the public and private sector, and privately contracted employment and training systems should be developed to open up the higher-wage positions in the primary sector of the urban economy.

What can the municipal government do to promote improvement in the secondary employment sector of low-wage, high-turnover, casual, dead-end jobs that comprise a considerable proportion of urban jobs and practically all the employment opportunities for slum-dwellers? Very little can be accomplished directly by local government. A great deal depends on other institutional forces, particularly the trade unions.

Union organization of these sectors of the urban economy would create stability and pressure to improve wages and working conditions. A classic example is the hospital workers in New York City, who have gained substantial improvements in their economic welfare as a result of aggressive union activities. Another example is the case of longshore and shipping in the port of New York City. In cooperation with the union the port operations are supervised by a two-state commission. The workers receive more steady employment, greater job protection, and higher wages under a stable hiring-hall system controlled by a strong union.

The economics of these industries encourages a casual, flexible, low-wage work force. Only strong institutional changes can stimulate employers to rearrange the employment relationship.

Extending the federal minimum-wage law to cover all workers, as well as higher unemployment-insurance taxes on employers, can place more pressure on employers. However, if these measures are undertaken on a local basis, they may stimulate an exodus of firms and economic activities to cities without such expensive laws. Moreover, it is difficult to calculate the disemployment effects of a substantial increase in minimum wages and coverage.

Municipal and state government can have a direct impact on two other sectors affecting the urban labor market, welfare and illegal activities. Local governments determine eligibility and payment levels under our current welfare system. Therefore, if local governments want to reduce welfare costs and case loads, they can affect the supply of labor and the unemployment rate. If states were

more liberal in supporting dependent populations, mothers with
dependent children or unemployed heads of families, unemployment
would decrease, particularly among young workers. If the incentives
offered by the Family Assistance Plan are strong enough to induce
people into the labor market—which will probably be the result in
some major cities, where an income of $2,400 for a family of four
will not be sufficient to live on, and states do not supplement their
income—they will probably raise unemployment rates in cities and
reduce future migratory flows from rural areas.

The most controversial area for local government policy is the
illegal activities of the work force in gambling, hustling, narcotics,
prostitution, theft, and so forth. There are three choices: (a) to
permit the status quo to continue, (b) to crack down on these activities,
and (c) to legalize some of them. The third course is the most controversial; however, it may also be the most desirable.

The advantages lie in the saving of funds and manpower in law
enforcement and adjudication; reduction in the corruption of public
employees; reduction in the huge profits of organized crime and in
the use of these funds to infiltrate and corrupt industries in the
urban economy; the very large employment effect of hiring disadvantaged minority group members of the urban labor force, many of
whom are already engaged in these activities; facilitation of medical
treatment of heroin addicts; reduction in addict crime; reduction of
overcrowding in prisons and juvenile homes; and increased tax revenues. These clear-cut benefits to the city and its residents from
the legalization of gambling, prostitution, and the medical treatment
of drug addiction should be considered in the determination of local
and state policy to improve employment opportunities and the quality
of life in our major cities.

Manpower Revenue Sharing

The new legislation in the field of manpower deserves special
attention because it focuses on giving the cities and states a larger
role in solving the unemployment problems of urban dwellers. Revenue sharing in the manpower field has some distinct advantages and
disadvantages. The controversy centers not on the need for revenue
in the cities and the availability of resources in the federal government but on the abilities of the respective levels of government to
deliver a vast array of services to the citizens of their respective
communities. The great diversity found among the factors influencing the urban labor market and in the structure of the urban
economy of various localities suggests that it would be beneficial
for local agencies and governments to play a major role in the

development of programs tailored to local problems and population. Programs and policies in transportation, information, discrimination, education, and training for subgroups of the urban labor force—such as youth, veterans, and the elderly; or blacks, Puerto Ricans, Mexican-Americans, and American Indians; or new foreign migrants, such as Chinese—may be more efficient at local levels than at the federal level of government.

On the other hand, manpower revenue sharing is probably inadequate to handle problems of mobility and migration, welfare, employment expansion, metropolitan growth and cooperation, housing, illegal activities, and their consequences for unemployment and poverty in the cities.

Moreover, there are some additional problems of revenue sharing and efficient use of funds on the local level. First, planning and evaluation require adequate data. The study clearly points up the paucity of local data for the most basic statistics, such as unemployment rates and earnings of subgroups of the labor force. Second, the objectives and commitments of local officials and agencies may not be identical to the will of Congress and the President. This is a particularly acute problem in the area of segregation and discrimination in employment and housing. Third, the responsibility of the federal government to provide full employment will be lessened with the shift of funds to state and local governments. Fourth, the local and state governments do not match the federal government in the quality of manpower and, consequently, the services offered and the programs developed and planned may be of lower quality. Fifth, there may be economies of scale in operating, planning, and evaluating programs that will be lost at the local level. Sixth, the assumption that local and state governments are more responsive to local problems and citizens and that this sensitivity guarantees better services, programs, and results needs to be carefully examined. Even if it proves to be valid, too much political sensitivity may limit experimentation and change in local programs and communities. In addition, patronage and corruption may subvert the programs for the benefit of the few at the expense of the many.

In conclusion, given the assumptions and problems inherent in revenue sharing, the manpower problems of urban dwellers and of the country as a whole would be best served by a joint effort of federal, state, and city officials and not by autonomous revenue sharing.

The federal government should assume a larger role in evaluating local and state manpower plans and existing programs, in operating diverse experiments and demonstration programs, in approving funds and providing performance incentives to state and local manpower agencies, in training personnel for local and state

government employment, and in collecting and disseminating information on labor market conditions. State and local governments
should have the responsibility of planning, designing, and operating
programs. There should be a partnership of federal and local government, combining local responsibility and operation with federal
funding and evaluation. This arrangement is likely to accomplish
national objectives with efficiency and responsibility.

In summary, city and state governments must recognize their
limitations in improving the employment prospects of urban dwellers.
Structural changes are required primarily on a national level, and
local governments can make only marginal changes, with nominal
results. Nevertheless, there is no excuse for not attempting to bring
about some positive change in the life of urban dwellers, and there
are devices available to policy makers for this purpose: (a) legiti-
mizing gambling, prostitution, and narcotics; (b) developing a large-
scale public employment program; (c) using government purchases
and construction to prevent employment discrimination; (d) developing
a powerful local antidiscrimination agency; (e) restructuring the
urban labor market, particularly the organization and stabilization
of the secondary market and the breaking down of barriers into the
primary market by union-management cooperation, upgrading, on-
the-job training, and cooperative education.

Finally, it should be clear by now that unless a concerted attack
is made simultaneously and with sufficient resources on the myriad
and complex institutional and economic forces that prevent minority
groups from competing in the labor market, the current piecemeal
and inadequate expenditures on social, manpower, and educational
programs will serve only to create great expectations and even
greater alienation, hostility, and frustration. The future of American
cities will be determined by the programs and policies affecting
the urban economy and the labor market for minority workers. The
social and political fabric of the nation is under attack because of
the injustices generated by an economy that deprives people of an
opportunity to participate in the benefits of prosperity. The gap between
ethnic groups in skills and education may be narrowing, but the opportunity structure continues to be closed, causing a widening of the
gap in material standards of living.

The solutions are known, the resources are available; all that
is needed is a commitment to change by the government and the
people. The future of our society and nation is at stake in the decisions
being made now. Full employment, rapid economic growth, effective
campaigns against racial discrimination, public employment for
all who are willing to work, a guaranteed income to support all who
are unable to work, a new system of education and training, a redistribution of population through large-scale mobility programs,

combining employment, housing, training, and wage-subsidies programs, all are required to meet the impediments in the metropolitan
labor markets and national economy. Time is running out. We must
reorder our priorities—$3 billion for training Americans compared
to $30 billion to kill Vietnamese, $2 billion to fight poverty compared
to $80 billion for defense. A man without a job or a child who is
hungry will never be free. We cannot defend military expenditures
in the name of freedom without extending the concept to include freedom from hunger and freedom to earn a living. Prominent Americans
warn us about the danger of a race war. The seeds of destruction
were sown across the country more than 200 years ago. The harvest
we may reap is destructive of our nation and all its great principles.
Revolution or repression; either will destroy our society. But there
is another path. We need to guarantee employment to all Americans.
We have the resources, and we have the knowledge. Do we have the
will to commit ourselves to this goal?

Definition of Standard Metropolitan Statistical
Areas as of December 1966

City	Central City County or Counties	Suburban Ring County or Counties
New York	Bronx, Kings, New York, Queens, Richmond	Nassau, Rockland, Suffolk, Westchester
Chicago	Cook	Du Page, Kane, Lake, McHenry, Will
Los Angeles	Los Angeles	
Philadelphia	Philadelphia, Camden (N.J.)	Bucks, Chester, Delaware, Montgomery, Burlington (N.J.), Gloucester (N.J.)
Detroit	Wayne	Macomb, Oakland
Baltimore	Baltimore City	Anne Arundel, Baltimore, Carroll, Howard
Houston	Harris	Brazoria, Fort Bend, Liberty, Montgomery
Cleveland	Cayahoga	Geauga, Lake, Medina
Minneapolis-St. Paul	Hennepin, Ramsey	Anoka, Dakota, Washington
Washington, D.C.	District of Columbia	Montgomery (Md.), Prince Georges (Md.), Alexandria City (Va.), Fairfax City (Va.), Falls Church City (Va.), Arlington (Va.), Fairfax (Va.)
St. Louis	St. Louis City	Franklin, Jefferson, St., Charles, St. Louis, Madison (Ill.), St. Clair (Ill.)

City	Central City County or Counties	Suburban Ring County or Counties
Milwaukee	Milwaukee	Ozaukee, Waukesha
San Francisco	San Francisco, Alameda	Contra Costa, Marin, San Mateo
Boston*	Suffolk	Essex, Middlesex, Norfolk, Plymouth
Dallas	Dallas	Collin, Denton, Ellis
New Orleans	Orleans Parish	Jefferson Parish, St. Bernard Parish, St. Tammany Parish
Pittsburgh	Allegheny	Beaver, Washington, Westmoreland
San Antonio	Bexar	Guadalupe
San Diego	San Diego	
Seattle	King	Snohomish
Buffalo	Erie	Niagara
Cincinnati	Hamilton, Campbell (Ky.), Kenton (Ky.)	Cleremont, Warren, Boone (Ky.), Dearborn (Ind.)
Memphis	Shelby	Crittenden (Ark.)
Denver	Denver	Adams, Arapahoe, Boulder, Jefferson
Atlanta	Fulton	Clayton, Cobb, DeKalb, Gwinnett
Indianapolis	Marion	Hamilton, Hancock, Hendricks, Johnson, Morgan, Shelby
Kansas City	Clay, Jackson, Wyandotte (Kans.)	Cass, Platte, Johnson (Kans.)
Columbus	Franklin	Delaware, Pickaway
Phoenix	Maricopa	
Newark	Essex	Morris, Union

*For this study employment data are reported for the entire counties of Essex, Middlesex, Norfolk, and Plymouth for the Boston SMSA and not portions of each county as specified in Standard Metropolitan Statistical Areas, 1967.

Source: Standard Metropolitan Statistical Areas, 1967, Executive Office of the President, Bureau of the Budget (Washington, D.C., 1967), Part II and Part IV.

Definitions of Variables

Variables	Definitions
C(P)	Property Crime Index
CIM	Cyclical Industrial Mix
D(R)	Discrimination Ratio
E(C)	Employment Change
E(CY)	Employment Change for Youth
EDL	Educational Demand for Labor
EG	Educational Gap—Cities
EG(S)	Educational Gap—Slum Areas
EG(Y)	Educational Gap—Youth
ESL	Educational Supply of Labor
ESL(NW)	Educational Supply of Labor—Nonwhites
ESL(S)	Educational Supply of Labor—Slum Residents
ESL(Y)	Educational Supply of Labor—Youth
H(TB)	Health—Incidence of Tuberculosis
IM(C)	Industrial Mix—Construction
IM(F)	Industrial Mix—Finance, Insurance, and Real Estate
IM(M)	Industrial Mix—Manufacturing
IM(R)	Industrial Mix—Retail
IM(S)	Industrial Mix—Services
IM(W)	Industrial Mix—Wholesale
LF%NW	Percent of the Labor Force That Is Nonwhite
LFPR	Labor Force Participation Rate
LFPR(F)	Female Labor Force Participation Rate
LFPR(NW)	Nonwhite Labor Force Participation Rate
LFPR(Y)	Youth Labor Force Participation Rate
M(DC)	Migration from a Different County
M(N)	Net Migration
M(NW)	Nonwhite Migration
NWUR	Nonwhite Unemployment Rate
N/WUR	Ratio of Nonwhite to White Unemployment Rates
OD	Occupational Distribution
RS	Residential Segregation
SD	Spatial Distribution
UR(A)	Adult Unemployment Rate
W(A)	Average Wage—Manufacturing
W(C)	Welfare Case Rate
W(P)	Welfare Payment Rate
WCxWP	Welfare Case Rate x Welfare Payment Rate

APPENDIX TABLE 1

City Unemployment Rates, 1960 and 1966, Equation 1 Variables

Equation 1 Variables	1960			1966		
	Regression Coefficient	Standard Error	T Value	Regression Coefficient	Standard Error	T Value
NWUR	0.27	0.09	2.96*	0.36	0.09	4.22*
H(TB)	0.04	0.02	2.38*	0.02	0.02	0.98
LFPR	-0.15	0.10	-1.47	-0.02	0.06	-0.32
EDL	-0.96	5.75	-0.17	-15.28	5.23	-2.92*
ESL	0.29	0.42	0.70	0.07	0.36	0.20
SD	0.01	0.02	0.78	0.02	0.02	0.93
M(N)	0.01	0.02	0.58	0.01	0.004	2.79*
E(C)	-0.02	0.03	-0.53	-0.10	0.04	-2.79*
CIM	0.02	0.06	0.28	-0.10	0.05	-2.12*
Intercept	16.91			193.26		
Adj R^2	0.74			0.76		
F Value	9.63*			9.96*		

*Significant at the 90 percent level.

233

City Unemployment Rates, 1960 and 1966,
Equation 2 Variables

Equation 2 Variables	1960			1966		
	Regression Coefficient	Standard Error	T Value	Regression Coefficient	Standard Error	T Value
CIM	0.05	0.07	0.70	-0.08	0.06	-1.28
H(TB)	0.06	0.02	3.70*	0.03	0.02	1.65
LFPR	-0.32	0.10	-3.32*	-0.12	0.08	-1.57
ESL	0.86	0.43	1.98*	-0.33	0.52	-0.63
EDL	-6.12	6.61	-0.93	-19.77	7.18	-2.75*
SD	0.02	0.02	0.88	0.03	0.03	0.84
E(C)	-0.03	0.04	-0.73	-0.08	0.05	-1.58
N/WUR	-0.34	0.55	-0.63	-0.02	0.28	-0.06
M(N)	0.01	0.02	0.33	0.01	0.01	1.72
Intercept	81.05			258.62		
Adj R^2	0.63			0.55		
F Value	6.17*			4.52*		

*Significant at the 90 percent level.

City Unemployment Rates, 1960 and 1966,
Equation 3 Variables

Equation 3 Variables	1960			1966		
	Regression Coefficient	Standard Error	T Value	Regression Coefficient	Standard Error	T Value
CIM	0.04	0.06	0.69	-0.08	0.06	-1.27
H(TB)	0.06	0.02	3.77*	0.02	0.02	1.04
LFPR	-0.39	0.10	-4.09*	-0.16	0.08	-1.89*
ESL	1.18	0.45	2.64*	-0.15	0.47	-0.32
EDL	-6.72	6.30	-1.07	-19.91	6.61	-3.01*
LFPR(NW)	0.03	0.02	1.57	0.03	0.03	1.00
SD	0.02	0.02	1.11	0.02	0.03	0.83
E(C)	-0.03	0.04	-0.89	-0.08	0.05	-1.71
M(N)	0.01	0.02	0.50	0.01	0.01	1.80*
Intercept	88.09			260.22		
Adj R^2	0.67			0.57		
F Value	7.02*			4.85*		

*Significant at the 90 percent level.

City Unemployment Rates, 1960 and 1966,
Equation 4 Variables

Equation 4 Variables	1960			1966		
	Regression Coefficient	Standard Error	T Value	Regression Coefficient	Standard Error	T Value
CIM	0.04	0.06	0.66	-0.08	0.06	-1.38
H(TB)	0.06	0.02	3.76*	0.03	0.02	1.69
LFPR	-0.33	0.09	-3.65*	-0.12	0.08	-1.62
ESL	0.90	0.42	2.12*	-0.31	0.45	-0.70
EDL	-5.62	6.47	-0.87	-19.91	6.61	-3.01*
SD	0.02	0.02	0.99	0.03	0.03	0.87
E(C)	-0.03	0.04	-0.76	-0.08	0.05	-1.71
M(N)	0.01	0.02	0.37	0.01	0.01	1.82*
Intercept	75.27			260.29		
Adj R^2	0.64			0.57		
F Value	7.10*			5.34*		

*Significant at the 90 percent level.

APPENDIX TABLE 5

City Unemployment Rates, 1960 and 1966,
Equation 5 Variables

Equation 5 Variables	1960			1966		
	Regression Coefficient	Standard Error	T Value	Regression Coefficient	Standard Error	T Value
CIM	0.08	0.03	2.87*	0.06	0.04	1.38
H(TB)	0.06	0.02	3.73*	0.04	0.02	1.70
LFPR	-0.33	0.09	-3.67*	-0.14	0.09	-1.54
EG	-0.91	0.42	-2.18*	0.21	0.53	0.41
E(C)	-0.04	0.03	-1.25	-0.04	0.05	-0.71
SD	0.02	0.02	1.10	0.02	0.03	0.46
M(N)	0.01	0.02	0.66	0.01	0.01	1.06
Intercept	18.38			7.68		
Adj R^2	0.65			0.40		
F Value	8.21*			3.46		

*Significant at the 90 percent level.

APPENDIX TABLE 6

City Unemployment Rates, 1960 and 1966, Equation 6 Variables

Equation 6 Variables	1960			1966		
	Regression Coefficient	Standard Error	T Value	Regression Coefficient	Standard Error	T Value
W(A)	3.68	0.74	4.97*	1.93	0.32	2.36*
LFPR	-0.32	0.08	-3.77*	-0.17	0.07	-2.30*
E(C)	-0.03	0.03	-0.91	0.03	0.05	0.63
W(C)	-0.16	0.14	-1.13	0.29	0.10	2.85*
M(N)	-0.01	0.02	-0.66	0.01	0.01	1.57
Intercept	15.94			6.31		
Adj R^2	0.60			0.44		
F Value	9.18*			5.05*		

*Significant at the 90 percent level.

APPENDIX TABLE 7

City Unemployment Rates, 1960 and 1966, Equation 7 Variables

Equation 7 Variables	1960			1966		
	Regression Coefficient	Standard Error	T Value	Regression Coefficient	Standard Error	T Value
W(A)	2.54	0.88	2.87*	1.38	0.99	1.39
LFPR	-0.29	0.07	-3.88*	-0.17	0.08	-1.98*
E(C)	-0.06	0.03	-2.09*	-0.02	0.06	-0.31
W(P)	0.04	0.02	1.85*	0.02	0.04	0.39
M(N)	0.01	0.01	0.67	0.002	0.01	0.40
Intercept	14.95			10.15		
Adj R^2	0.63			0.25		
F Value	10.36*			2.61		

*Significant at the 90 percent level.

City Unemployment Rates, 1960 and 1966,
Equation 8 Variables

Equation 8 Variables	1960			1966		
	Regression Coefficient	Standard Error	T Value	Regression Coefficient	Standard Error	T Value
D(R)	-0.42	0.76	-0.56	0.06	0.44	0.14
EDL	-12.31	2.58	-4.77*	-14.32	4.57	-3.13*
H(TB)	0.03	0.01	2.34*	0.03	0.02	1.61
RS	-0.10	0.04	-2.49*	-0.10	0.06	-1.85*
SD	0.01	0.02	0.64	0.03	0.03	1.04
C(P)	-0.0001	0.0005	-0.12	0.0002	0.001	0.34
Intercept	154.91			184.37		
Adj R^2	0.64			0.45		
F Value	8.92*			4.62*		

*Significant at the 90 percent level.

APPENDIX TABLE 9

City Unemployment Rates, 1960 and 1966,
Equation 9 Variables

Equation 9 Variables	1960			1966		
	Regression Coefficient	Standard Error	T Value	Regression Coefficient	Standard Error	T Value
OD	-0.20	0.40	-0.45	0.16	0.28	0.57
EDL	-12.25	2.62	-4.67*	-14.39	4.53	-3.17*
H(TB)	0.03	0.01	2.48*	0.03	0.02	1.60
RS	-0.10	0.04	-2.62*	-0.12	0.05	-2.13*
SD	0.01	0.02	0.61	0.03	0.03	1.05
C(P)	-0.0001	0.0005	-0.10	0.0002	0.001	0.28
Intercept	154.20			186.19		
Adj R^2	0.64			0.46		
F Value	8.86*			4.73*		

*Significant at the 90 percent level.

APPENDIX TABLE 10

City Unemployment Rates, 1960 and 1966, Equation 10 Variables

Equation 10 Variables	1960			1966		
	Regression Coefficient	Standard Error	T Value	Regression Coefficient	Standard Error	T Value
IM(W)	-0.49	0.23	-2.18*	-0.66	0.30	-2.18*
IM(R)	-0.18	0.17	-1.08	-0.43	0.17	-2.44*
IM(F)	-0.36	0.22	-1.63	-0.32	0.31	-1.05
IM(C)	-0.34	0.25	-1.37	-0.57	0.39	-1.45
IM(M)	-0.12	0.12	-1.01	-0.29	0.16	-1.79*
IM(S)	-0.09	0.17	-0.55	-0.35	0.21	-1.71
Intercept	23.99			39.56		
Adj R^2	0.39			0.20		
F Value	3.71			1.97		

*Significant at the 90 percent level.

APPENDIX TABLE 11

City Unemployment Rates, 1960 Equation 11 Variables

Equation 11 Variables	1960		
	Regression Coefficient	Standard Error	T Value
W(A)	3.55	0.68	5.25*
LFPR	-0.27	0.07	-3.82*
M(DC)	-0.09	0.05	-2.00*
E(C)	0.01	0.03	0.46
Intercept	13.78		
Adj R^2	0.65		
F Value	13.80*		

*Significant at the 90 percent level.

APPENDIX TABLE 12

City Unemployment Rates, 1960, Equation 12 Variables

Equation 12 Variables	1960		
	Regression Coefficient	Standard Error	T Value
W(A)	3.53	0.64	5.50*
LFPR	-0.39	0.08	-4.95*
M(NW)	0.53	0.20	2.66*
E(C)	-0.04	0.02	-2.56*
Intercept	18.64		
Adj R^2	0.69		
F Value	15.93*		

*Significant at the 90 percent level.

APPENDIX TABLE 13

Nonwhite City Unemployment Rates, 1960 and 1966, Equation 1 Variables

Equation 1 Variables	1960*			1966		
	Regression Coefficient	Standard Error	T Value	Regression Coefficient	Standard Error	T Value
D(R)	-5.87	2.65	-2.22**	1.09	1.09	1.00
C(P)	-0.002	0.001	-1.50	-0.002	0.001	-1 72**
ESL(NW)	-1.85	0.97	-1.91**	-1.36	0.74	-1.82**
LF%NW	-0.13	0.06	-2.10**	-0.11	0.06	-1.92**
WCXWP	-0.01	0.01	-0.65	0.0001	0.004	0.03
H(TB)	0.02	0.05	0.39	0.13	0.05	2.61**
RS	-0.03	0.12	-0.26	-0.16	0.12	-1.30
Intercept	43.11			32.56		
Adj R^2	0.24			0.35		
F Value	2.07			2.89		

*1960 figures apply only to male nonwhite unemployment rates.
**Significant at the 90 percent level.

Nonwhite City Unemployment Rates, 1960 and 1966,
Equation 2 Variables

Equation 2 Variables	1960			1966		
	Regression Coefficient	Standard Error	T Value	Regression Coefficient	Standard Error	T Value
W(H)	6.11	1.34	4.57*	1.20	1.67	0.72
LFPR(NW)	-0.29	0.09	-3.03*	-0.24	0.06	-3.69*
CIM	0.15	0.05	2.75*	0.21	0.08	2.78*
E(C)	-0.03	0.03	-1.00	0.10	0.07	1.27
M(NW)	-0.40	0.35	-1.17	-0.01	0.01	-0.70
SD	0.03	0.03	1.12	0.01	0.05	2.24*
Intercept	3.88			3.90		
Adj R^2	0.77			0.51		
F Value	16.23*			5.44*		

*Significant at the 90 percent level.

APPENDIX TABLE 15

Nonwhite City Unemployment Rates, 1960 and 1966,
Equation 3 Variables

Equation 3 Variables	1960			1966		
	Regression Coefficient	Standard Error	T Value	Regression Coefficient	Standard Error	T Value
W(A)	7.35	1.34	5.46*	2.33	1.53	1.53
LFPR(NW)	-0.36	0.10	-3.60*	-0.26	0.06	-4.11*
IM(S)	-0.19	0.13	-1.39	-0.38	0.13	-2.88*
E(C)	-0.05	0.07	-0.67	0.04	0.08	0.58
SD	0.01	0.04	0.31	0.09	0.04	2.11*
M(N)	0.01	0.04	0.20	-0.005	0.01	-0.43
Intercept	16.29			21.90		
Adj R^2	0.70			0.52		
F Value	11.60*			5.62*		

*Significant at the 90 percent level.

APPENDIX TABLE 16

Slum Employment Rates, 1960 and 1966, Equation 1 Variables

Equation 1 Variables	1960			1966		
	Regression Coefficient	Standard Error	T Value	Regression Coefficient	Standard Error	T Value
W(A)	6.99	2.92	2.39*	1.73	2.46	0.70
LFPR	-0.27	0.18	-1.49	0.14	0.22	0.67
M(N)	-0.09	0.09	-0.97	0.05	0.15	0.36
W(C)	-0.52	0.47	-1.11	0.31	0.46	0.67
E(C)	0.09	0.17	0.51	0.20	0.18	1.14
Intercept	10.97			-8.10		
Adj R^2	0.19			0.03		
F Value	1.35			0.80		

*Significant at the 90 percent level.

APPENDIX TABLE 17

Slum Employment Rates, 1960 and 1966, Equation 2 Variables

Equation 2 Variables	1960			1966		
	Regression Coefficient	Standard Error	T Value	Regression Coefficient	Standard Error	T Value
W(A)	5.74	2.72	2.11*	2.18	2.30	0.95
LFPR	-0.21	0.17	-1.19	0.19	0.20	0.93
M(N)	-0.02	0.06	-0.26	0.03	0.14	0.18
E(C)	-0.02	0.14	-0.17	0.12	0.13	0.94
Intercept	8.03			-8.04		
Adj R^2	0.16			0.07		
F Value	1.36			0.93		

*Significant at the 90 percent level.

APPENDIX TABLE 18

Slum Employment Rates, 1960 and 1966,
Equation 3 Variables

Equation 3 Variables	1960			1966		
	Regression Coefficient	Standard Error	T Value	Regression Coefficient	Standard Error	T Value
W(A)	6.26	3.08	2.03*	5.50	2.05	2.69*
W(P)	-0.04	0.10	-0.42	-0.24	0.08	-3.06*
E(C)	-0.02	0.15	-0.14	-0.17	0.14	-1.22
LFPR	-0.16	0.22	-0.73	0.29	0.16	1.87*
M(N)	-0.02	0.06	-0.23	0.21	0.12	1.73
Intercept	5.45			-9.87		
Adj R^2	0.10			0.47		
F Value	1.04			3.19		

*Significant at the 90 percent level.

APPENDIX TABLE 19

Slum Employment Rates, 1960 and 1966,
Equation 4 Variables

Equation 4 Variables	1960			1966		
	Regression Coefficient	Standard Error	T Value	Regression Coefficient	Standard Error	T Value
IM(S)	-1.93	0.82	-2.34*	1.05	0.43	2.47*
IM(M)	-0.24	0.34	-0.72	1.56	0.29	5.36*
IM(F)	0.12	0.42	0.28	3.54	0.58	6.06*
IM(W)	-0.42	0.98	-0.43	-1.69	0.69	-2.44*
IM(C)	-0.21	0.58	-0.37	7.77	1.08	7.17*
IM(R)	0.03	0.37	0.09	-1.63	0.25	-6.41*
Intercept	54.22			-90.14		
Adj R^2	0.48			0.82		
F Value	2.85			10.98*		

*Significant at the 90 percent level.

Slum Employment Rates, 1960 and 1966,
Equation 5 Variables

Equation 5 Variables	1960			1966		
	Regression Coefficient	Standard Error	T Value	Regression Coefficient	Standard Error	T Value
EDL	-33.25	7.04	-4.73	-22.32	16.10	-1.39
H(TB)	0.16	0.04	4.10*	-0.19	0.07	-2.82*
RS	- 0.19	0.06	-2.97*	-0.45	0.13	-3.54*
OD	5.20	1.83	2.85*	1.00	0.89	1.13
SD	0.01	0.03	0.31	-0.001	0.005	-0.25
C(P)	- 0.0002	0.001	-0.20	-0.003	0.001	-2.53*
Intercept	393.66			330.85		
Adj R^2	0.75			0.45		
F Value	7.44*			2.61		

*Significant at the 90 percent level.

APPENDIX TABLE 21

Slum Employment Rates, 1960 and 1966,
Equation 6 Variables

Equation 6 Variables	1960			1966		
	Regression Coefficient	Standard Error	T Value	Regression Coefficient	Standard Error	T Value
EDL	-47.70	23.58	-2.02*	36.17	74.20	0.49
M(N)	-0.22	0.11	-1.98*	-0.18	0.27	-0.68
E(C)	0.42	0.22	1.94*	0.23	0.24	0.99
SD	-0.06	0.06	-0.97	-0.01	0.01	-0.83
CIM	-0.06	0.23	-0.26	0.20	0.47	0.42
ESL(S)	0.15	0.69	0.22	0.75	1.27	0.59
Intercept	564.01			-448.95		
Adj R^2	0.43			0.26		
F Value	2.42			0.29		

*Significant at the 90 percent level.

Slum Employment Rates, 1960 and 1966,
Equation 7 Variables

Equation 7 Variables	1960			1966		
	Regression Coefficient	Standard Error	T Value	Regression Coefficient	Standard Error	T Value
EDL	-10.00	16.00	-0.63	-30.78	6.32	-4.87*
ESL(S)	-0.44	1.25	-0.35	-0.42	0.64	-0.67
H(TB)	0.09	0.08	1.19	-0.19	0.04	-4.59*
RS	-0.001	0.14	-0.01	-0.52	0.09	-5.96*
SD	0.01	0.05	0.26	-0.01	0.01	-0.02
D(R)	-1.49	6.04	-0.25	-3.09	2.35	-1.31
Intercept	123.65			438.46		
Adj R^2	0.09			0.69		
F Value	0.96			6.12*		

*Significant at the 90 percent level.

APPENDIX TABLE 23

Slum Employment Rates, 1960 and 1966,
Equation 8 Variables

Equation 8 Variables	1960			1966		
	Regression Coefficient	Standard Error	T Value	Regression Coefficient	Standard Error	T Value
EDL	-13.89	12.73	-1.09	-33.07	7.49	-4.41*
ESL(S)	-0.77	0.96	-0.80	-0.36	0.51	-0.70
H(TB)	0.13	0.06	2.18	0.18	0.05	-3.49*
C(P)	0.001	0.001	1.47	-0.002	0.001	-3.32*
RS	-0.03	0.10	-0.30	-0.49	0.10	-4.74*
SD	0.04	0.05	0.80	-0.001	0.01	-0.48
Intercept	168.59			468.50		
Adj R^2	0.26			0.71		
F Value	1.53			6.34*		

*Significant at the 90 percent level.

APPENDIX TABLE 24

Slum Employment Rates, 1960 and 1966, Equation 9 Variables

Equation 9 Variables	1960			1966		
	Regression Coefficient	Standard Error	T Value	Regression Coefficient	Standard Error	T Value
ESL (S)	1.22	1.66	0.73	-0.34	1.11	-0.31
EDL	0.59	20.49	0.03	-30.95	22.81	-1.36
SD	-0.01	0.10	-0.08	0.01	0.01	0.40
E(C)	0.28	0.34	0.83	0.05	0.14	0.34
M(N)	-0.16	0.19	-0.84	0.19	0.20	0.98
LFPR(F)	-0.17	0.24	-0.71	0.21	0.23	0.94
CIM	0.32	0.21	1.51	-0.17	0.23	-0.74
Intercept	-17.83			387.52		
Adj R^2	0.11			0.03		
F Value	0.99			0.83		

APPENDIX TABLE 25

Slum Employment Rates, 1960 and 1966, Equation 10 Variables

Equation 10 Variables	1960			1966		
	Regression Coefficient	Standard Error	T Value	Regression Coefficient	Standard Error	T Value
EG(C-S)	-1.17	1.48	-0.79	0.52	1.16	0.45
SD	-0.003	0.08	-0.04	0.004	0.01	0.29
E(C)	0.27	0.29	0.93	0.12	0.14	0.86
M(N)	-0.15	0.16	-0.96	0.03	0.16	0.17
LFPR(F)	-0.17	0.23	-0.76	0.30	0.23	1.34
CIM	0.31	0.13	2.40*	0.10	0.14	0.70
Intercept	3.48			-10.98		
Adj R^2	0.20			0.08		
F Value	1.30			0.59		

*Significant at the 90 percent level.

APPENDIX TABLE 26

Slum Youth Unemployment Rates, 1966,
Equation 1 Variables
(a)
Ages 14-19 and 16-19

Equation 1 Variables	14-19			16-19		
	Regression Coefficient	Standard Error	T Value	Regression Coefficient	Standard Error	T Value
IM(C)	20.34	7.43	2.74*	18.38	7.43	2.47*
IM(M)	3.95	1.60	2.47*	3.61	1.60	2.55
IM(R)	-4.72	1.61	-2.92*	-4.14	1.61	-2.57*
IM(W)	-0.04	2.23	-0.02	0.97	2.23	0.44
IM(F)	8.22	3.65	2.25*	6.99	3.65	1.92
IM(S)	3.74	2.22	1.69	3.25	2.21	1.47
Intercept	-271.16			-249.86		
Adj R^2	0.76			0.78		
F Value	4.13			4.67		

(b)
Ages 20-24 and 14-24

Equation 1 Variables	20-24			14-24		
	Regression Coefficient	Standard Error	T Value	Regression Coefficient	Standard Error	T Value
IM(C)	10.64	4.60	2.31	11.00	6.28	1.75
IM(M)	2.43	0.99	2.45*	2.52	1.35	1.86
IM(R)	-1.98	1.00	-1.99	-2.29	1.36	-1.68
IM(W)	0.09	1.38	0.06	0.69	1.88	0.37
IM(F)	4.19	2.26	1.86	3.30	3.08	1.07
IM(S)	2.19	1.37	1.60	2.95	1.87	1.57
Intercept	-168.82			-172.42		
Adj R^2	0.75			0.73		
F Value	4.02			3.65		

*Significant at the 90 percent level.

APPENDIX TABLE 27

Slum Youth Unemployment Rates, 1966, Equation 2 Variables

(a)
Ages 14-19 and 16-19

	14-19			16-19		
Equation 2 Variables	Regression Coefficient	Standard Error	T Value	Regression Coefficient	Standard Error	T Value
E(C)	-0.01	0.28	-0.03	-0.15	0.29	-0.52
W(A)	12.89	4.62	2.79*	14.45	4.66	3.10*
LFPR(Y)	-0.28	0.40	-0.69	-0.40	0.30	-1.36
M(N)	-0.20	0.25	-0.79	-0.09	0.24	-0.39
W(P)	-0.30	0.16	-1.86	-0.43	0.16	-2.62*
Intercept	14.83			23.39		
Adj R^2	0.65			0.70		
F Value	3.35			4.07		

(b)
Ages 20-24 and 14-24

	20-24			14-24		
Equation 2 Variables	Regression Coefficient	Standard Error	T Value	Regression Coefficient	Standard Error	T Value
E(C)	-0.37	0.11	-3.36*	-0.31	0.19	-1.58
W(A)	7.04	1.76	4.01*	8.20	3.60	2.28*
LFPR(Y)	0.32	0.15	2.06	0.09	0.30	0.29
M(N)	0.21	0.10	2.13*	0.05	0.16	0.33
W(P)	-0.32	0.06	-5.51*	-0.45	0.11	-3.96
Intercept	-12.65			13.59		
Adj R^2	0.87			0.75		
F Value	10.48*			4.89		

*Significant at the 90 percent level.

APPENDIX TABLE 28

Slum Youth Unemployment Rates, 1966, Equation 3 Variables

(a)
Ages 14-19 and 16-19

Equation 3 Variables	14-19			16-19		
	Regression Coefficient	Standard Error	T Value	Regression Coefficient	Standard Error	T Value
E(CY)	0.01	0.17	0.03	-0.04	0.17	-0.25
W(A)	12.78	4.50	2.84*	13.71	4.57	3.00*
LFPR(Y)	-0.28	0.40	-0.69	-0.34	0.29	-1.20
M(N)	-0.21	0.33	-0.63	-0.12	0.33	-0.35
W(P)	-0.30	0.12	-2.46*	-0.38	0.12	-3.10*
Intercept	14.77			20.11		
Adj R^2	0.65			0.69		
F Value	3.35			3.83		

(b)
Ages 20-24 and 14-24

Equation 3 Variables	20-24			14-24		
	Regression Coefficient	Standard Error	T Value	Regression Coefficient	Standard Error	T Value
E(CY)	-0.12	0.11	-1.05	-0.13	0.15	-0.87
W(A)	6.63	3.09	2.14*	7.42	4.15	1.79
LFPR(Y)	0.20	0.26	0.79	0.12	0.38	0.32
M(N)	0.17	0.22	0.77	0.09	0.28	0.32
W(P)	-0.22	0.08	-2.74*	-0.37	0.11	-3.45*
Intercept	-9.15			10.63		
Adj R^2	0.62			0.65		
F Value	2.97			3.36		

*Significant at the 90 percent level.

APPENDIX TABLE 29

Slum Youth Unemployment Rates, 1966, Equation 4 Variables

(a)
Ages 14-19 and 16-19

Equation 4 Variables	14-19			16-19		
	Regression Coefficient	Standard Error	T Value	Regression Coefficient	Standard Error	T Value
EG(Y)	-7.76	4.50	-1.73	-12.48	3.70	-3.37*
SD	0.003	0.06	0.05	0.09	0.05	1.64
E(CY)	0.40	0.17	2.42*	0.07	0.17	0.43
M(N)	-0.99	1.32	-0.75	1.09	1.31	0.84
LFPR(F)	-1.04	1.05	-0.99	-2.37	0.84	-2.83*
CIM	0.57	0.33	1.72	1.03	0.19	5.38*
Intercept	35.16			73.89		
Adj R^2	0.66			0.88		
F Value	2.78			8.65		

(b)
Ages 20-24 and 14-24

Equation 4 Variables	20-24			14-24		
	Regression Coefficient	Standard Error	T Value	Regression Coefficient	Standard Error	T Value
EG(Y)	-1.42	1.85	-0.76	-2.99	6.12	-0.49
SD	-0.01	0.01	-1.04	-0.03	0.02	-1.36
E(CY)	0.13	0.11	1.25	0.32	0.18	1.75
M(N)	-0.64	0.50	-1.27	-1.42	0.62	-2.28
LFPR(F)	0.13	0.16	0.84	-0.26	0.59	-0.44
CIM	0.59	0.18	3.35*	0.86	0.27	3.17*
Intercept	-22.43			-9.76		
Adj R^2	0.77			0.54		
F Value	4.45			1.96		

*Significant at the 90 percent level.

APPENDIX TABLE 30

Slum Youth Unemployment Rates, 1966, Equation 5 Variables

(a)
Ages 14-19 and 16-19

Equation 5 Variables	14-19			16-19		
	Regression Coefficient	Standard Error	T Value	Regression Coefficient	Standard Error	T Value
E(CY)	-0.16	0.23	-0.70	-0.25	0.22	-1.14
W(A)	15.04	6.79	2.22*	14.10	6.14	2.30*
LFPR(Y)	-0.34	0.46	-0.75	-0.47	0.31	-1.51
UR(A)	-0.08	1.38	-0.06	0.35	1.26	0.28
W(P)	-0.36	0.17	-2.11	-0.44	0.16	-2.84*
Intercept	15.46			26.66		
Adj R^2	0.60			0.70		
F Value	2.79			3.98		

(b)
Ages 20-24 and 14-24

Equation 5 Variables	20-24			14-24		
	Regression Coefficient	Standard Error	T Value	Regression Coefficient	Standard Error	T Value
E(CY)	-0.27	0.03	-9.52*	-0.30	0.13	-2.32*
W(A)	-1.07	1.08	-0.99	4.27	4.28	1.00
LFPR(Y)	0.40	0.06	7.06*	0.10	0.26	0.39
UR(A)	1.41	0.18	7.06*	0.82	0.71	1.15
W(P)	-0.20	0.02	-8.60*	-0.40	0.10	-4.07*
Intercept	-11.67			16.13		
Adj R^2	0.98			0.80		
F Value	88.16*			6.58		

*Significant at the 90 percent level.

APPENDIX TABLE 31

Slum Youth Unemployment Rates, 1966,
Equation 6 Variables
(a)
Ages 14-19 and 16-19

Equation 6 Variables	14-19			16-19		
	Regression Coefficient	Standard Error	T Value	Regression Coefficient	Standard Error	T Value
EDL	-83.20	66.65	-1.25	-90.40	71.50	-1.26
D(R)	3.20	3.43	0.93	3.26	3.68	0.89
H(TB)	0.29	0.50	0.59	0.38	0.53	0.71
C(P)	0.001	0.01	0.24	0.002	0.01	0.33
RS	-0.15	0.63	-0.24	0.03	0.68	0.04
SD	0.01	0.02	0.37	0.004	0.02	0.18
Intercept	1023.35			1098.01		
Adj R^2	0.32			0.30		
F Value	1.16			1.10		

(b)
Ages 20-24 and 14-24

Equation 6 Variables	20-24			14-24		
	Regression Coefficient	Standard Error	T Value	Regression Coefficient	Standard Error	T Value
EDL	-84.47	35.87	-2.36*	-97.29	45.25	-2.15*
D(R)	-0.43	1.84	-0.24	0.21	2.33	0.09
H(TB)	0.08	0.27	0.30	0.15	0.34	0.45
C(P)	0.001	0.003	0.35	0.002	0.004	0.56
RS	0.08	0.34	0.24	0.30	0.43	0.69
SD	0.005	0.01	0.39	0.01	0.02	0.44
Intercept	1028.31			1167.25		
Adj R^2	0.47			0.51		
F Value	1.64			1.80		

*Significant at the 90 percent level.

APPENDIX TABLE 32

Slum Youth Unemployment Rates, 1966, Equation 7 Variables

(a)
Ages 14-19 and 16-19

Equation 7 Variables	14-19			16-19		
	Regression Coefficient	Standard Error	T Value	Regression Coefficient	Standard Error	T Value
EDL	-163.76	51.01	-3.21*	-208.39	73.50	-2.84*
ESL(Y)	-13.61	7.64	-1.78	-20.87	13.56	-1.54
H(TB)	0.08	0.38	0.21	0.19	0.43	0.44
C(P)	0.004	0.004	1.06	0.01	0.004	1.60
RS	-0.83	0.68	-1.23	-0.79	0.85	-0.94
SD	0.02	0.02	1.32	0.03	0.02	1.40
Intercept	2213.91			2822.28		
Adj R^2	0.57			0.51		
F Value	2.14			1.78		

(b)
Ages 20-24 and 14-24

Equation 7 Variables	20-24			14-24		
	Regression Coefficient	Standard Error	T Value	Regression Coefficient	Standard Error	T Value
EDL	-64.24	29.56	-2.17	-101.89	53.07	-1.92
ESL(Y)	3.35	3.15	1.06	-0.62	9.64	-0.06
H(TB)	0.04	0.23	0.17	0.14	0.33	0.43
C(P)	-0.0003	0.002	-0.14	0.002	0.003	0.75
RS	0.20	0.31	0.64	0.26	0.85	0.31
SD	-0.002	0.01	-0.17	0.01	0.02	0.46
Intercept	741.52			1232.84		
Adj R^2	0.61			0.51		
F Value	2.39			1.80		

*Significant at the 90 percent level.

CHAPTER 1

1. Manpower Report of the President, 1971, U.S. Department of Labor (Washington, D.C., 1971).

2. Statistical Abstract of the United States, 1971, U.S. Bureau of the Census (Washington, D.C., 1971), Table No. 527.

3. Statistical Abstract of the United States, 1963, U.S. Bureau of the Census (Washington, D.C., 1963), Table No. 14.

4. 1960: Statistical Abstract of the United States, 1963; 1966: Bill Publications Incorporated, Sales Management: Survey of Buying Power (New York City, June 10, 1967); Current Population Reports, U.S. Bureau of the Census, Series P-25, No. 427, "Estimates of the Population of Counties and Metropolitan Areas, July 1, 1966: A Summary Report" (Washington, D.C., 1969). The population is reported by city for 1960 and 1966 and includes the city of Long Beach with Los Angeles, the city of Oakland with San Francisco, and the city of Kansas City, Kansas, with Kansas City, Missouri.

5. See Lloyd Reynolds, The Structure of Labor Markets (New York: Harper & Brothers, 1951).

CHAPTER 2

1. See Black Americans: A Decade of Occupational Change, U.S. Department of Labor, Bureau of Labor Statistics, Bulletin 1731 (Washington, D.C., 1972).

2. Manpower Report of the President, 1971, U.S. Department of Labor (Washington, D.C., 1971).

CHAPTER 3

1. Manpower Report of the President, 1971, U.S. Department of Labor (Washington, D.C., 1971).

2. Statistical Abstract of the United States, 1971, U.S. Bureau of the Census (Washington, D.C., 1971), Table No. 348.

3. The Hudson Institute, "The New York State Drug Study," Vol. I (mimeo., 1971).

CHAPTER 4

1. There is a growing literature on urban labor markets and unemployment and poverty problems of slum residents. For an interesting discussion of the problems of labor market segmentation and dual labor markets see the following: Bennett Harrison, "Education, Training, and the Urban Ghetto" (unpublished Ph.D. thesis,

University of Pennsylvania, 1970); Peter Doeringer, "Ghetto Labor Markets: Problems and Programs," Discussion Paper No. 35, Program on Regional and Urban Economics, Harvard University, 1968; and Michael J. Piore, "On the Job Training in a Dual Labor Market," in Arnold R. Weber et al., eds., Public-Private Manpower Policies (Madison, Wis.: Industrial Relations Research Association, 1969).

2. Manpower Report of the President, 1971, U.S. Department of Labor (Washington, D.C., 1971).

3. See Black Americans; A Decade of Occupational Change, U.S. Department of Labor, Bureau of Labor Statistics, Bulletin 1731 (Washington, D.C., 1972), p. 12.

4. See Gary S. Becker, The Economics of Discrimination (Chicago: University of Chicago Press, 1957) and Lester Thurow, Poverty and Discrimination (Washington, D.C.: The Brookings Institution, 1969).

5. The Hudson Institute, "The New York State Drug Study," Vol. I (mimeo., 1971).

6. John Kain, "Housing Segregation, Negro Employment and Metropolitan Decentralization," Quarterly Journal of Economics (Harvard University) (May 1968).

CHAPTER 5

1. These national figures and the ones that follow are from the Manpower Report of the President, 1971, U.S. Department of Labor (Washington, D.C., 1971).

2. Ivar Berg, Education and Jobs: The Great Training Robbery (New York: Praeger Publishers, 1970).

3. Supplement to Health of the Army: Results of Examinations of Youths for Military Service 1966, U.S. Department of Defense, Office of the Surgeon General, Department of the Army (Washington, D.C., 1968).

CHAPTER 6

1. The Hudson Institute, "The New York State Drug Study," Vol. I (mimeo., 1971).

2. Ibid.

3. See an imaginative paper written by Mark Moore on the "Economics of the Heroin Industry" in the Hudson Institute, "The New York State Drug Study," Vol. IV.

4. Fred J. Cook, "The Black Mafia Moves into the Numbers Racket," The New York Times, April 4, 1971.

5. Ibid.

6. Ibid.

7. Reported in The New York Times, April 27, 1971.

CHAPTER 7
1. Nation: Manpower Report of the President, 1971, U.S.
Department of Labor (Washington, D.C., 1971), Tables A-1, A-3,
and A-7. Cities: Monthly Labor Review, U.S. Department of
Labor, Bureau of Labor Statistics Vol. XCI, No. 5 (May 1968).
Unpublished data supplied by the U.S. Department of Labor,
Bureau of Labor Statistics, 1968. Special tabulations prepared
by the Bureau of the Census, based on annual averages from the
"Current Population Survey of 1967."
2. Ibid.

CHAPTER 8
1. Employment and Earnings, U.S. Department of Labor,
Bureau of Labor Statistics, Vol. XVIII, No. 7 (Washington, D.C.,
1972), Table A-1.
2. Ibid., Table A-6.
3. Manpower Report of the President, 1970, U.S. Department of Labor (Washington, D.C., 1970).
4. Manpower Report of the President, 1971, U.S. Department of Labor (Washington, D.C., 1971).
5. Ibid.

STANLEY LAWRENCE FRIEDLANDER is an Associate Professor of Economics at the City College of the City University of New York, where he specializes in labor economics and urban problems. He is currently serving as Executive Director of the North Atlantic Regional Manpower Advisory Committee of the departments of Labor and Health, Education and Welfare and as Vice Chairman of the National Manpower Policy Task Force Associates.

Professor Friedlander received his Bachelor of Arts degree from the City College in 1959, his Master of Arts degree from the University of Illinois in 1960, and his Doctor of Philosophy Degree in 1964 from the Massachusetts Institute of Technology. As a student at MIT, he received the Westinghouse Fellowship and the MIT Doctoral Dissertation Fellowship. His research at MIT culminated in his first book, entitled Labor Migration and Economic Growth: A Case Study of Puerto Rico, published by MIT Press.

Professor Friedlander was appointed to a position as a Senior Staff Economist on President Johnson's Council of Economic Advisers in 1966-67, where he specialized in labor, manpower, education, and urban problems. Since then, he has served as a consultant to numerous private and governmental agencies, including the U.S. Budget Bureau, the Council of Economic Advisers, the Governor of Puerto Rico, the Puerto Rico Planning Board, and the Hudson Institute.

This present study was undertaken while Professor Friedlander was a senior research associate at the Conservation of Human Resources Project of Columbia University.

ROBERT SHICK is currently a Research Associate at the Conservation of Human Resources Project, Columbia University, and has been there, except for one year, since completing his graduate work in economics at Indiana University. During the year 1970-71, Mr. Shick lived in Puerto Rico and worked for the Puerto Rican government on problems relating to social and economic policy.

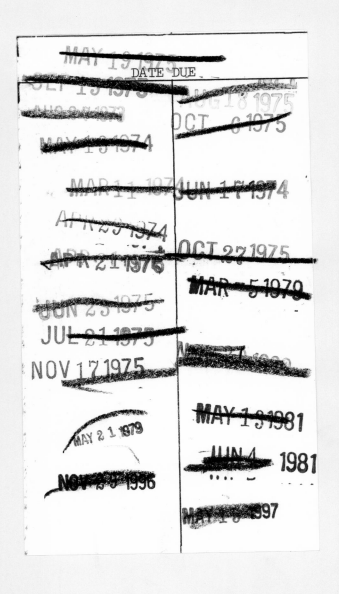